Trees on Mars

Trees on Mars
OUR OBSESSION WITH THE FUTURE

Hal Niedzviecki

SEVEN STORIES PRESS
New York • Oakland

Seven Stories Press
140 Watts Street
New York, NY 10013
www.sevenstories.com

College professors may order free examination copies of Seven Stories Press titles. To
order, visit http://www.sevenstories.com/textbook or send a fax on school letterhead
to (212) 226-1411.

Book design by Elizabeth DeLong

Library of Congress Cataloging-in-Publication Data

Niedzviecki, Hal, 1971-
  Trees on Mars : our obsession with the future / Hal Niedzviecki.
     pages cm
  ISBN 978-1-60980-637-8 (pbk.)
  1. Twenty-first century--Forecasts. 2. Future, The. 3. Information technology--Social
aspects--United States. 4. Disruptive technologies--Psychological aspects. 5. Future,
The--Psychological aspects. 6. High technology industries--Social aspects--United
States. 7. Technological innovations--Social aspects--United States. 8. United States-
-Social conditions--21st century. 9. Social prediction--United States. 10. United
States--Civilization--21st century. I. Title. II. Title: Our obsession with the future.
  CB161.N52 2015
  973.93--dc23

                                2015025042

Printed in the United States

9 8 7 6 5 4 3 2 1

Returning is not possible/And going forward is a great difficulty.
—KOFI AWOONOR, Ghanaian poet, novelist, and critic shot
dead in the Al-Shabab raid on the Westgate Mall in Nairobi

Contents

PART III: The Case Against the Future

PART IV: The End

A Winning Future

"The first step in winning the future is encouraging American innovation."[1] I find these words on WhiteHouse.gov in a section dedicated to "a strategy for American innovation." Attributed to a 2011 speech by United States president Barack Obama and garlanded with the requisite multimedia slide show/report, they are part of an overall package designed to convey the sense of concerted purpose the White House brings to "winning the future." The White House isn't alone in naming future as a priority. In 2005, six years before the Obama speech and two years before Steve Jobs was to unleash the awesome power of the iPhone on an eager world, British Prime Minister Tony Blair opined in a speech that the world was "fast forwarding to the future at unprecedented speed." He then asked the all-important question: "How do we secure the future for our party and for our country?"[2]

Over the last decade or so, "securing" morphed into "winning" and statements that once seemed at least a touch hyperbolic have become utterly the norm. Say that a main priority for a city, region, country, or even the entire human race is to be first to secure, win, or own the future, and people from widely different ideological and cultural backgrounds are likely to nod their heads in auto-pilot agreement. After President Obama used the words "innovate" or "innovation" more than ten times in his January 2011 State of the Union address, a *Time* magazine article noted that "on this issue, at least, Republicans seem in sync. . . . Everyone wants innovation and agrees that it is the key to America's future."[3] We have reached, as of 2011 or more likely some years before, a rare point of seemingly incontrovertible concord: there is a race to the future, and we must run it.

But do we know what, exactly, we've agreed to? The more we accept and advance what has become, over the last decade, an oft-repeated mantra around the world, the more we are fundamentally redefining humanity. Consider what these now de facto statements regarding the race to the future take as a given. First, there's the notion that tomorrow is now almost entirely under human control. As such, the future is no longer a collective, all-encompassing unknowable that governs the fate of all creatures on Earth; instead it's a looming time to come that we can moderate more or less at will.

Furthermore, we have somehow come to agree that this shapeable, attainable future is something we have to compete with each other to own. No longer to be considered as simply part of the endless weave of time, the future has been recast as a finite resource: there is only so much future to go around. In this new, now seemingly uncontroversial version of the future, nations, communities, and individuals all battle each other for prime territory in the time to come.

As we'll explore in this book, these two now-default notions represent a very different understanding of the universe than the one that dominated humanoid thinking for most of the time bipeds have walked the planet. Although often couched, as President Obama's words certainly were, in the quotidian of the commercial enterprise, what we're really dealing with here is a vast systemic shift in our collective consciousness. This is an entirely new way of apprehending our place in the cosmos.

How and why did we agree to embrace the notion that we are all tiny little gods, diminutive Olympians slugging it out to win the right to monopolize the future? How did we come to agree on the present as an impediment, a piddling problem to be solved on the way to the future? These are hard questions to answer, largely because we aren't really aware that we *have* embraced this shift and all that it implies. I'm hardly the first person to note that technological innovation has displaced both pop culture fantasy and religious conviction as the primary site of our projections. CNN segments on people camping out overnight to be first to acquire the latest iPhone remind us just how anxiously we now await the arrival of new totems of the future. They adjoin and accompany *Wired* cover stories trumpeting the personal drone revolution and *Fast Company* profiles of twenty-four-year-old multimillionaire app inventors. But despite the mainstream prominence techno-disruptive-futurism receives, there is little to no coverage that puts these phenomena in context. Nobody seems to mention how utterly different this approach to life is. Nobody asks how and when and why we reframed the future as something individuals can and should own and then placed the attainment of the future on a pedestal, effectively telling each other: look to this for all that matters.

Still, as we'll see in the coming chapters, educational institutions at all levels now advance this perspective; bureaucracies and politicians now make decisions that privilege this ideology; and our pop culture and media now relentlessly depict the future as a winnable, contested space. All the same, nobody actually comes out and says exactly what this means. Governments aren't sending official notices advising that we should stop ordering our lives around the past (doing things the way they've always been done), or the present (adapting to circumstances as they arrive), and start focusing exclusively on getting to the future first. An all-encompassing ideology is washing over us like a tidal wave, and we're pretty much treating it like a fun-loving must-see blockbuster consumer culture spectacle—the next *Star Wars*–My Little Pony–goji berry–craft beer craze, the first *Jaws*.

A new era emerges with the arrival of a dogma that is so compelling and overwhelming that human life and thought shapes itself to that ideology. It's happened before with various religious, political, and economic systems, and it is happening now. In this book, I will argue that an ideology has arrived and the systemic shaping of the social order that defines our lives is in progress. But, at the same time, unusually for such a large shift in the collective belief structure, the move to the future has been barely noticed; the tectonic plates ever so slowly bumped up against each other deep under the Astroturf of contemporary culture until, all of a sudden, the landscape around us changed so dramatically it was like it hadn't changed at all. Suddenly everything is different, every single one of us is affected, and yet the world looks (mostly) the same and it's hard to pinpoint exactly what changed or why.

Still, this is no short-lived fad. The rise of future as organizing principle is having deep, lasting effects on our families, our communities and our mental and physical environments. This new faith in disruptive futurism is an ideology and, increasingly, a governing system that, at its core, rejects stability, continuity, even community; in many ways, it is a complete restating of what we should desire and aspire to, what we should believe in and live for. As a result, it would be hard to underestimate its impact, despite its surreptitious arrival in the form of a kind of benevolent mission creep. Beset with an ideological pressure neatly dovetailing with addictive, increasingly personalized technologies that reach deeper and deeper into daily life, we find ourselves enabled in new ways, and yet all too familiarly struggling to live up to expectations. How can *you* change the world today? We are at least as much terrorized as we are empowered by this now-omnipresent question. As we'll see, this is not some so-called future shock to be met by leading the populace into awareness of the potentiality of a new era. We are all too aware of our supposed potential as change agents. But despite what we're being told and shown and taught, we are not instinctively able to embrace ongoing, constant flux in pursuit of future. As this book proceeds, it will become increasingly evident that though we are superficially eager to adopt the trappings of the superhero cum technologist, we remain culturally and psychologically ill-equipped to deal with our new role. There is surprisingly little in the four–and-a-half million or so years humanoids have spent on Earth that has prepared us to deal with the increasingly globalized presumption that each and every one of us should be running a race to the future.

We sense that some bad or at least some very difficult and confusing thing is happening. But we struggle to pinpoint its source, like the occupants of a house beset by a rotten smell emanating from somewhere under the floorboards. There's nothing to post to Instagram, upload to YouTube, share on Facebook. The tidal wave came and went so fast, we didn't even know it hit us. All the same, it reordered and continues to reorder. Some are even now being confronted with the fact that their lives and communities have been lost or diminished—though they didn't notice it at the time. The high-octane race to future, ever sweeping past us in relentless after-shocks, is creating expanding waste zones fit only for future losers—beaches after the tsunami. Despite this, and, indeed, because of it, the future glitters and beckons like never before. Cast adrift, we continue to swim to it to the extent that we are able. Ahead, we are told, lie endless archipelagos of abundantly provisioned tropical islands. There is one for each of us; we just need to get to them. Keep swimming, we are implored, and we do—though this promised future never seems to get any closer, and in our weakest moments we wonder if it is even really there.

PART I

Our Lives in the Age of Tomorrow

CHAPTER 1

Chasing Tomorrow
Dispatches from our Obsession with the Future

I'm lurking in the Startup America room when I meet Mara Lewis. It's crowded, a hive of activity. There's a three-hour waiting list to get a fifteen-minute sit-down with a start-up expert who can advise you on everything from attracting funding to marketing your app. Everywhere I look, there are people in T-shirts sporting brands you've never heard of. They don't exist yet. The women of New York's dormify.com—a new online retailer specializing in customized designs for the dorm rooms of seventeen- to twenty-two-year-olds—huddle in a corner strategizing. The team of clickwithmenow.com occupy an entire long table. I make eye contact and am loaded up with business cards and a pitch from the entourage of this St. Louis–based start-up who provide single-click web co-browsing (click on a button and invite someone to join you on your browser—they see what you see and can even type and move the mouse). At the core of the company are two guys who used to work at health insurance company Blue Cross Blue Shield. As they tell it to me, it was there that they had a eureka moment—realizing the pressing need for a tool that would solve the problem of a company looking for "a simple way for its customers to share information about insurance policies with their loved ones."

The venue is the Austin Convention Center, ground zero for SXSWi, a.k.a. South by Southwest Interactive. A spin-off of the annual music festival, this is the place where thousands of start-up aspirants come to join their peers for three days in Texas. A festival pass buying the right to listen in on panel discussions about the latest technologies, learn more about potential competitors and, most importantly, pitch to potential investors, costs $1,095. There are lots of people willing to pay—attendance at SXSWi was around 32,000 in 2014, double the attendance of the combined music and film festival from which the tech conference originally sprang.[1] In the Startup America room, the vibe is gleaming cheeks and spotless T-shirts fresh out of the box; the mood is frenetic, dialed-down frantic; the would-be digi-entrepreneurs have paid their money and they're looking for their return. They've got their eyes on the prize. As long as they think I can help them get the word out, they're interested. As soon as their message has been delivered, they are on their way.

Mara Lewis is sitting on a stool at the end of a long high table alternating between checking her text messages and scanning the packed room. She's tall and thin with long brown curly hair and an easy smile. She is sporting a shiny new "Stopped.at" black V-neck T-shirt. What's Stopped.at? I want to know.[2] Stopped.at, Lewis quickly informs me, is a new way to think about and conduct search. "The problem we're solving is search," she tells me. "How do you grow the web efficiently? We're building an algorithm that extracts the many from a website and ties it to the individual. We're building a concrete understanding of online identity."

It only takes a few minutes of conversation before I realize that Stopped.at is much more than the intense gleam in twenty-nine-year-old Mara Lewis's brown eyes. Stopped.at, a web start-up in a long stage of embryonic testing, is Lewis's baby. She can feel it in her, kicking and urging her along. It's part of her. It's her life and her passion. As with all start-ups, there is a foundational story, an "ah-ha" moment. Mara had been thinking about the need for a new kind of search for some time. "But the final tipping point," she explains to me, "was hearing my friends talking about this website and I hadn't heard about it." Her best friends were online checking things out and she was missing out. It was an inconceivable situation for self-described web "nerd" Lewis, who proudly tells me that she is "connected ten to fifteen hours a day." It's the start-up dream. A problem perceived. A pattern that needs disruption. And so, Stopped.at.

Mara Lewis describes the service to me. Once a user has signed up, they drag the Stopped.at bookmarklet to their browser. As they use the web, they "check in" by passing their mouse over the bookmarklet. The more they check in, the more Stopped.at's algorithm learns the interests of the user. Then it can suggest new sites, apps, or services the user might be interested in. And of course it can track where you check in online and make that information available to your friends so you never again have to blindly surf the web alone. Is Stopped.at a good idea? Does it work well? Will people take to it? Can it make money? I have no idea. What captures my attention is Lewis herself. She shimmers with intensity. Talking about her project, she focuses on me like bringing me onside is the only thing that matters. "I want to change the way people discover things," Lewis tells me. "I know I'm not solving world hunger, it's not going to feed the children. As an entrepreneur you have to recognize what you're good at—I'm good at organizing and sharing. We live in this online world. We need to be more transparent in this, our new environment, where business happens, where relationships happen."

I ask her about her life as a start-up developer. A complex project like this is a long road. Lewis tells me she's been working on Stopped. at for just about two-and-a-half years. She's recently launched a very early beta version.

"I haven't had a salary or paycheck in three years. I walk dogs, do babysitting, I moved into a small apartment. I sold some jewelry. I'm really good at making my dollars stretch." I ask her to estimate how much in earnings she thinks she may have forgone to develop Stopped. at. She estimates the dollar figure at around $100,000. And, she tells me, she's already put in $15,000 of her own cash. A lot of people in Mara's life are struggling to relate to her passion. "It's difficult. I feel like an outcast. My friends don't get it—I weep in my pillow for ten to fifteen minutes once a week. Why are you doing this to yourself? My boyfriend and parents are worried. Am I crazy? It becomes your identity. There is no plan B for me."

This is, I find out, actually Mara's third start-up. Originally from New York but now living in San Francisco, she developed the other two when she was barely in her twenties. The first was a video tutoring tool she invented while still in college to help out her sorority sisters. The second was a video-sharing application that evolved into a service for live online jam sessions. "It did well," Lewis tells me, "but it wasn't changing the world."

Changing the world. That's Lewis's modest goal. As she tells it, her start-up is not about the money or even the fame. It's about change and disruption. "What we're doing right now," she says. "It has the potential to alter the future."

o o o o o o

Google the word "innovate" and be confronted with twenty-five million links.[3] They lead to a steady stream of titles, web sites, articles, and conferences. A Canadian competition challenged university-age entrepreneurs to "create new value" out of the "everyday household object," the coffee cup. The winners got to go to the 2012 Global Entrepreneurship Conference in Liverpool and hear Sir Richard Branson tell the crowd, "I had a dream. I'm living it," and eBay's Martha Lane Fox explain, "We believed the world would shop online, we proved it."[4] Innovate Washington, Innovate Calgary, Innovate America, Innovate 3D, InnovatelikeEdison, they all exist to do one thing: promote "innovation." There is even an "Innovate Rotary!" blog exploring how you can create "thriving, growing, high-impact Rotary clubs." I read a post on the blog asking: "Does Your Club Have a Growth Mindset?" The blog is written by Rotary leader and management consultant Greg Krauska. In it, he laments the fact that even successful clubs that have been rewarded with trophies can lose their vibrancy if they don't keep changing, upgrading, innovating. Writes Krauska: "Unless a club is focused on where its next success will come from, it can get stagnant." What's the solution? The solution is to "adopt a growth mindset."[5] The solution is to look to the future.

Stock markets surge and recede on rumors of what Apple and Microsoft have in the pipeline or what a gas company announces they'll be able to frack out of the ground through technologies to be developed in the next decade; metropolises release lavish reports trumpeting their status as a "new tech hubs"; politicians eagerly crow about every last cent they invest in "innovation." Magazines trumpet special "the future of" issues and even museums and art galleries are trying to get into the future business, with exhibits like the London-based Design Museum's *The Future is Here* demonstrating the techniques and technologies that add up to the arrival of a "new industrial revolution."[6] When Apple released last quarter numbers for 2011, the *Wall Street Journal* headline read: "Apple Reports Blowout Earnings; Shares Surge After Hours."[7] A *Globe and Mail* article was even more instructive: "As the company that invented smartphones spirals downward, the company that reinvented them is soaring."[8] Blackberry, much maligned for failing to keep up with the pace of "innovation," is out. Apple, with its seemingly effortless ability to know what we will want before we even get around to wanting it, is in. But look out, Apple. A mere handful of years after the death of Apple co-founder and CEO Steve Jobs, grumbling about even that company started to surface. "Apple is sacrificing innovation on the altar of shareholder value," warns the headline of a piece written by a prominent business columnist. The article chastises Apple for "fiddling with updates of existing products" instead of focusing on coming up with the next game-changing revolution in personal technology.[9]

A search of annual and quarterly reports filed with the United States Securities and Exchange Commission shows corporations mentioned some form of the word "innovation" (defined by *Webster's* as "the introduction [presumably in the near future] of something new,") 33,528 times in 2012, a 64 percent increase from five years before. Apple and Google mentioned innovation twenty-two and fourteen times respectively. Procter & Gamble used innovation twenty-two times, Scotts Miracle-Gro chimed in with twenty-one innovates, and Campbell Soup Co. easily bested Google, employing the innovate buzzword eighteen times.[10]

At the same time, the number of entities registering trademarks and applying for patents has skyrocketed. In the 1980s, there were around 10,000 trademarks registered every year in the Unites States. By 2010, US entities were registering something in the range of 300,000 trademarks per year.[11] Words and phrases ranging from "Technolift" to "Meetings Ideas" and "Tamper Proof Key Rings" now enjoy the protection of the US government as more and more people try to come up with creative ways to claim ownership over the brand-building slogans that might just be the future.[12] Similarly, in 1980 there were 104,329 patent applications filed with the United States and 66,170 patents issued. By 2012, there were more than half a million patent applications filed—542,815 to be exact—and 276,788 patents issued.[13] And this isn't just a US phenomenon: through most of the 1980s and early 1990s, the worldwide number of patents stayed roughly the same, with around 400,000 filed per year. But by 2010 the number of patents filed around the world exceeded 800,000. In the new era of future, the number, notes an economist, "reaches new heights almost every year."[14] There are so many new patents and trademarks being issued because money is pouring into start-up ventures from all directions. Ever more anxious to get to the future first, investors compete to fund, and thereby own percentages, in the best new ideas. From bionic organs to a plan to mine distant moons to yet another app to help college kids coordinate their social lives, there's a roster of eager multimillionaires looking to get even richer—in the future. According to the National Venture Capital Association, 2012 was a banner year with venture capitalists pouring $29.4 billion into around 4,000 new companies, an increase of 7 per cent over the previous year.[15] Since then, it's been nothing but go go go for those with the money to gamble on owning a slice of the future. PricewaterhouseCoopers LLP and the National Venture Capital Association report that venture capitalists invested $48.3 billion in 4,356 deals in 2014, an increase of 61 percent in dollars and a 4 percent increase in deals over 2013. Internet-specific companies ($11.9 billion) and investments in the software industry ($19.8 billion) account for the bulk of the investments.[16] The intent of all this activity is nicely summarized by an ad on the back cover of a magazine. The ad features a sleek, silver, futuristic BMW poised in mid-rotation in the midst of a nearly empty anonymous city. The headline for the BMW i3, which features an "open-pore eucalyptus wood dashboard" and is supposedly the "first all-electric vehicle to achieve sustainability without compromising luxury, design or performance" reads: "We didn't predict the future. We built it."[17]

Strategy& (formerly Booz & Company) strategist Alexander Kandybin estimates that Fortune 100 companies are paying innovation consultants $300,000 to $1 million for work on a single project, spending anywhere from $1 million to $10 million a year each. Four out of every ten executives say their companies now have a chief innovation officer, according to a study released by Capgemini Consulting.[18] Many companies, like petroleum monolith Royal Dutch Shell, one of the world's biggest corporations by revenue, have entire well-funded departments devoted to getting to the future faster. Royal Dutch Shell has a twelve-person unit called GameChanger tasked with one thing and one thing only: "to identify potentially disruptive business ideas," to figure out what's going to happen before it happens, to own the future.[19] "There isn't a business in America that doesn't want to be more creative in its thinking, products, and processes," goes the marketing pitch for the book *The Art of Innovation* by Silicon Valley design bigwig Tom Kelley of IDEO. "At many companies, being first with a concept and first to market are critical just to survive."[20]

The emphasis the global corporation—the primal and primary institution in our society, the lion in our jungle—has put on seeking to know and shape the future over the last decade cannot be overstated. At Facebook, recently hired engineers are "encouraged to change something small on the site as early as the first day, so they can feel as if no product is ever really done."[21] At Google, programmers and technologists are expected to spend as much as 20 percent of their time pursuing their own pet projects for changing the future of the company and the world. "It's all about the long term," went the title of Amazon CEO Jeff Bezos's first letter to shareholders way back in 1997.[22] Everything is about shaping the future. Everything is about "visionary product insight." If the new media monoliths of the twenty-first century can be said to have put forth one cohesive vision, it's this: own the future, or the future will own you. Or to put it another way: own the people who will shape the future, or they might end up owning you.

Economist Enrico Moretti writes in his book *The New Geography of Jobs*: "Globalization and technological progress have turned many physical goods into cheap commodities but have raised the economic return on human capital and innovation. For the first time in history, the factor that is scarce is not physical capital but creativity."[23] It's not strength we admire and seek to emulate in order to be seen as successful in our society. It's not speed, not any singular talent, not even technical ability or sheer smarts. It's creativity; it's innovation. It's the unique, highly specific yet totally vague skillset that will allow us to know and shape future.

In this climate, future-focused think tanks and consultancies mushroom. Entities like the Push Institute ("pushthefuture.org"), Technology Futures, The Foresight Institute, and Institute for the Future issue ever more-lavish directives on seizing the coming day. Consulting firms, companies, and leading tech organizations release their annual proclamations on the future. These include Frog Design, an industrial design company that has worked with Apple and Sony, and its annual "Tech Trends" report; the World Economic Forum's annual "Top 10 Emerging Technologies" report; Accenture's "Technology Vision" report; Deloitte's annual "predictions for the technology, media, and telecommunications (TMT) sectors"; and consulting firm Gartner's annual "Gartner Predicts—Gartner's Predictions for the Year Ahead."[24]

These and many more missives are dispensed at must-attend conferences. Among others, there's Virtual Edge Summit, TEDx, MIT Sloan Tech Conference (2014 theme: "Disrupting Life"), and, of course, SXSWi where I meet Mara Lewis. At these gatherings, CEOs, academics, scientists, designers, engineers, techies, politicians, and even priests peddle apps, websites, podcasts, books, and predictions. They all have a common goal: to seize the future. To own what is coming next.

o o o o o o

At one of these ubiquitous conferences, I meet Patrick Tucker, an author, conference organizer, and self-proclaimed futurist. Fifty years ago, that label, *futurist*, would have conjured up the image of pocket protectors and awkward gatherings of like-minded outcasts wishing the Star Trek tricorder into real life. But Tucker, with his careful stubble, sleek rumpled suit and styled hair, doesn't come close to fitting that mold. When I meet him at a downtown Toronto hotel bar, he greets me with relaxed congeniality. Between sips of mineral water, the Washington DC–based associate editor for the World Future Society's magazine *THE FUTURIST* tells me about his then book-in-progress (now published under the title *The Naked Future: What Happens in a World that Anticipates Your Every Move?*), and the World Future Society annual conference, then coming up in Toronto.

The conference—with the tagline "Dream. Design. Develop. Deliver."—is a five-day who's who of speakers in fields ranging from international security to agriculture to education. Around a thousand people gather to listen to professors, company presidents, senior leaders, founders, and executive directors. The conference is similar to hundreds happening across the world every year, many of them now fixtures in popular consciousness identified solely by their acronyms— TED, SXSWi, etc. But the World Future Society conference adds a unique twist to the thriving business of future-first gatherings; their annual event also offers multiple seminars on the future of the "future" business—tutorials and panels that don't just expound on the future of agriculture or security or microchips, but also prepare others to be future espousers and expounders.[25] There's a seminar, for instance, that shares "the approach that futurists use to anticipate and influence the future" taught by Peter C. Bishop, chair of the Studies of the Future graduate program at the University of Houston and member of the Association of Professional Futurists. I hadn't before seen "futurist" skills on the agenda at a tech conference before, nor did I realize that you could now earn a university degree in futurism, so I ask Patrick Tucker about it.

"Everyone should be a futurist," he tells me enthusiastically. "You should embrace the idea that you are a futurist. You will feel better and be more confident about the future. All the trends that scared you, they suddenly portend great success, advancement, progress."[26]

As Tucker sees it, we all need to develop the skills of futurism.

Having the ability to envision the future ("anticipate") and even take steps to bring the future into being ("influence") is essential to succeeding and thriving in the coming decades. Tucker fleshes out this vision over the course of the next hour. "Now," he says, "the vast majority of young people understand that companies are things you start, they are not permanent at all, they have a lifespan which can be very short." Tucker explains that someone who approaches work with this attitude is "going to negotiate their future and is going to be increasingly suspicious of anything that gets in the way of moving on to the next opportunity." This ever-hungry, ever-advancing "worker," Tucker proudly explains, now "owns the future, including all the risks and all the uncertainty."

We own the future—we take the risks and we reap the rewards. Stuffed shirts flanked by walls of diplomas can no longer be an impediment to our success. In the future envisioned by Tucker, corporations can't hire or fire us, governments can't restrict us, and institutions either need to adapt to this new reality or get out of the way. Tucker points to universities doing things like dispensing lectures on astrophysics via YouTube. You want an education? It's out there, yours for the taking. As he puts it:

> Institutions we created to help us prepare for the future have been rendered somewhat conspicuously obsolete—we are really tied into maintaining these education institutions but at the same time in the coming decades more and more institutions will realize what MIT and Stanford found out: you want to be the first one to make education free as much as possible. This changes our relationship with the future. . . . Gaining acceptance into a certain institution will wane in importance.

Gaining acceptance into a certain institution will wane in importance. There are no impediments to our success, no barriers other than those we impose on ourselves. It's a beautiful vision. But what does this look like in the real world? I ask. Tucker is effusive with examples of people using the combined interactive possibilities of the Internet, home robotics and computing power to *anticipate* and *influence* the future. In Manhattan an enterprising fellow (illegally) installs a sensor in the sewer system that allows him to predict with astonishing accuracy when toilets will overflow in his neighborhood; a professor uses Twitter feeds, news reports, and Facebook updates to accurately predict the location of Osama bin Laden (albeit after the raid in which he was killed); amateur stock traders buy and sell shares based on real-time data garnered from studying Twitter feeds and the number of times people search for "unemployment benefits" on Google; a group of graduate students build, yes, an early prototype of what they believe will become the first functioning Star Trek tricorder.

"There are more and more areas of the future becoming transparent to more and more people," Tucker enthuses. He speaks of how this shift will usher in an age of self-confidence and do-it-yourself enthusiasm—the rise of new generations who instinctively and ably read the digital tea leaves. "And then," says Tucker, "you are reacting to the future the way everyone does at Silicon Valley, the way everybody does at TED. I see these people all the time, and they are looking at these things in a far different way from a guy laid off at an auto parts manufacturer in Michigan."

This perpetually young, plugged-in populace 2.0 has instant access to everything from a total scan of their genetic code to the best beaches in Thailand to the best-informed sentiments behind economic shifts. You can't be laid off—you knew to leave that company five years ago. The World Future Society conference program confirms Tucker's vision: more people from more disparate disciplines are taking up the futurist mantle. There are not just the expected programmers and think-tankers, but also industrial designers, investors, border security professionals, career bureaucrats, and even people at the pinnacle of the corporate world like conference keynote speaker Brian David Johnson, the director of Future Casting and Experience Research for Intel Corporation. For the most part, these are highly successful people who start their own businesses, solve their own problems, create and reject authority as they see fit, and never take their eyes off the big picture—the what-is-going-to-happen-next. They are the sleek, fit, freethinking, permanently connected postmodern man. They are the new model replacement for old, slow, Cro-Magnon Detroit autoworker watching helplessly as the tides of change *he could have anticipated* swap his job with a robot installed in a foreign factory.

o o o o o o

Patrick Tucker's vision is very quickly becoming the mantra of the mainstream. It is, quite simply, what more and more people, from our prominent thinkers/doers to young people just starting out in life, believe to be true. Twenty-three-year-old Tom Greany, who dropped out of London's Imperial College to work for Silicon Valley company Bump Technologies, summarizes our perceptions neatly: "To me," he tells a journalist, "the choice was to help create the future, or sit on the sidelines and think about it."[27]

There's plenty more where this comes from. Cheryl Wakslak, psychology professor at the University of Southen California Marshall School of Business in Los Angeles, tells me how the hype around apps and the techno-future is affecting her students. "The students in business school are wildly overconfident," she tells me. "They are very ambitious and willing to think in broad ways."[28]

In addition to the almost superhuman doses of confidence around their ability to succeed and change the world, Wakslak reports an underlying tension—anxiety that they aren't pushing forward into the future with enough zeal. "Working with these kids in the business school environment, a lot of them feel guilty for being conservative—'I want to be responsible but I should be doing something more, I've got this good job, and I should be doing something more . . .'" This is the urgency around getting to the future first. "People are supposed to be on a global stage," says Wakslak. "Different generations have felt that way, but today I think it seems very realistic to them." For past generations, the idea that you could go from college student to billionaire in a few years would be farfetched at best. But these kids, infused with mass media representations of the ideology of future-first, fully believe not only that it can be done, but that getting rich will be a mere by-product of reshaping the planet.

"You have to be more than who you are, you have to live on a larger platform," says Wakslak, explaining what she's hearing from her students. One example of that, Wakslak notes, is the rise of the "reflected life." "Kids growing up in today's generation are constantly documenting their experience. It's different—how does that change their sense of self when everything becomes a story that you are telling?"

The story we're telling is all about the future. A 2014 national survey by the Pew Research Center and *Smithsonian* magazine asked Americans about their perspectives on the future. The results show an impressive consensus—the future is coming, and it's going to be great. In fact, three in five Americans (59 percent) "feel that technological advancements will lead to a future in which people's lives are mostly better." How enthusiastic are we about the future? Consider:

- Fully four in five (81 percent) of us "expect that within the next fifty years people needing new organs will have them custom grown in a lab."
- Half (51 percent) of us "expect that computers will be able to create art that is indistinguishable from that produced by humans."
- More than one in four of us (39 percent) "expect that scientists will have developed the technology to teleport objects fifty years from now."
- One in three (33 percent) expect that "humans will have colonized planets other than Earth."
- One of every five people (19 percent) surveyed even believed that "humans will be able to control the weather in the foreseeable future."[29]

We're so hyped about the future that we'd be willing to dive into it right now if we could. An astonishing one quarter of people asked (26 percent) say they "would get a brain implant to improve their memory or mental capacity if it were possible to do so." What's the overall takeaway from the survey? We have "long-term optimism" for the future that is inextricably intertwined with "high expectations for the inventions of the next half century."[30] Today we are more enthusiastic, optimistic, and demanding of the future than any people ever before. "Contemporary life is overloaded with visions of the future," note two professors of philosophy in a column. "Whereas Friedrich Nietzsche bemoaned the surplus of historical sense, crushing old Europe under the weight of its past, we are now suffering from an obsession with what lies ahead."[31] "The word 'innovation' has become a buzzword and it's been drained of much of its meaning," notes bestselling Steve Jobs biographer Walter Isaacson.[32] All around us, writes critic Thomas Frank, there are "TED talks on how to be a creative person." There are "'Innovation Jams' at which IBM employees brainstorm collectively over a global hookup," and "'Thinking Out of the Box' desktop sculptures for sale at Sam's Club."[33]

Language matters. Language shapes how we see things. A famous psychology experiment provides insight into the way words and ideas on the surface enter our collective mental infrastructure. In the study, students were given a series of words to organize into a sentence. Half the students had words we tangentially associate with the elderly—words, for instance, like Florida (which became the name of the study). All the students were then asked to walk down the hall to another room. The students who had been given the Florida grouping of words walked down the hall at a noticeably slower pace. They were subconsciously influenced by the set of words they had read.[34]

Amazon, Apple, Facebook, Twitter, Skype, Google. These companies are not *just* the new middlemen, the monopolistic cultural arbitrators of their day, the new judges, the new Hollywood, the new record company A&R. They are also our touchstones, verbs, and identities. They *are* the twenty-first century. And they are not just offering us momentary fame and fortune decided on by the whims of boardroom executives. They are offering us something much deeper, something that now shapes us on the granular, on the cellular level. They offer permanent connection to the ever-flowing tide of pop culture, to the possibilities of shape-shifting ourselves right into the future.

In 2006, inspired by the empowering possibilities of connectivity, the *Time* magazine Person of the Year was "You." The 2010 *Time*

Person of the Year was Mark Zuckerberg.[35] "You" aren't good enough anymore. The rhetoric of special, of human hubris, continues to push into new terrain. Today it's not just the present that we are repeatedly urged to shape and control; today, the future, too, is something that individuals are being told to contest, buy, sell and bring into being. We used to talk about living in the moment—carpe diem; just do it. A consume-now, think-later mentality boiled down to any number of 1980s-era slogans. But even that doesn't cut it anymore. Pursuing your dreams with wild abandon, seizing the day, living fast and dying young, going big or going home—that's not big enough anymore. Achievement in the age of the Internet has been super-sized. Rags-to-riches is now app-to-global domination. More and more, owning the future permeates our psychological space.

The future-now ideology shapes our mental landscape, and our mental landscape shapes how we think things should look and feel in physical space. "Headphones are the new cubicle," says Duncan Logan about his office venture RocketSpace, which charges $700 to $800 a month for desk space, a 20 percent premium over other similar rental spaces in San Francisco. Amenities include free beer and coconut water, fast Internet, bowls of candy, and an informal speaker series that features Twitter executives and venture capitalists. But what really attracts the young start-up bucks is the main amenity—being crammed in next to other people who think and work the same way. Duncan Logan personally vets all the companies seeking space to ensure that they are legitimate up-and-coming could-be-the-next-big-thing start-ups. "I was here until 10:30 the other night, and so was the guy at that company, and them over there," Michael Perry tells a reporter. Perry has a four-person start-up that connects corporations to their brand's most vocal supporters. "When I was working alone, I thought I had a billion-dollar idea," he says. "Here, everybody thinks they have a billion-dollar idea, and they're hammering away. That's inspiring."[36]

The RocketSpace look—long tables, ceilings dangled with cables, hardwood floors, a notable absence of partitions—is the look of the permanent future: a crowded yet empty space ready at an instant for change, for disruption, for the what-is-to-come. There are more and more spaces that look like this in every city in North America, spaces that deliberately set out to physically evoke the ethos of constant change. The casual observer might think the haphazard décor is about saving money, but these spaces are deliberately constructed. Companies actually pay to have their offices stripped away to virtually nothing. When Facebook took over the former headquarters of Sun Microsystems they hung wires from the ceiling, removed walls and put "people in close proximity," all to give "the space an unfinished look."

Meanwhile, over at Twitter there are couches adorned with pillows crocheted with the words "Home Tweet Home" set among "irregular soft cubes," the whole setup meant to function as an "impromptu meeting area." At Twitter HQ, you have to make a formal request for a stationary phone at your desk, otherwise it's assumed you'll use your cell, which the company pays for. The main dining area is known as the Commons, an open area designed to encourage "chance meetings." Writes a reporter ruminating on the Twitter complex: "Here, as at many other tech companies, is a sense that nothing is permanent, that any product can be dislodged from greatness by something newer. It's the aesthetic of disruption: We must all change, all the time."[37]

Mental space changes, physical space changes and even the tools that we use to bridge the two are changing. From 3-D Printing to file sharing, more and more of our tools exist in the so-called cloud so they can be accessed by anyone from anywhere. These are the tools we need to live in permanent connection, ready to change and be changed. A start-up called Quip, headed by Bret Taylor, age thirty-three, who previously helped build Google Maps and served as Facebook's chief technical officer, is creating cloud-based word-processing software designed entirely for mobility and collaboration. It's the stuff the people in RocketSpace are going to use to reinvent the world. Quip is Google Docs meets social media meets whatever mobile device you happen to have on hand. "Its files and documents are meant to be collaborative products," explains a reporter, "which anyone in a group can jump into and change around. Trappings like instant messaging along one side of the screen and Facebook-like photos of others currently working in one's files drive home values of change, and getting products out fast." The physical, the mental, the virtual. For Quip's Bret Taylor, the quest for the future works best when it all comes together, when the workplace and the software and the mental process all reflect each other: "Seeing who is working on what, chatting with them or deciding to collaborate, that is what we have here. Workplaces are changing, so expectations are changing."[38]

Expectations change. Redesign your city, your park, your life, your policies, to be about more than just the prosaic present. An artist team doing an elaborate installation in a London, UK, park says: "We wanted to encourage people to see their lives, the future, the city as an idea that they can positively participate in the writing of."[39] Bay Area's Marin County holds a public forum: "Choosing the Future We Want: Environmental, Equity and Climate Solutions for Marin."[40] When the Rio+20 Earth Summit in Brazil wrapped up in summer 2012, its delegates titled its nonbinding agreement, "The Future We Want"—an evocation of a near future "we" can all have input into, perhaps through the sweep of a finger down the luminescent screen of a third grader's iPad. "The future we want can be ours—if we act now," exhorts United Nations Secretary-General Ban Ki-moon at the start of the 67th General Assembly Session in Fall 2012.[41] Or as Barack Obama implored us in what seemed like a groundbreaking campaign in 2008: *Change.*

But Obama very quickly went from hero to not-quite-zero: just another president, forced by the strictures of the job to spend far too much time in the present. How quickly we turned on him. When he represented "change" he was our hero. But then he became mired in the present, in the time *before* change. Our heroes are no longer those who seized the day, the warriors and tycoons and presidents and pop stars of yesteryear who shone so bright in the moment. The new heroes are the ones who are perpetually on the cusp of seizing tomorrow. "Growing Numbers of Start-Ups Are Worth a Billion Dollars," a headline in the *New York Times* all but screams.[42] "There is a swagger," goes another article. "Tech boosters don't have to bray that the industry is changing the world. Everyone knows, because it really is."[43] "Hard to believe," notes a tech columnist, "but there was once a time when the visionaries worked for the government." The writer goes on to list the men (interestingly, only men) and companies at the forefront of change, noting, "The wild dreamers these days work for technology companies."[44]

ounder Jeff Bezos is a hero. The late Steve Jobs, whose
hy was a best seller throughout 2011 and who was all but
after his death, is a hero. A six-year-old given the "Most
Like., Be the Next Zuckerberg" award at the Seattle Startup Weekend for his ideas about a water-dissolving sticker business is a potential
hero. ("He was definitely the youngest and most articulate entrepreneur in training that I know of at a Startup Weekend," Marc Nager,
the executive director of Startup Weekend, tells a tech commentator.)[45]
A promo e-mail I receive goes: "Want to be a marketing leader? Use
the entrepreneurial techniques that made Mark Zuckerberg a success,
says Ekaterina Walter, best-selling author of *Think Like Zuck*." Even
the unlovable likes of Facebook's Mark Zuckerberg is a hero. Here's
a glowing assessment of Zuckerberg in the *New York Times* on the eve
of Facebook's multibillion dollar IPO: "Mr. Zuckerberg's success is an
object lesson in what works in crowded, competitive Silicon Valley:
Remain in charge, stave off potential predators and expand the company so quickly that no one can challenge the boss."[46] (Note: speedy
constant expansion—keeping everyone in a constant state of change—
that's the way you stay on top.)

Or consider this portrait of Napster founder Sean Parker (who was
also involved in the early days of Facebook) in the *New York Times*
Sunday Styles section. The piece fawningly cites his $20 million Man-
hattan mansion, his reputation as a polymath, and his $2.1 billion net
worth. It concludes with Parker lecturing the 950 guests of a charity
ball—including, we are told, Kim Kardashian and Ivana Trump—on
what area he believes cancer research scientists should be focusing on.
Socialite fundraiser-organizer Denise Rich is convinced: "The impression of him changed that night," she says. "This man had so much
substance."[47]

Both pieces give a brief nod to the well-documented fact that neither
of these men is particularly well-liked. But so what? Here's the real
point: Mark Zuckerberg invented and rules over Facebook. Sean Parker
invented file-sharing service Napster and was an early investor in Facebook. Both men start visionary companies at the drop of a hat. They
can do no wrong. They are the new rock stars. They see the future. As
Facebook investor Paul Madera, managing director at Meritech Capital

Partners, is quoted as saying of Zuckerberg: "He always knew before the rest of us what Facebook could be."[48]

He knew before the rest of us. Mere mortals live in the now. Presidents and elected officials, besieged by the moment, are no longer heroes (at least not for long). Soldiers, dogged by the questionable morality of the wars they fight, can no longer be heroes. Even in pop culture soldiers are portrayed as dinosaurs, archaic creatures caught in situations beyond their control. The Oscar-winning *The Hurt Locker* portrays its "hero" as a pathological risk-taker; the hit TV series *Homeland* has returning prisoners of war "turned" into Muslim terrorists; the Cold War show *The Americans* creates antiheroes out of CIA agents and puts undercover spies—dogged soldiers of the Soviet Union—one good offer away from defecting. These are not heroes; they are mice and men, buffeted by the present, unable to own the future. Sports stars are mired in doping scandals, concussions, and televised specials devoted to covering which absurdly inflated contract they are going to accept from which team. Injured, traded, getting older every year—they seem like the heroes of yesteryear, as dwarfed by the vagaries of now as the rest of us.

Even scientists and engineers toiling in their laboratories, slowly and painstakingly coming up with the formulas and reactions and equations that might lead to new cures and technologies, are forgotten in our rush to celebrate the new innovator-technologists. As billionaire Russian technology investor-entrepreneur Yuri Milner said in an interview, "In the last 50 years, we have evolved from a world where Einstein was the biggest celebrity to a world where the most famous scientist is not in the top few hundred celebrities in the world."[49] Hero worship has always reflected what a society most values. In the case of twenty-first century postindustrial society, the message is clear: the now is not where you want to be. If you want to truly achieve at the highest levels of our society, you have to be altering the future. "People in tech, when they talk about why they started their company, they tend to talk about changing the world," notes Joe Green, a roommate of Mark Zuckerberg at Harvard who now leads a Silicon Valley–funded political advocacy group. Reid Hoffman, founder of LinkedIn, describes it like this: "I can make a multibillion-dollar company with a little bit of investment. Why can't the whole world do that?"[50] Speaking about his company's research into the driverless car, Google cofounder Sergey Brin says: "We want to fundamentally change the world with this."[51]

New Yorker writer Jill Lepore notes, "The eighteenth century embraced the idea of progress; the nineteenth century had evolution; the twentieth century had growth and then innovation. Our era has disruption."[52] Or, as Jeff Bezos once told Charlie Rose: "Amazon is not happening to book selling. The future is happening to book selling."[53] You can't resist the future, you can only take advantage of it. As a result, "not knowing the future," notes Brendan Keenan, business columnist for the *Belfast Telegraph*, "is now widely taken as a sign of inadequacy."[54]

o o o o o

The effects of future fervor are more than apparent back at the SXSWi conference where I meet Mara Lewis. It's the kind of place where people go to great lengths to get just a few minutes of alone time to pitch a potential investor. One LA-based start-up hopeful won a contest earning her twenty minutes of driving around Austin with a venture capitalist in a tiny red-and-black electric BMW (we can presume it featured a eucalyptus dashboard). She promptly cashed in all her frequent flier miles to buy a ticket on a red-eye flight that brought her in a few hours before her big chance and brought her back out a few hours after. In the end, she didn't get an offer of funding, but it wasn't a total loss—the VC did favorite the tweet she sent out about their drive.[55]

At SXSWi, I sit in on three packed public pitch sessions, though I easily could have sat in on that many every day of the weeklong conference. The pitches I watch are high pressure and, by now, fairly predictable. They go like this: someone with an idea like Mara Lewis's new way to search—or, say, an app that lets you order your drink at the bar before you get there—takes the stage to deliver a two-minute, or, at most, ten-minute pitch to a panel of encouraging but skeptical venture capitalists. Of the three sessions I go to, one is the finals for students who entered a start-up competition aimed at undergraduates.

One is for more advanced entrepreneurs also competing in the finals of a start-up contest. And one is put on by Startup America and just features a lineup of people—anyone who could afford a SXSWi pass and wants to pitch. Again and again, they get up to the microphone and passionately extol, for instance, the virtues of their new way to connect business travelers to yoga classes. There are so many people pitching so many ventures that the VCs, overwhelmed and swarmed, end up prescribing generic advice and their business card to just about everyone. "The advice was very high-level, and the investors didn't even remember my pitch ten minutes later when I went up to speak with them after the event," recalls one person who pitched at SXSWi a few years back and now works for someone else's start-up.[56]

I meet students pitching a new-way-to-connect-up-with-your-friends app; I meet the guy pitching the bartender app; I meet a woman who has launched an app aimed at helping people with their eating disorder (I listen, amazed, as she describes her bitter feud with the other eating disorder app developer, her sole competitor). I listen to a group developing a new way to buy health care services offered à la carte by doctors and hospitals so you can shop, right there in your doctor's office, for the best price on that MRI. In each case, there is considerable skepticism about the idea's capacity to succeed in the marketplace. In each case, the creators tell me they will soldier on regardless. As one student developer tells me, if this particular idea doesn't pan out, he'll just go on to the next idea. He's even got plans to develop an incubator in his hometown. It'll be a think tank where others can gather with their ideas. He has no money, no financing, hasn't even graduated from college yet, but that isn't stopping him from proclaiming that he'll very soon be, himself, at the head of a venture capitalist firm, investing in the best and brightest ideas, investing in future.

After a lukewarm reception to his pitch at an open cattle-call session, I catch up with Ryan Konicek. Ryan—twenty-three years old, handsome and informal in jeans and a T-shirt, and living in Milwaukee, Wisconsin—has the kind of face you can imagine superimposing on a quarterback or the star of an action movie. He tells me a team of eight people in their twenties built the app he is pitching, called Tappr, which lets you order a drink on your mobile device from anywhere in the bar (or even, presumably, before you have arrived). The app then sends a text to your phone when your drink is ready. You flash your phone at the bartender as you pick up your beverage, somewhere along the way your credit card gets charged, and presto—the "problem" of having to stop what you're doing in order to go and reload your drink is solved. When I catch up with Ryan, I find out that the app has already been launched and a few bars in Milwaukee are using it. "We launched the product before we started testing it," Ryan tells me. "The philosophy is to get it out into the market as quickly as you can."[57] This is similar to Mara Lewis's plan and the reason that, at the time I met her, you could already use a beta version of Stopped.at, though it hadn't been officially launched. In fact, I learn that this is the norm with apps and start-ups—launch something as soon as possible. The idea stems from the fact that because there are so many other app makers and developers, some of them are very likely to be building something similar to yours; so you want to launch as soon as possible and stake a claim to your territory. Get to the future before the future gets to you. The only problem, as both Lewis and now Ryan Konicek are finding out, is that if your start-up launches before it is fully functional, people might not want to use it. After the responses he got at the pitch session at SXSWi and recent experiences with app functionality problems in actual bars and restaurants, Ryan laments adopting the future-now strategy popularized in hundreds of books and articles about building and launching start-ups. "We should have tested it," he tells me. "Everyone thinks if you build it they will come . . ." He's spent eight months of time and estimates his sweat equity at $15,000 in personal labor done after his day job as part of an innovation team for a health care company. Alas, all that work and energy and investment, and Tappr seems destined for the dustbin before it's even been fully completed. "What's next?" I ask Ryan. Back to the day job? Ryan is shaking his head before I even ask him the question. "I want to build my own business," he tells me. "As a team our goal is to make a product that has a positive impact on society, that can change the way people behave. If we do really well with this, we can help other people start up."

Like everyone else I meet at SXSWi, Ryan won't be deterred by a dose of reality. If Tappr isn't the answer, they will just have to come up with something else. And along the way, of course, they will change the world.

"There are now hundreds of thousands of app developers," prominent investor and former programming innovator Brian Singerman tells me.[58] Singerman was the imaginative force behind iGoogle and Google Alert. He then left Google to become an angel investor, eventually joining forces with the venture capital firm Founders Fund. I reach him on the phone and ask him for a snapshot of the start-up scene as he sees it. "There's definitely an element of a lottery ticket to it," he says to me. "I'm not saying no one will succeed, but it will be a tiny, tiny fraction." So what draws them to such a risky venture? "People think that right now with this frothy environment the safe thing to do is to start a start-up," he says. "'Oh I'll just get bought,' they think. It's not true. A few months ago I was talking to someone, a guy who had a started a company, and the guy actually said, 'I'm doing this because I think it's the safest way to feed my family.'" Singerman, who has had a firsthand look at the difficulties of taking any kind of tech start-up to the point at which it will be an enticing target for a buyout from Facebook or Yahoo!, is incredulous at the attitude he is now encountering. He told me that hearing the entrepreneur talk so dispassionately about his start-up represented one of the lowest moments in his career as a venture capitalist. From his point of view, it just doesn't make sense. Even someone who is entirely passionate and willing to sacrifice everything is unlikely to end up with millions of dollars in the bank, let alone achieve change-the-world status. The competition is fierce and cruel. Venture capitalist Marc Andreessen, of the Silicon Valley firm Andreessen Horowitz, notes that he gets 3,000 pitches a year and his company funds just twenty of them. "Our day job is saying no to entrepreneurs and crushing their dreams," he says.[59]

The odds of success are daunting, but this doesn't seem to deter anyone. Clearly, the rhetoric of owning the future is far more powerful than the reality. Mantra coalesces into belief even though the competition to "alter the future" intensifies every day. Mara Lewis had her chance to pitch the judges at the SXSWi Dolphin Tank. But she didn't win. She came in second. Six months later and Stopped.at disappears from the web. I ask around—no one I know has ever heard of it. A

Google search reveals no reviews, no discussion. As I perform several more fruitless searches, I think back to what Mara Lewis told me at the conference: "There is no plan B."[60]

CHAPTER 2

Teaching Future
Why Schools are Teaching Change and Preaching Tech

In a high-security Manhattan building that houses the regional head-quarters of technology and telephony companies, including Google's New York City offices, I walk into a large open-concept office jammed with desks and flanked by glassed-in meeting rooms. The look of the space—wide open, chaotic, customizable—is familiar to me from my visits to high-tech firms across North America. Everything from the cords dangling from the exposed ceiling to the translucent conference areas oozes innovation. Only, this isn't the already too-cramped offices of a Silicon Valley start-up. This is the temporary home of Cornell Tech, university of the future.

Cornell Tech is, in many ways, the brainchild of former New York City mayor Michael Bloomberg. Bloomberg held a competition for proposals for a new educational facility on Manhattan's Roosevelt Island. The contest was part of an initiative called *Applied Sciences NYC* launched by Mayor Bloomberg in 2011. As such, it was open only to educational facilities dedicated to technological entrepreneurship and innovation, with the stated aim of growing the city's innovation sector and adding to New York's status as a high-tech hub. Upstate New York's Cornell University won the bid by proposing a partnership with the acclaimed Israeli university Technion, a world leader in technological research. The group edged out competitor Stanford and took possession of the island. The award came with $100 million from the City of New York, and has attracted various private and public donors plus substantial investment from Cornell to come up with the rest of the estimated two billion dollars needed to build the two million–square-foot, ultra-state-of-the-art institution. Once built, the campus will host graduate students taking programs at the Joan and Irwin Jacobs Technion–Cornell Innovation Institute (described as the centerpiece of Cornell Tech). There will also be a Postdoctoral Innovation Fellows Program aimed at supporting individuals seeking to "commercialize their research ideas . . . while taking advantage of the entrepreneurial network of Cornell Tech and its proximity to New York City–based markets."[1]

Indeed, partnerships with New York–based tech firms, including Google, are the core of Cornell Tech. "One of the most exciting components of the Cornell/Technion proposal is the innovative, industry-linked curriculum 'hubs,'" enthused then New York City Deputy Mayor Robert K. Steel. "Consider the mold broken," the Cornell Tech website announced before proclaiming the institution "ready for students, faculty, and partners who want to change the world." Cornell Tech's Roosevelt Island official campus will open in 2017, though construction will continue for quite a while after that. But for now, the postdoc program and a smattering of graduate students enrolled in programs like a two-year degree in Connective Media "designed to train the entrepreneurial engineers and technologists needed to drive the digital transformation of publishing, advertising, news and information, and entertainment," are operating out of the Google building in Chelsea.[2]

So that's where I meet up with the two men charged with putting this program together. Joining me in one of the exposed meeting rooms is Daniel Huttenlocher, dean of Cornell Tech, and Adam Shwartz, director of the Postdoctoral Innovation Fellows Program. I ask them why everything I read about Cornell Tech emphasizes that this institution will take a completely different approach to education. Is higher education in a shambles? Do we need the totally different approaches they are promising? Huttenlocher tells me that we are in a time analogous to the period just after "the first wave of the industrial revolution."[3] As Huttenlocher sees it, back then, the universities were busy drilling their students in Latin and Greek while the world was changing seismically and irrevocably. There were no engineering schools, let alone programs teaching business or management. "And it became clear that what was happening in academics was not all that connected to needs of the age." Similarly, today, "the ways people need to be educated are changing fast and not being met by today's education system."

So, the next obvious question: how are things going to be different here? Huttenlocher tells me that Cornell Tech will be relentlessly multidisciplinary. Nobody will be working in some abstract silo. It's all about connecting with the real world. "There will be not just a change in the role of discipline, but also a change in engagement between the academic and real worlds including corporate, nonprofit, etc. We bring people in from industry as part of the everyday of what we're doing. We have people from industry here doing clinics, workshops, teaching in courses, being part of a rich active network of advisors . . . everyday engagement between the academic and corporate worlds." Huttenlocher points out that even the physical space of this first small "campus" has been set up to look and feel like a start-up. "We have a completely open floor plan, faculty sitting out in open cubes. That," Huttenlocher says seriously, "is hard to do if you hire older faculty."

At the mention of the youthful nature of most of the faculty, Adam Shwartz cuts in for the first time, playing the joker to Huttenlocher's straight man. "I'm the oldest on campus," he quips. The two men briefly debate the question. Sporting thin, graying hair and the intense look of a man ready and willing to pounce, the Israeli Shwartz, a Technion professor of electrical engineering who looks to be in his late fifties, easily wins the argument. And the message has been delivered to the journalist in the room: crusty fuddy-duddies stuck in time need not apply to Cornell Tech. That done with, Dean Huttenlocher picks up where we left off. He tells me about the chasm in higher education between practice and research and the need for new institutions like Cornell Tech that can close the gap. I ask him for an example of how that gap can be closed, and he talks about students forming teams and becoming involved in "all of the parts of building an early stage project" including "interacting with companies" and looking at issues like marketing and fundraising.

Shwartz jumps in here: "Traditionally, activity like that would be in business school. If you go to engineering school then this aspect is completely missing. At Technion, you tell them, 'Let's do something applied.' They immediately push back and say, 'No no, let's just teach them the fundamentals.' A guy at Harvard Computer Science moved from Harvard to Google, and people said he's nuts but, actually, he said, 'Here, if you have an idea you have to wait two years until you are ready to start working with it.'"

Huttenlocher breaks in, careful to emphasize that it's not all going to be education applied to the development of product-based technology. There will still be plenty of room to teach core practices. Shwartz listens impatiently then says: "We're not claiming that you don't need to do fundamental research. There are people doing it and that's wonderful—there are places that work only with the theoretical stuff and that's really important. But the part that's missing is what we do here: to develop it, to try it."

By the time our hour is up, I'm getting a pretty good picture of how Cornell Tech will be approaching education differently and why its brain trust thinks this is necessary. The programs will be short—one or two years. The concentration will be on applying knowledge, on taking things out into the real world. The outcome will be graduates who will have the fundamentals needed to be technological innovators while also knowing how to develop, pitch, raise money, start a business. The six postdocs Shwartz will supervise each year will be treated as if they are already in early start-up mode. In lieu of tuition, Cornell Tech plans to take a small percentage of whatever business its postdocs go on to start. Figuring that the credibility and expertise they get at Cornell is worth roughly $150,000, "if the postdoc decides to create a spinoff, that $150,000 would be converted to equity in the resulting start-up company—roughly 5 percent for a start-up that got a few million dollars in initial funding."[4] Right now, this model will apply only to the postdocs, but if it works, Shwartz has said that they might very well end up applying it to all students at Cornell Tech and even Technion.

This is the new, lean, mean, future-first world of education. You get the tools to succeed in shaping the future now, and the institution gets a small slice of your action. Incentive to go out into the world and change something is baked right into the pie. Your goal as a student is to introduce relentless, potentially profitable change by any means and for any reason. Adam Shwartz excuses himself; he has to introduce a technical talk happening around the corner in another, larger meeting room. I ask him if I can tag along, get a sense of the day-to-day presentations happening on campus. He shrugs amenably, jokes apologetically that I probably won't understand much of it, and off we go.

The talk, attended by twenty or so students and faculty, is presented by Vivek Farias, a youthful and enthusiastic associate professor/Robert N. Noyce Professor of Management at the Massachusetts Institute of Technology (MIT) Sloan School. Farias is a graduate of the Information Systems Laboratory in the Department of Electrical Engineering at Stanford University. After my conversation with Huttenlocher and Shwartz, I'm excited to see all of this in action. What crucial problems are Farias and his students at MIT grappling with that the students at Cornell Tech can learn from and build on? Farias launches into his talk, which, he announces, is called Modern Revenue Management. His research is a partnership—as it turns out, precisely the model for the way Cornell Tech wants their students to do things. Farias talks about how he worked with a start-up called JumpTap that, as Farias put it, "had a lot of money and a lot of data." (JumpTap has since been acquired by a similar company called Millennial Media.) Farias and his students were given access to the data in order to delve deeper into the "problem" of operating revenue management systems for media sites. Farias, still in introduction mode, gives us a bit of background. He tells us that airlines were the first to introduce revenue management, noting that "the first start-ups in the space are from the early '90s and they are behemoths today: Sabre Holdings, JDA, all the dynamic pricing in airlines are using tech from these guys. Over the last ten years it started to make its way into retail—DemandTech—doing revenue management via SASS, IBM bought them two years ago for 500 million . . . Profit-Logic, they got bought by Oracle for 200 million. . . ."

Okay, I get the point. There's gold somewhere in these hills. But I'm still not sure what exactly it is he's building that might one day solve a pressing problem and earn a half-billion-dollar payday. Then, finally, Farias begins to get to the nuts and bolts of the issue. Paraphrasing Farias's talk, it's something like this: if you go to the *New York Times* website, they can tap into various datasets that reveal you are a sports car lover and show you an ad for a new Porsche. Or Farias, who is a proud new father, will see an ad for a Baby Bjorn sling. But that's pretty crude. So the problem that needs to be resolved is how to maximize what is known about a visitor to a web portal—what ad should someone see when and how many times?—while factoring in the different levels of payment the advertisers are offering the *New York Times* per view or click. There are, apparently, hundreds, if not thousands, of factors to consider when pondering a system that can deliver the best return to the host site, which includes not overly barraging the visitor with repetitive targeted ads. Therefore what follows is a very detailed analysis of how Farias is attempting to solve this "problem," complete with charts and graphs and mathematical equations. "How do you even figure out the relative amount of traffic that you have across these different types? What's the trade-off between the granularity of this modeling and estimating what this supply might look like? You can use statistics, but the statistical risk is gigantic."

Adam Shwartz is right. I don't understand most of the talk. But even though I'm basically packing up my laptop and preparing to sidle out of the room with my tail between my legs, I get at least one thing: This is the way of the college of the future: research and technology and commerce all mixed together so that it's impossible to see where one ends and the other begins. The needs of the commercial world identified and met before you've even written your first essay on Shylock or wondered out loud in a buzzed stupor if there really might be a god. In the future-first education model, so-called problems are being identified and companies and products are being created in near-lockstep. The world is changing, the future is coming, and Cornell Tech's island plans to be a hothouse where students can learn the principles of surviving and thriving in the new world order of identifying problems, disrupting weaknesses, and, most importantly, getting there first.

o o o o o o

Our institutions are under enormous pressure to adapt to the new realities of the future era. First and foremost, the mantra holds that anything impeding access to the future is a thing that needs to be done away with. Change or be left behind. Respond to the imperatives of the future or become obsolete. Education is ground zero for attempts to implement changes that reflect this new agenda. Why education? Because education is the intersection of a wide array of interlocking forces—state, corporate, and the myriad aspirations of families and students all collide in the educational system. As such, it's particularly vulnerable to newly pervasive ideology. Everyone—from governments to bureaucrats to corporations looking to hire and graduates looking to be hired—wants the education system to be preparing students to function successfully in society. And while this doesn't mean the same thing to all the stakeholders, this preparation is increasingly coming to mean giving students specific skills that identify them to prospective employers as change agents ready to reshape the future. When colleges and universities, and even, as we'll see, middle and high schools, examine the best way to outfit graduates with the skills they need to succeed economically, increasingly they're landing on the permanent future agenda. They're asking the question—how can we reshape what we're doing so that our graduates are prepared to take part in the race to the future?

As a result, colleges and universities are falling all over themselves to introduce new courses, programs, and degrees that will prepare students to get to the future first. More and more educational institutions are remodeling century-old programs of study to give students the future cred they need. Cornell Tech is reinventing how academic institutions approach science and technology, but they're hardly alone in doing so. The places where we send our young people are now increasingly concerned with being seen as institutions able to churn out the new creatives of the knowledge economy. "Our CEO mastered social networking 2,000 years before Mark Zuckerberg was born," proclaims a billboard marketing the Jesuit-founded University of San Francisco.[5]

"Chapman University," goes a banner ad, "where innovation and discovery come into focus."[6] The colleges all want to graduate people who will be desired by the gold standard companies like Google and Amazon, not to mention the thousands of other companies and institutions seeking to inject the orthodoxy of change into their corporate DNA.

We've already talked about Cornell Tech, and I briefly touched on University of Houston's graduate program, offering the tongue-twisting Master of Science in Futures Studies in Commerce degree. So let me tell you about the decision of Utah's Brigham Young University (BYU) to rename their humanities program "Humanities+." Humanities+ (echoing Google's social media network Google+) is a program that not only offers the traditional humanities—i.e., a course of study in literature or philosophy or European history—but also internships, overseas trips, and direct partnerships with their business school. The stated aim of Humanities+ as articulated on the BYU website is to prepare students to work for governments, nongovernmental organizations, and "high profile companies." BYU notes that in the "globalized marketplace recruiters are turning directly to humanities majors." Why? Apparently it's because of their "leadership abilities, communication skills and, above all, their intellectual flexibility and creativity."[7]

An entire, newly conceived course of study from an acclaimed degree-granting institution designed around the notion that our primary (primal) twenty-first century institutions want students who are able to shape and predict the future, students who have the skills needed in the age of permanent change. And this is no one-off anomaly. There are an increasing number of these types of reinventions. For instance, the University of Southern California (USC) opened a new program in 2014 with the slogan, "The degree is in disruption." The USC Jimmy Iovine and Andre Young [a.k.a. Dr. Dre] Academy for Arts, Technology, and the Business of Innovation is, according to the program's website, "a transformational presence" with a "focus on invention and conceptual thinking, drawing on the talents and influences of leaders from across industries to empower the next generation of disruptive inventors and professional thought leaders."[8]

Even departments and professions once considered virtually sacrosanct are getting into the act of teaching innovation. Michigan State

University has reconfigured its law school to focus on business and technology and encourage its students to think of themselves as potential start-up entrepreneurs. "Legal education has been stronger on tradition than innovation," says Joan W. Howarth, dean of the Michigan State University College of Law. "What we're trying to do is educate lawyers for the future, not the past."9 It's difficult to teach reinvention and future, but the universities are doing their best. If they can't unveil entirely new high-tech hub island offshoots, they can at least rebrand and recreate their degrees and course offerings to cluster around technology-related themes and applications. Consider the rise of the Digital Humanities. Digital Humanities (DH) is a popular new interdisciplinary field that is now being offered by universities across the US, Canada, and the UK. At Michigan State University for instance, students can earn a bachelor of arts degree in DH, which amounts to "reading and learning about, exploring, researching, analyzing, arguing about, and critiquing the ways in which digital tools, technologies, and spaces have transformed—and are continually transforming—work in the humanities. Students also create, design, craft, mash, mix, and produce using digital tools, technologies, and spaces."10 A Harvard Digital Humanities Initiative website describes DH as "referring to the various applications of information technology to research and teaching about human society and culture."11 Or, more specifically, instead of learning the humanities, you learn to analyze and critique the way digital "tools" are "continually transforming" the humanities. Over the last decade, DH programs and offices have proliferated. The National Endowment for the Humanities has created an Office of Digital Humanities to help fund projects. The Mellon Foundation is providing large grants to several universities including a 2013 grant of one million dollars to the University of Rochester to develop a graduate fellowship in DH.12 The authors of the handbook *Digital Humanities* talk about the field's arrival as nothing less than transformational: "We live in one of those rare moments of opportunity for the humanities, not unlike other great eras of cultural-historical transformation such as the shift from the scroll to the codex, the invention of movable type, the encounter with the New World, and the Industrial Revolution."13 Scholar Jerome McGann, long an advocate of using computing in the humanities, suggests that the primary goal of the Digital Humanities will be to reshape the institution: "Here is surely a truth now universally acknowledged: that the whole of our cultural inheritance has to be recurated and reedited in digital forms and institutional structures."[14] In other words, notes *New Republic* senior editor Adam Kirsch in an essay, "Here is the future, we are made to understand: we can either get on board or stand athwart it and get run over."[15] Kirsch quotes from an article called "What Is Digital Humanities and What's It Doing in English Departments?" In that piece, Matthew Kirschenbaum, professor of English and associate director of the Maryland Institute for Technology in the Humanities at the University of Maryland, writes that "the construction of 'digital humanities' . . . increasingly serves to focus the anxiety and even outrage of individual scholars over their own lack of agency amid the turmoil in their institutions and professions."[16]

In a five-year capital campaign concluding in 2011, Stanford University raised $6.2 billion—"surpassing by more than $2 billion any other single higher-education campaign."[17] Flush with Silicon Valley money, "Stanford built a new medical school, business school, engineering center, institute of design, interdisciplinary law building, environment and energy building, center for nanoscale research and technology, cognitive and neurobiological imaging building, bioengineering center, automotive innovation facility, and concert hall. The university gave birth to more than five thousand companies and licensed eight thousand inventions that brought in $1.3 billion in royalties."[18] "Everybody sits around their dorm rooms late at night talking about their next project," is how one Stanford student describes his experience of the Bay Area campus bursting with tech-savvy students eager to make their mark. "Everyone feels like they have an opportunity to do the next great thing."[19]

At Stanford, the number of computer science majors has more than tripled in the last five years, making that major the most popular on campus. In fact, computer science is so popular that in 2015 Stanford announced a new degree—CS+X, double majors in computer science and either English or Music. The idea is to give students the opportunity to differentiate their computer programming skills from their peers by also having a background in the arts. "Pretty much everyone who majors in computer science at Stanford gets a job," notes Jennifer Widom, chair of Computer Science at Stanford. "But those [in these new programs] might get more offers, or more interesting offers."[20]

Others might say that Stanford is just trying to throw a bone to the starving dog of its humanities departments. At Stanford, 45 percent of the faculty teaches in the humanities, but only 15 percent of the students are taking their classes. Similarly at Harvard, there has been a 20 percent drop in students studying humanities over the last decade.[21] Seeking to emulate Stanford, universities scramble to reimagine themselves as high-tech centers as attractive to students as they are to corporate and government funders. "There's an overwhelming push from the administration at most universities to build up the STEM [Science, Technology, Engineering, Math] fields," says John Tresch, a historian of science at the University of Pennsylvania. "Both because national productivity depends in part on scientific productivity and because there's so much federal funding for science."[22] As a result, anything not STEM, not Stanford and Cornell Tech–like, is slowly being starved out. Consider that even as Stanford builds bigger, better labs and research facilities, the overall University of California system of public colleges and universities—once considered the best in the United States, if not the world—has had its budgets repeatedly cut. In 2011, just as Stanford was wrapping up its record-setting six billion dollar capital fund, California public colleges and universities were dealing with 13 percent less in state money than they had in 1980 (when adjusted for inflation). Between the 2010–11 and 2011–12 state budgets, public colleges and universities in California lost another $1.5 billion, "the largest such reduction in any high-population state in the country."[23] This decline was more severe than in the rest of the US, but it follows a pattern. Despite the fact that everyone and anyone in a leadership role talks about the clear relationship between higher education, prosperity, and owning the future, in 2014 higher education spending in the United States was actually notably lower than it was in 2008, with spending per full-time-equivalent student at $6,105, well below the $7,924 mark in 2008 (without even factoring in inflation).[24]

As a result, if you're not doing future on campus, you are probably facing cuts. The plight of the humanities has gotten so bad that the American Academy of Arts and Sciences issued a report decrying decreased funding for humanities and "calling for new initiatives to ensure that they are not neglected amid the growing money and attention devoted to science and technology."[25] But in the age of future, it's an uphill battle. Harvard and Stanford aren't exactly cash-strapped and won't be cutting—as the much smaller Edinboro University of Pennsylvania did—their entire programs of degrees in German, philosophy, and world languages and culture.[26] Nevertheless, overall, the humanities are in big trouble—nationally, the percentage of humanities majors hovers around 7 percent, half the 14 percent share in 1970.[27] One example of how precipitous the decline is: at the University of Maryland in suburban Washington, DC, the number of English majors rose between 1996 and 2011 from 641 to 850 students. But in 2012, the numbers started to drop dramatically. By 2014, the English department had lost 363 majors—about 40 percent—"and the numbers continue to fall." William Cohen, professor and current department chair, told a reporter via e-mail that at least part of the decline is "cultural, as reflected in declines among humanities majors nationally. There seems to be a perception (however unfounded) among some students and their families that the employment prospects for humanities majors are not as great as in some other fields."[28]

The decline is reaching a near-crisis level, but only for universities and faculty members desperate to stave off the inevitable primacy of science and technology—those portals to the future. To be frank, nobody else really cares. As Florida Governor Rick Scott put it, "You know, we don't need a lot more anthropologists in the state. It's a great degree if people want to get it, but we don't need them here. I want to spend our dollars giving people science, technology, engineering, math degrees. That's what our kids need to focus all their time and attention on."[29] The message isn't subtle: the past is a wasteful luxury; building the future is the only thing that matters. The real action is in STEM and everybody knows it.

o o o o o o

In our bottom-line society, it's not surprising that the education system is at the forefront of the many institutions seeking to adopt a future-first agenda. A major part of the appeal of the future era, the reason it has imbued so many with such a sense of purpose in such a short period of time, is that it does, indeed, offer real opportunity at a time when what once seemed to be a clear-cut path to career is becoming increasingly entangled and overgrown. In other words, a driving force of our enthusiasm for permanent future comes down to the now-(in) famous Bill Clinton campaign slogan: "It's the economy, stupid." Students want jobs, universities want graduates who can get jobs, and the high-tech trade is the only industry that seems to be growing, not shrinking.

Rates of employment are stagnant, a situation unlikely to change in any meaningful way. At any given time, with some fluctuation for year-by-year economic conditions, it's fair to say that around 10 to 15 percent of the population of the US, or some forty to fifty million Americans, are unemployed or significantly underemployed.[30] In fact, the number could be even higher than that. For instance, in June 2013, economist John Williams, who runs the newsletter *Shadow Statistics*, put the real number of just unemployed Americans at a staggering 23.3 percent of the population.[31] But there remains one place where demand for employees seems insatiable and that's the IT companies, the innovation companies, the companies who have positioned themselves as being at the forefront of future.

In 2011, a middling bad year for an economy that has barely managed to trudge along since the great crash of 2008, Google, with annual global revenue of *$38 billion*,[32] hired around 6,000 workers in the United States.[33] The job market is awful but the innovation companies are constantly complaining they can't find the talent they need. Managers at tech companies are increasingly willing to hire people who, previously, no company would touch with a ten-foot-long search query. Neil Rae, an executive at the tech company Transcom, tells a *New York Times* reporter that their quest to "fill technical-support positions" has shifted away from college graduates to "kids living in their parents' basement." Companies are more and more willing to hire from less prestigious universities and the ranks of the dropouts and disaffected gamers. In New York City, a study estimated that more than half of the city's 300,000 or so tech workers don't have a college degree.[34]

There's a lot at stake, since shortages seem endemic. A 2014 analysis of available jobs by the Georgetown University Center on Education and the Workforce finds that "the most in-demand jobs are for applications software developers and computer systems analysts."[35] The US Department of Labor predicted that the number one sought-after employee in 2016 will be the Network Systems and Data Communications Analyst. There will be positions for more than half a million of them, double the 260,000 employed in the field ten years earlier. Fourth most sought-after job title? It's Computer Applications Software Engineers. (Second- and third-fastest growing job categories are personal care workers and personal aides to take care of the septuagenarian baby boomers and their nonagenarian parents. Until the robots get up to speed on making appropriately sympathetic noises to stories about the good old days, people willing to change adult nappies can expect steady, un-world-changing employment.)[36]

The numbers are clear. If you don't want to be spoon-feeding Ativans crushed into blended meatloaf for slightly above minimum wage, you should probably look to a career somehow related to owning the future. But be careful. Even many STEM careers no longer guarantee a path to secure employment. A survey of American PhDs in biology and life sciences found that only 14 percent of them had secured an academic position within five years of completing their degree. (Traditionally, this would be the expected career path with this kind of degree—a lifetime of doing and teaching science at a lab in an academic institution.) Paula Stephan, an economist at Georgia State University who studies the scientific workforce, tells a reporter that despite the ongoing emphasis on getting more young people to enter the STEM fields, "the supply of scientists has grown far faster than the number of academic positions."[37]

All is not completely lost for those whose mechanical or technical aptitude is limited to app downloads and status updates. You don't have to be a systems engineer or a programmer to get into the high tech game (though that would certainly help). Of the 6,000 positions Google filled in the US in 2011, around 4,000 of those hired were people with degrees in the liberal arts. (The BYU plan makes perfect sense.

Google will hoover up those grads like a robot vacuum cleaner set to stun.) But Google isn't hiring just anybody with an enticing joint BA in philosophy and women's studies from a brand name university. The richest and most desirable employers like Google are looking for very specific, yet weirdly vague, talents in their new hires. A posting by Google for a "Product Manager" talks about "eyes focused squarely on the future." The company is looking for people with the ability to consistently "bring innovative, world-changing products to market." This means you should be "flexible," "experienced," and able to "drive numerous initiatives" while having "visionary product insight" and a "great insight for developing compelling products." Insight is the key, oft-repeated word here, in case you didn't notice. It's code for someone who can come up with the ideas that will shape the future. For Google, and, increasingly, just about every other company in the world, staying one step ahead of what's going to happen is the sweet spot. Job descriptions for those positions can be paraphrased as: we are looking to hire a person who can figure out what's coming next and build it before anyone else does. "The No. 1 thing we look for," notes Laszlo Bock, "is general cognitive ability, and it's not IQ. It's learning ability. It's the ability to process on the fly. It's the ability to pull together disparate bits of information."[38]

The most successful job candidates, explains Eleonora Sharef, age twenty-seven and cofounder of HireArt.com, a website that acts as a middleman between companies and job seekers, are "inventors and solution-finders."[39] These people are relentlessly "entrepreneurial." "Many employers today," writes *New York Times* columnist Thomas Friedman, "don't care about your résumé, degree, or how you got your knowledge, but only what you can do and what you can continuously reinvent yourself to do."[40] Now there's a tongue-twister for the post-industrial job interview: *what can you continuously reinvent yourself to do?*

This raises the question: are new programs and degrees a cure for the whiff of obsolescence, or are they just cologne poured over the ever more rank odor of decay? For an ever-increasing subset of both prospects and employers, the university has become something like a moldering zombie—still trundling along, but already dead. The skills needed in the age of future either can't be taught, won't be taught, or are better taught on the job. Is it too late for the university? There are, in fact, many who think that the time is right for the university system to be put out to pasture. Consider the receptive response that the twenty-year-old leader of the UnCollege movement Dale J. Stephens has received. Already author of a book published by Penguin—*Hacking Your Education: Ditch the Lectures, Save Tens of Thousands, and Learn More Than Your Peers Ever Will*—he finds himself in the enviable position of traveling the globe touching down at the hippest tech conferences talking about how to succeed (i.e., get to the future faster) by thumbing your nose at higher education. Typical Dale can be found in a *Forbes* magazine Q&A in which he tells Gen Y what they need to do: "Don't expect going to school to get you a job, and understand that if you want to be successful you're going to have to hustle and create opportunities for yourself."[41]

Dale's wisdom is echoed by the hiring guru at Google, Laszlo Bock: "G.P.A.'s are worthless as criteria for hiring, and test scores are worthless. . . . We found that they don't predict anything." Accordingly, Bock points out, at Google the proportion of people working at the company without a college degree continues to increase. Zuckerberg didn't need college, Bill Gates didn't need college, and maybe you don't either. "Too many colleges," Bock says, "don't deliver on what they promise. You generate a ton of debt, you don't learn the most useful things for your life. It's [just] an extended adolescence."[42]

In 2013, the presidents of 165 universities issued a joint statement calling on President Obama and Congress to deal with the supposed "innovation deficit." "Our nation's role," they wrote, "as the world's innovation leader is in serious jeopardy. The combination of eroding federal investments in research and higher education, additional cuts due to sequestration, and the enormous resources other nations are pouring into these areas is creating a new kind of deficit for the United States: *an innovation deficit.* Closing this innovation deficit—the widening gap between needed and actual investments—must be a national imperative."[43] There was a kind of desperation, even hysteria, underpinning the joint statement. There may be an innovation deficit, but this is more about the university presidents' needing to respond to the future ideology, an ideology impatiently hostile to the notion of an education system—any system really—that slows us down, that puts roadblocks on the highway to the future. They know that, increasingly, higher education is being seen as part of the problem rather than part of the solution. It is in this climate that the presidents seek to make their universities more about innovation and change. They band together and demand money to reinvent themselves as change agents teeming with future Facebook interns.

They have to do this, because in the tech sectors that increasingly dominate our perceptions, consensus is emerging: college is a big waste of time and money. Dale Stephens got his start when he was "selected out of hundreds of individuals around the world" to be a 2011 Thiel Fellow. The notion of the Thiel fellowship—a kind of unscholarship dreamed up and funded by PayPal founder, now billionaire venture capitalist, Peter Thiel—is exactly the kind of challenge that the university presidents are desperately trying to respond to. Thiel funds students not to go to university. Instead, those accepted into his program are moved to San Francisco and given money and advice in order to pursue their dream ideas in the form of start-up companies hell-bent on disruption. It comes full circle: the result of Dale Stephens's Thiel fellowship is UnCollege, the social network and advocate site for those who choose not to pursue higher education.

And if you do go to university? Well, there's plenty of enticement to give up on your degree and start chasing the future. "Here in Silicon Valley, it's almost a badge of honor," says Mick Hagen, age twenty-eight, about being a college dropout. He dropped out of Princeton in 2006 and moved to San Francisco to start the mobile app Undrip. Hagen now recruits from the undergraduate ranks and says that other tech companies also do this. They are essentially pitching students to drop out and come work for them. The students are getting the message. Consider the rise of the campus hackathon, weekend programming sessions in which groups of students, jacked up on energy drinks and donuts, compete to come up with and program some new piece of tech. These once-fringe events are increasingly popular on campuses across the country. In 2014, there were only forty of them. As of 2015, there were around 150. The longest-running hackathon, as of this writing, happens at the University of Pennsylvania and hosts 1,200 students from across the country each semester. "A few years ago, hackathons weren't really that popular—it was sort of a subculture," Kathryn Siegel, a junior at the Massachusetts Institute of Technology, tells a reporter. "There's been an enormous explosion." That's hardly surprising. The events are a potent cocktail of rewards now and later. "We want you to build the future of television!" announces a representative from DirecTV, sponsor of a Stanford hackathon. If you do, you might win a zero-gravity flight, or a trip to Paris, or a flat-screen TV or, even better, a job offer. Tech firms and venture capitalist companies are all over these events. "We want to find the next Mark Zuckerberg and the next Jack Dorsey," says Andy Chen, a partner at Kleiner Perkins Caufield & Byers, the venture capital firm that sends its people to twenty or more hackathons every year. "If you're not at a hackathon, you're at a disadvantage," Chen explains. "What you learn in class isn't necessarily as applicable to the work force." Nobody needs to worry about the college hackathoners getting distracted by their homework: "What's really cool about this atmosphere is that it's pretty easy to say 'Screw it' when it comes to schoolwork," says Vikram Rajagopalan, a sophomore from the University of Michigan. "Pulling out a textbook is very frowned upon."[44]

As far as Mick Hagen is concerned, students who drop out of college are actually more desirable than those who stay in school. "College puts a lot of constraints, a lot of limitations around what you can and can't do," Hagen said. "Some people, they want to stretch their arms, get out and create more, do more."[45] College is constraining. Come with us and "create" and "do." Stretch out your arms and create Undrip, "a mobile iOS app that algorithmically surfaces the best and most interesting content from your social feeds." Alas, the app ran out of money and closed shop in 2013, a victim, according to its in memoriam web presence, of a lack of "explosive growth to attract additional capital." Mick Hagen's not heading back to Princeton. According to his website, he's already collected just short of a million dollars—and no doubt several more college drop-outs—for his next start-up venture launching soon.[46]

o o o o o o

Universities aren't the only educational institutions under pressure to alter how they do things in order to get to the future faster. In a speech to the California Charter Schools Association, Netflix Chief Executive Officer Reed Hastings outlined his vision for what he claims to be a faltering, if not completely failing, public school system. Summarized, he has this to say: public schools should be steadily replaced by charter schools that also put in a place a new governance model of appointed, rather than elected, school boards. "The importance of the charter school movement is to evolve America from a system where governance is constantly changing and you can't do long-term planning to a system of large non-profits . . . The most important thing is that they constantly get better. Every year they're getting better because they have stable governance—they don't have an elected school board."[47]

The old way is slow and has impediments to change like democratically elected school boards that aren't necessarily filled with visionaries. The new way is based in data and can continually and rapidly evolve. Like so many very rich techno-titans, Hastings is willing to spend money to get to the future faster. He's put millions of dollars into Rocketship Education, an outfit that creates and runs charter schools based on a "blended" education model. Rocketship, according to their website, "reimagines the traditional school system for today's needs, and tomorrow's opportunities." At Rocketship, which runs eight charter schools in the San Jose area and is promising new schools opening soon in at least three other cities around the country, kids spend a bunch of time in front of computers taking in "personalized" lessons, and then work with teachers and their peers on group projects. This, according to Rocketship, is all about "creating a flexible space where teachers leverage tools—tutors, online learning programs, and their peers—to engage kids in a truly personalized learning experience. Innovation is in our DNA."[48]

The reflexive shift of the educational system to future-first is part fear, part hope, part pragmatism (there's gold in them hills!). At the high school and even primary school level, we see, again, how the rhetoric is being turned into reality. At the World Future Society Conference I meet Amy King, an administrator at a public school in Elk Rapids, Michigan, an isolated community in Northern Michigan that's a four-hour drive from Detroit. She tells me that the school system, which teaches 1,400 students from kindergarten to twelfth grade, is part of a state program to issue almost every student an iPad. I ask her why. She tells me it's because the school is trying to "motivate them to be self-driven, to provide them with opportunities." They are concerned that their students are not "ready for the future." Moving forward, they'll try to "integrate the technology into every curriculum." Amy notes that the problem is particularly urgent for her community, which feels like it is being left behind, "being in the middle of nowhere." And so the school needs "to do things to show our kids what the real world is like." Administrators view the iPad program as part of educating today's students for the technology-dependent world they'll graduate into.

I hadn't heard about the give-every-kid-a-tablet thing before, but when I get home and start looking into it, I find out it's a full-on trend: iPads are already used by at least 8 million kids in schools around the United States.[49] In Los Angeles, somehow the problem is similar to the one in rural Michigan. Kids are being left behind by the future. The answer there, too, is to roll out the iPad to every student. Thus the second-largest school district in the United States announced in 2013 that it would give every student in its schools an iPad. The initial deployment will cost about one billion dollars. The rollout started with the devices going out to forty-seven schools. But it hit a snag when students immediately broke through the security features and started visiting Facebook during class. The school board delayed the rest of the rollout for a year, but now it's back in full swing. Similarly, Florida's Miami-Dade County Public Schools recently halted a plan to hand out devices to seventh and ninth graders, though it's still on the table once they figure out how to avoid an LA-like educational disaster. Their new model is San Diego, which is gradually handing out iPads to all its students over a six-year period.[50] Meanwhile, in North Carolina, Guildford County's twenty-four middle schools have signed up with Amplify, a New York–based division of Rupert Murdoch's News Corporation that sells tablets, training, and educational software to school boards. Amplify is run by Joel Klein, chancellor of New York City's public schools from 2002 to 2011, who frequently asserts the need for the for-profit program because, as his popular refrain goes, "K–12 isn't working." Education, according to Klein, is "ripe for disruption."[51]

But the overall pressure on the educational institution to adapt to the needs of the permanent future isn't about objective improvement. It's about the subjective rhetoric regarding the imperative of seizing the coming tomorrow. It's not as if universities conducted a long-term study and determined that the digital humanities—or a program that replaces classroom time with business school partnerships in which students work on hypothetical start-ups—leads to happier, more intellectually stimulated or even higher-paid graduates ten years down the road. Of course, universities need students to keep paying tuition, so it makes sense for them to do what they think they need to do in terms of attracting as many applicants as possible. But public education has a captive audience of students who have to be there. There's no objective reason, then, to pander to rhetoric about owning the future. In which case, iPads must really be helping these kids, right? I mean, why else would they spend so much money and time on these programs? Following this train of thought, I do a search for studies that conclude that tablets in the schools improve educational outcomes. I don't find any. But I do find a study that concludes the exact opposite. In the early 2000s, Duke University economists Jacob Vigdor and Helen Ladd "tracked the academic progress of nearly one million disadvantaged middle-school students" before and after they were issued laptops that connected to the Internet. Over five years, they discovered that reading and math scores actually went down. "Students who gain access to a home computer between the 5th and 8th grades tend to witness a persistent decline in reading and math scores," the economists wrote. After being issued laptops, the students' grades went down and stayed down for the entire duration of the study.[52] "There are already several randomized, controlled trials of schools with and without One Laptop per Child," notes Kentaro Toyama, a self-described "recovering technoholic" and former Microsoft Research Executive who worked for the company in India overseeing projects aimed at using technology to alleviate conditions leading to poverty. Now a professor at the University of Michigan and author of *Geek Heresy: Rescuing Social Change from the Cult of Technology*, he tells an interviewer that, "[g]enerally, what most of these studies show is that schools with laptops did not see their children gain anything in terms of academic achievement, in terms of grades, in terms of test scores, in terms of attendance, or in terms of supposed engagement with the classroom."[53] Why would One Tablet, One Child be any different?

Perplexed by this finding, I reach out to California-based Larry Cuban, longtime high school teacher, university professor, and author and researcher into technology in education. Larry Cuban tells me that there have been constant pressures to use technology in the classroom since the 1950s. Things that have been tried range from radio programs to instructional television. The aim is always the same—to achieve a kind of Holy Grail of reducing costs by replacing teachers with technology while improving outcomes. However, technology has not yet achieved any of these goals. But surely, I press Cuban, with the Los Angeles school board spending as much as one billion dollars to give every student a tablet there must be some kind of study that shows this is efficacious for educational outcomes? Cuban's answer is curt and to the point: "Do kids learn more? The evidence being on standardized tests, there is no evidence for it at all. There are only a few studies and the studies are designed with methodologies that are not persuasive to a larger audience. It is not done rigorously."[54] So why go through all the trouble and expense? "It's been adopted because of the hype and all the rhetoric around it," Cuban tells me. Similarly, responding to the introduction of iPads to LA school kids, Leslie Wilson of the One-to-One Institute, a nonprofit that provides technology guidance to schools and districts nationwide, says, "I haven't seen anything like this in the ten years I've been doing this work. Did they have a desired goal beyond the ever present, 'We want our kids to be twenty-first–century learners?' Why do we want every child to have an iPad? Because it will do what?"[55]

As Cuban explains it, the decisions are made based on politics and appearances. Politicians, school districts, community leaders, even parents, want to be seen doing things—making visible improvements, keeping up with the times—so they introduce flashy technologies. First laptops, and now tablets, for every student. It's got nothing to do with education and everything to do with the thinking that pervades the permanent future. Says Larry Cuban: "That is the ideology, the theory that kids need to have these devices and software for college and career."

It needs to be noted that all of this is happening against a background of deepening, systemic poverty. In Antrim County, home of Elk Rapids, Michigan, 17 percent of the population is living in poverty, and the under-eighteen poverty rate is an astonishing 30 percent.[56] Meanwhile, Los Angeles County has the highest poverty rate of California and one of the highest in the entire country, sitting at 18 percent of the population, and something in the range of 25 percent for those under eighteen. It is certainly worth asking, in the absence of evidence that the dispersal of tablets improves educational outcomes and thus prospects for prosperity down the road, whether spending millions of dollars on these programs is the best way to help the children and teens born into and likely fated to live their lives far below the poverty line.[57]

A paradox emerges, the paradox that we will come to recognize as being the heart of life in the age of future. In the educational context, the paradox is that a field traditionally about transmitting past knowledge is increasingly attempting to teach not what we already know, but *what we don't know.* Trying to teach people to create and prepare for the future—an unknowable—is a bit like teaching the blind to describe what they see. The paradox at the heart of changes in the field of education can be restated as the bigger paradox at the heart of life in the future era. When I say that the ideology of chasing the future has infected our most important institutions, I mean that institutions that formerly relied on the accumulated knowledge of the past for guidance and meaning are increasingly looking to the future ideology for direction and substance. In the fast-forward present, everyone from politicians to corporate middle managers to sixth-grade teachers want to be soothsayers and game changers. Institutions ignore proven methodologies, preferring instead to spew buzzwords like "change" and "insight" with a fervor once reserved for God and country or at least predictability and stability.

Education is just one of the primary institutions being challenged and changed by the era of permanent future. The corporate, governmental, and educational sectors are so increasingly intertwined that in many ways they are all one big institution. In the age of permanent future, this giant amalgam is attempting the impossible: at once defending its turf, and actively lending its awesome authority to the notion that each and every one of us has to own the future. The results are incongruous, confusing, and at times exhilarating. It's fascinating to watch as institutions with traditions going back thousands of years fall over themselves to embrace ideologies and policies that seem to suggest their own eventual demise. The ideology of permanent future is (not so) slowly but surely taking root in the institution.

CHAPTER 3

The Group Just Slows Us Down
Future vs. Institution

As I write this, there are 306 teams vying to be the first in the world to build a working tricorder. (I know, I know . . . again with the Tricorder!) If you're thinking Star Trek's Spock rubbing a device emitting a sound like a transistor radio stuck between AM channels over the red uniformed chest of a prone Enterprise minion, you are on the right track. That's pretty much the thing teams from the US and all over the world are competing against each other to build. It's a device "designed for consumers that would provide the ability to capture information on about 15 different health conditions and also be able to interpret that information for consumers plus be able to capture vital signs in real time and be able to stream those wirelessly."[1] Whoever builds this thing first is the winner of the Qualcomm Tricorder XPrize and a purse of $10 million.

The XPrize Foundation was officially launched in 1994, then made its mark in 1996 when its founder, tech entrepreneur, and futurist utopian Peter Diamandis announced a $10 million prize to be awarded to the first group to build a private spaceship capable of carrying three

people and flying two times within two weeks to the open space frontier. This prize was awarded in 2004 to a team funded by former
Microsoft CEO Paul Allen. The fanfare of giving out the first prize was
a public relations bonanza to Diamandis and his XPrize. Corporations
lined up to sponsor further prizes including the 2007–2010 Progressive Insurance Automotive XPrize, the 2010–2011 Wendy Schmidt Oil
Cleanup XCHALLENGE, and the ongoing 2007 Google Lunar XPrize.
Since then, prizes are coming at a furious pace. Among them include
three new ocean-related XPrizes to be launched before 2020, whose
goals, apparently, will be determined by crowdsourcing public opinion.
The message of the XPrize Foundation is as unambiguous as its crowdsourcing marketing exercises: this is how you get to the future.

Ten years ago, we might have dismissed the XPrize as an outsized
personal obsession, an outlier that doesn't actually represent any kind
of systemic change in how we think about future collectively and individually. After all, XPrize founder Diamandis is a pundit, speaker, TED
Talk regular, and author of iconic Silicon Valley text *Abundance: The
Future is Better Than You Think*. In other words, he's a professional
future-first prophet—someone who has made a career out of preaching that creativity leashed to science and technology will solve our
problems. (I get his mass e-mails for "abundance-minded thinkers"
complete with pithy zingers like "Women, we're entering your age of
abundance. Men, it's time to join the movement.") Once upon a time,
his entire line of thinking—not to mention his organization—would
have been dismissed as fringe. But the profusion of admirers, copy-cat
visionaries, and similar approaches to fostering technological research
clearly shows how the message of rapid-fire tech solutions to overarch-
ing global problems is one we very much want to hear.

As a result, the XPrize Foundation, located in Southern California, is
the leader in what is becoming the increasingly more common practice
of offering large cash prizes to the first team to achieve a technological
goal on a relatively short timeline. (In the case of the Tricorder XPrize,
the teams have about one-and-a-half years to build their devices.) But
on a deeper level, the XPrize Foundation's efforts are evidence of the
way the thought process of permanent future is becoming embedded
in the systems and institutions of society on many levels. That is, the

Tricorder XPrize is further evidence for the increasing prevalence of the cultural idea that we need new institutions and systems whose explicit and even only mission is to intervene as directly as possible in the future with the ultimate goal being domination over the what-comes-next. What we see when we look at the XPrize is, again, the philosophy of future first embodied in real life, and altering our institutions on the most elemental level. If institutions ranging from colleges to governments can't get us to the future fast enough, then we need to replace them with newer, better institutions. Or maybe, we don't need institutions at all.

o o o o o o

To learn more about the XPrize philosophy, I reach Mark Winter via Skype. Winter is the senior director of the Qualcomm Tricorder XPrize Challenge. He has had a thirty-year-plus career in Silicon Valley working for companies including Adobe and Apple. Most recently he was a founder and executive vice president of a company providing wireless monitoring of blood glucose levels for people with diabetes. I ask Winter to tell me how the XPrize works. "We as a foundation have a pipeline of great challenges that are not addressed by market forces successfully yet. And we'll shape those into an idea and then talk to business leaders and others about that and it starts to shape itself up into an idea that not only addresses a major challenge or opportunity but also is something that satisfies the interests a large sponsor might have like the Qualcomm corporation."[2]

Not only, Winter explains to me, can the XPrize provide otherwise nonexistent market incentives to solve a problem, it can also help change the system in general, eliminating barriers that might be preventing market forces from addressing an issue. Winter uses the example of private space flight to illustrate the way XPrize has advanced an entire industry. "The FAA was saying initially, 'There will be no private space flight.' Today there not only is private space flight supported on a regulatory level, but look at all the companies entering that space, largely born out of Peter Diamandis's vision of a space industry that is private." Winter sees a similar progression down the road when the Food and Drug Administration (FDA) is asked to come to terms with the rise of the handheld tricorder. "We're really trying to follow the same pattern in a health care space. We have a close affiliation with the FDA. They are believers in helping to create this migration to personal medical technology, that is the important role for them to play."

As far as the XPrize is considered, the best thing government agencies and other institutions can do is to believe—believe that these kinds of competitions will cut through the red tape and get us to the future first. And, it seems, governments are coming around. "There has been a massive expansion of government competitions," Mark Winter tells me. "There was actually an act passed during the first Obama administration that focused on creating or allowing federal agencies to run their own incentive-based competitions. Some of our great successes have been the model that is now being followed by government. We believe there is a trend toward using incentive-based competitions to get the best ideas out that we can in order to solve challenges. We're working closely with governments and actually supporting that process, we probably know more about designing these competitions than any other organization in the world."

The plainspoken, jovial Winter points out to me that the XPrize model is being rapidly adopted. Exhibit one is of course the ongoing growth of XPrize and its many sponsors. And exhibit two is, as Mark Winter mentioned, the astonishing number of diverse departments of the United States government now running various XPrize-like challenges. At the forefront is the once-secretive but increasingly public federal agency known as the Defense Advanced Research Projects Agency (DARPA). DARPA has run a bunch of challenges already, including one on the subject of driverless cars. As I write this, the agency is developing a new challenge with a two million dollar prize. The goal of the challenge is to develop "fully automatic network defense systems. DARPA envisions teams creating automated systems that would compete against each other to evaluate software, test for vulnerabilities, generate security patches and apply them to protected computers on a network."[3]

Okay, it hardly seems surprising that government departments developed expressly to be experimental in their approach and aggressive in their timelines would eagerly adopt these kinds of competitions. But then there's the State Department with their Innovation in Arms Control Challenge asking, "How Can Technology Support Future Arms Control Inspections?";[4] the Department of Labor, asking for someone to "create an innovative tool that lets an informed consumer find out if a business is obeying the law when it comes to paying workers properly";[5] and even the National Endowment for the Arts, offering a $60,000 reward for coming up with a way to "present arts data artfully."[6] There are also regular contests emerging from the Department of Justice, the Environmental Protection Agency, the Department of Energy, and the Centers for Disease Control and Prevention. To keep track of it all, there's a nicely presented and regularly updated federal government website—Challenge.gov. Then there's exhibit three—organizations and ad hoc groups following XPrize's example by problem solving via high-tech development achieved outside of the traditional institutions. These groups aren't sitting around waiting for the government to get its act together. The pools of money being directed by the "innovative" tech sector working largely outside of academia and government are becoming something more like a decent-sized lake. The modestly named Bill and Melinda Gates Foundation famously offered a Reinvent the Toilet Challenge, doling out $400,000 in prize money in 2011 for a toilet that could bring sanitation for the 2.5 billion people in the world without access to electricity and running water.[7] They have also partnered with the XPrize to offer a prize for an effective means of diagnosing tuberculosis in the developing world. Then there's the annually awarded Hult Prize. The goal of this prize is to "identify and launch the most compelling social business ideas—start-up enterprises that tackle grave issues faced by billions of people." Winners receive one million dollars in seed capital, as well as mentorship and advice from the international business community.[8] In 2013, the winning team, coming out of McGill University in Montreal, took home the prize for a business aiming to promote and cultivate the consumption of insects (a.k.a. micro livestock) to alleviate world hunger.[9] Then there's the Smart Tech Foundation, which has launched the Smart Tech Firearms Challenge. They're offering winners a funding package including $50,000 to "apply user authentication technologies to a fire-arm," and $100,000 to develop and refine a prototype.[10] This fund was initiated by Ron Conway, a prolific angel investor (Google, Facebook, Twitter, Zappos), and entrepreneurs Jim Pitkow and Don Kendall. "We looked at this and said there's been a systemic failure in the level of innovation and capitalization in this area," Pitkow told *Fast Company.* "Well, we know how to foster innovation."[11] There are even other groups competing in the all-important personal medical diagnostic tool space. Mike Lazaridis, one of the founders of BlackBerry maker Research In Motion announced a $100 million fund to invest in medical tricord-ers.[12] Another pool of money for tricorders doesn't bother Mark Winter: "What we hope is that some of the teams coming out of this competition will actually be in the position to access that money."

The Lazaridis fund isn't a contest, per se, but it is an end-run around traditional methods of funding new technologies and research. In the past, when the rich wanted to foster research and development in science and technology, they gave to a university or a hospital and were content to have their name affixed to a plaque over a new laboratory. Now, the rich are actively pursuing their causes in very specific ways that all share one particular characteristic: immediate application in the world; being first to usher in the future. They pursue these hyper-specific upgrades via contests, investments, and even the founding of their very own labs and not-for-profit research spaces and corporations operating outside the traditional university/hospital structure. "Billionaires With Big Ideas Are Privatizing American Science" goes the headline of a *New York Times* article that estimates America's billionaires could spend around $125 billion over the next ten years trying to fast forward the future. Modest goals include North Dakota oil man Harold Hamm's plan to "eradicate diabetes in our lifetime" and Utah billionaire Jon M. Huntsman's plan to direct his money toward "making sure cancer is vanquished."[13]

Though each organization running a contest or funding and pursuing research has its own goals, there is an unmistakable shared vision. It's a vision of technological upgrade that can cut through institutions and solve just about every problem. Pursue the prize whether you're a bunch of underfunded PhD students, a bunch of government scientists, or just inventors working out in the garage. Institutions don't matter. Regulations are just in the way. We need to be relentlessly pursuing the future until we finally get it right. It's a vision in which we engineer away intractable problems. Tech can intervene in just about everything from gun deaths to lack of sanitation to the slow pace of tricorder development (after all, it's been, like, fifty years since this thing debuted on *Star Trek*). It's the belief—even within government agencies themselves—that traditional, organizational approaches take too long and cost too much. Instead, if we want to get to the future faster and better, we need to put our faith in individuals and what Jim Pitkow of the Smart Tech Foundation calls his organization's preference for "free market alternatives."[14] This attitude is epitomized in a quick anecdote: When the president of the United States touched down at a famous Silicon Valley company, a mid-level employee decided against attending his speech. "I'm making more of a difference than anybody in government could possibly make," he told a colleague.[15]

o   o   o   o   o   o

As institution-busting challenge models expand, traditional funding for research shrinks. A 2012 article in the *Journal of the American Medical Association* sums it up this way: "Biomedical science in the United States faces an unprecedented, dismal situation, with application success rates for NIH extramural research projects at an all-time low."[16] This was *before* the 2013 budget sequestration which forced the National Institutes of Health to trim a further $1.5 billion from its budget and led to at least 640 fewer research projects being funded by the organization.[17] No wonder a group describing themselves as a "coalition of business, higher education, scientific, patent, and other organizations" representing old school institutions like the Aerospace Industries Association, the American Heart Association, the American Society for Microbiology, Industrial Research Institute, Institute of Electrical and Electronics Engineers, and fifty or so similar organizations all but begged Congress to restore lost research funding. Like the university presidents demanding funding to help transform their campuses into innovation hubs, these institutions fear their obsolescence and seek funding to stave off the new anti-institution methodology taking hold. Appearing at a 2014 United States Senate Committee on Appropriations Hearing on "Driving Innovation Through Federal Investments," the umbrella organization released this statement: "While U.S. federal R&D investment was once on a consistent growth path, we are today coming nowhere close to that. Projected U.S. investments fall far short of GDP growth and even further below China's rate of investment."[18] Following this came a 2015 report out of MIT called "Future Postponed," which makes the case for massive increases in basic research funding and details fifteen areas where increasing funding could foster American innovation. The report, put together by a high-powered committee of scientists, was necessary because, as committee chair and MIT physicist Marc Kastner told journalists, science funding is "the lowest it has been since the Second World War as a fraction of the federal budget."[19]

It's a strange situation. Despite—or perhaps because of—the rhetoric of future, the government is struggling to maintain or, as one might expect, increase funding for scientific research. Part of this is obviously the result of the bizarre world of congressional lawmaking, but another part of it emerges from a sensibility that the really important stuff is getting done regardless. Maybe the government doesn't need to fund research laboratories and institutions the way they used to? After all, we've got private companies and innovation institutes circulating millions of dollars in prize money. Google and XPrize are on the case. The future, it seems, is being taken care of through means other than traditional investment in the usual institutions.

When I was a kid in the 1970s and '80s, the launch of a spacecraft was still a big deal. In the mid-'80s I recall a TV rolled into my Maryland classroom, several classes crowded together onto the floor so we could watch Christa McAuliffe become the first teacher to go to space. Instead, we all watched in numb shock as the Challenger exploded seventy-three seconds after liftoff, killing McAuliffe and the other six crew members. It was a terrible, tragic end to an optimistic, adventurous era whose peak was the 1969 triumph of putting a man on the moon.

The 1986 Challenger mission wasn't just a horrible blow to NASA and America—in many ways it would eventually prove to be the end of government-controlled space exploration, as the space shuttle program never really recovered from what turned out to be a technical malfunction triggered by the outside temperature during launch time.

Before that fateful, fatal moment, the pursuit of future was done by the institution in full view of the public who gathered in their schools and living rooms to watch the power of the collective launch men and women into space. The Teacher in Space program was an excellent example of how we thought about future and its attainability. The program's ostensible mission was to get more young people excited about the sciences, but its overall effect was to entrance us with the allure of the national project and pull us into the optimistic orbit of can-do nationalism. McAuliffe was supposed to deliver a school lesson from space. The whole thing was part of a program Ronald Reagan launched in 1984 in which teachers would be selected to go to space then return to the classroom, the idea being to stimulate interest in science and technology among young people in school and, eventually, help win the space race and the Cold War. Kids around the country, myself included, gathered in classrooms to watch her ascent. Instead, we watched the descent not just of the remains of the shuttle, but of the remains of a whole idea—that institutions had a lock on the future.

Over the last few hundred years, institutions have held sway when it came to massive technological projects. Of course there were individual inventors, but by far the most extensive technological research, development, and implementation projects were mounted by either governments or corporations acting as government proxies. Game changing shifts ranging from railroads to telephone wires to the interstate highway system, the nuclear bomb, space exploration, and of course the infrastructure that would become the Internet all were developed under the auspices of government institutions. Modern governments have pretty much always seen developing and maintaining technological prowess as an essential aspect of their role as stewards of the nation-state.

In the midst of the Cold War, techno-achievement as orchestrated by entire nations became a crucial part of the rhetorical battle. After the 1957 *Sputnik 1* launch sent the first man into space, many around the world, including anti-Communists, "came to believe that the Soviet Union had indeed cracked the problem of innovation and use of new technology."[20] It was the Soviet success in space that allowed Khrushchev to declare that the Soviet Union would inevitably triumph over capitalism. After all, the country's technological prowess, unfettered by the relentless competition and money grubbing of the West, was increasingly renowned. In his book *The Shock of the Old*, British historian David Edgerton recounts an old Soviet-era joke: An inventor goes to the ministry and says: "I have invented a new buttonholing machine for our clothing industry." "Comrade," says the minister, "we have no use for your machine: don't you realize this is the age of the Sputnik?"[21] "Much more," writes Edgerton, "has been invested by governments in invention in aviation than in shipping, or in nuclear power than other energy technologies."[22] Up until now, culture and progress had always been intertwined. The national institution sets the agenda, decides what kinds of technologies to pursue, and makes that decision both for scientific and political/cultural reasons.

Looking back now at the twenty-year period of the space race we can see how it captivated people around the world and set up what would be the greatest shared arrival at the "future" ever known to humanity. First *Sputnik*, then America's answer: tens of millions watching the *Apollo* lunar landing on live TV (this, coming only twenty years after the introduction of television as a mainstream commodity in the United States and elsewhere, itself can be considered a futuristic moment). And when Neil Armstrong uttered those famous words, there was a sense of both commonality and exceptionalism. "One small step for [a] man, one giant leap for mankind." Future was still a collective project, something aspired to by the entire human race (though some countries—most notably the United States, would of course do future better and get there first). Future was not (yet) your burden to achieve. Future lay on all our shoulders and was the responsibility of the nation and its institutions. Progress was to still to be found in the collective exercise of the commons, in the decisions of the government as representative of the people's will. Then the shift: what was once seen as a collective enterprise for the betterment of humanity became something

individuals could and should seek to own and control. "A few generations ago," notes David Brooks in a *New York Times* column, "people
grew up in and were comfortable with big organizations—the army,
corporations and agencies. . . . Now nobody wants to be an Organization Man. We like start-ups, disrupters and rebels . . . people assume
that big problems can be solved by swarms of small, loosely networked
nonprofits and social entrepreneurs."[23]

As just one example of this general shift, today we have a whole
new conception of space travel. A company called Planetary Resources
(backed by billionaire investors including Google's Larry Page and Eric
Schmidt) is promising to mine moons and asteroids. Richard Branson's Virgin Galactic is offering $250,000 zero-gravity flights and has
its eye on space tourism and suborbital trips with zero friction and
gravity—New York City to Tokyo in two hours. Jeff Bezos of Amazon
works out vigorously every morning in preparation for the moment
when Blue Origin, the space exploration company he founded on
300,000 acres of land in rural Texas, is ready to send him into orbit.[24]
And, as we've already touched on, entrepreneur/tech-cheerleader Peter
Diamandis has partnered with Google and launched the Google Lunar
XPRIZE competition, a $30 million prize for the first private entity
that can land a robot on the Moon, get it to travel at least 500 meters,
and transmit images and information back to Earth. Twenty-six groups
have entered.[25] In the meantime, Paypal's founder Elon Musk, now
head of California's SpaceX, celebrated what is now generally seen as
the first successful launch of a privately developed manned spacecraft
on a fee-paying mission. The mission was to resupply the International Space Station and their client was the United States government.
Fee-paying missions on behalf of America have become necessary
because for the first time in half a century, the United States government no longer has the capability to organize its own manned flights
to space. NASA has mothballed the space shuttle and there is no new
spacecraft in the works capable of flying to the space station.[26] Manned
space exploration—the ultimate metaphor for future—has become
another territory for individuals to own, control and disrupt.

Back in 1986, it would have been inconceivable to imagine that
space exploration would be ceded, more or less, to the private sector.

Of course the US government is still pouring a lot of money into space exploration as the main buyer for SpaceX's services—SpaceX has a $1.6 billion contract to ship cargo to the international space station, and a $2.6 billion contract to fly astronauts to the space station starting in 2017.[27] But it's the difference between renting and owning; the US now has to rent its space expertise and facilities from private corporations. (Including Google, which made a one billion dollar investment in SpaceX in early 2015, no doubt influenced by what one article describes as Google founders Larry Page and Sergey Brin's personal interest in space exploration.) Overall, contracting out to private companies may be a net benefit in terms of optimizing what the money achieves, but it sends a very different overall message to the country; nobody is gathering school children in classrooms to watch Elon Musk cheer on the next landmark fee-paying mission.

□ □ □ □ □ □

I'm suspicious by nature, especially of grand sweeping theories of how things were way back when. So I decide to call up Matt Novak. Novak is a self-described amateur historian and futurist best known for his popular and often very funny blog *Paleofuture*, which lived on the website of the Smithsonian Institute and now resides on Gizmodo.com.[28] *Paleofuture* chronicles what people in the recent past thought about the future. Novak blogs about advertisements, commercials, TV shows—*The Jetsons!*—newspaper articles, 1960s time capsules, letters to the year 2000, and so much more.

I reach Matt Novak via Skype in his hometown of Los Angeles. He listens attentively to my theory about the move to a different conception of future in which individuals are empowered and even required to pursue the time to come. But he's not convinced. He warns me about making blanket statements about a certain generation and their conception of the future. Though we view the 1950s and 1960s as a time of great collective optimism and enthusiasm for the future in general and space travel in particular, that wasn't necessarily the case. As he tells me, "For the adults of the time, only once did public support of the *Apollo* space project go over 50 percent. Most people didn't believe it was worth the money to go to the moon, approval rates hovered at between 35 to 45 percent through 1960s, and only once did it go to 51 percent, right after we landed on the moon. Part of the reason we have this impression is because people like my parents were talking about how great things were, and part of the reason they thought that was because they were kids."[29]

Nevertheless, Novak in many ways is buttressing my argument. There was, in the 1950s and '60s, a conception of a collective project known as future. People agreed generally we should move to it together, as a nation or a group of nations with shared commonalities, or even as a planet. They did not necessarily agree on exactly what direction the country should go in, what aspect of future we should concentrate on. President Kennedy and his administration thought it was the moon. Clearly many Americans disagreed, but no one was saying: Let's just let the rich fund the future. Let's just get out of the way and let people fight amongst themselves for the chance to own progress. It wasn't necessarily the optimism about future we imagine those living in the age of Neil Armstrong to have had, but it was a pervasive attitude, a general agreement that the future could only be reached together, individuals collectively part of an overall march toward progress, leaders up front, showing the way. Matt Novak's *Paleofuture* archive reminds me just how much the future-as-national project narrative was advanced by the prevailing popular culture of the time. In the 1930s, '40s, '50s, and even '60s, the future was not just pursued by the primary institutions, it was also pushed forward by the first great wave of pop culture coming to us in the form of science fiction movies, radio plays, cartoons, sci-fi paperbacks, and theme parks. Even a "futuristic" style of architecture sprang up to evoke this Jetsons-like coming age. It was called Googie (sound familiar?), "a style," as Matt Novak explains, "built on exaggeration; on dramatic angles; on plastic and steel and neon and wide-eyed technological optimism."[30] Googie became particularly popular with the developing highway culture of the day: gas stations and drive-in restaurants and motels featured sweeping roofs and neon curves. Robot maids, rocket ships, airplane cars in every garage—the future swirled around as a new kind of benevolent magic. The future, in development by the nation's experts, required nothing more of the average individual but to enjoy speculating on its possible arrival in fifty to a hundred years.

When futuristic theme park zone Tomorrowland opened as part of Disneyland in 1955, its featured partners included leading "future-oriented" corporations like Monsanto and American Motors. The message of fun and adventure and passive entertainment was underscored by Walt Disney himself: "Tomorrow," he announced, "can be a wonderful age. Our scientists today are opening the doors of the Space Age to achievements that will benefit our children and generations to come. The Tomorrowland attractions have been designed to give you an opportunity to participate in adventures that are a living blueprint of our future."[31] In Tomorrowland, we find an evocation of the utopian, institutionally managed, collective future to come. "A '60s kid," writes the cultural critic Tim Appelo, "could cherish the illusion of evolution as progress, especially if he was watching Tomorrowland's all-robot drama the Carousel of Progress."[32] We are giving you the opportunity to participate in the future, said Walt and his partner companies. You don't create it or own it—you buy a ticket to the Carousel of Progress. The general message put out to the average person is that everything you need will be developed by "our scientists" for you. If you're not a scientist or an astronaut, you should pretty much be sitting back and enjoying the ride.

o   o   o   o   o   o

Tomorrowland was just following the rhetorical script of the industrial age. Throughout the nineteenth and well into the twentieth century, the future-as-national-spectacle was showcased in major cities from Paris to Chicago to London. These "World" Fairs featured the technological advances of future and promised more to come. They were attended by millions who came from all over the globe in the first age of global tourism to see everything from early prototypes of the fax machine to armaments powered by steam. They were the Superbowls of tech and they dwarfed by a wide margin the Vegas electronics tradeshows of today. Even the architecture of these spectacles was meant to instill a sense of awe. London's 1851 Great Exhibition of the Works of Industry of All Nations was housed in a massive greenhouse-like building dubbed The Crystal Palace. It was large enough to contain fully grown trees and sculptures—a futuristic structure deliberately envisioned as a statement of national power and an example of mankind's dominance over the natural world.

Chicago's 1893 World's Columbian Exposition was an even larger spectacle. An astonishing twenty-seven million people attended from all over the United States and the world, encountering such shimmering visions as the world's largest conveyor belt. By the next Chicago World's Fair, held in 1933, we see that despite a global depression and a brutal world war, not much had changed where the future was concerned: it was still coming, still something to be admired from afar. Officially named A Century of Progress International Exposition, its theme was technological innovation and the motto was "Science Finds, Industry Applies, Man Conforms."[33] The attitude was clear from these festivals: the future was proceeding and the millions need do nothing but pay their taxes, buy their tickets, and get ready to "conform" to what was just around the corner. The citizenry didn't create or own the future, they admired it and eventually got over being afraid of it so they could get used to how much better technological change was making their lives. At the 1933 fair, General Electric showcased its lauded research department with an elaborate display featuring all-electric kitchens with refrigerators, washers and dryers, and, most impressively, air conditioning. But the highlight for the audience was a speech–controlled train that could back up, stop, and move forward on command. The whole experience happened in a pavilion called the "House of Magic."[34]

The prevailing attitude—future-as-passive-spectacle in which the forces of government and industry shape the time to come while "man conforms"—continued even up through the 1950s and '60s, the dawn of the computer age and the golden age of a certain kind of future-longing we now look back at with nostalgia. Consider something like this 1956 ad in *Scientific American* for General Motors New Direction Ball Bearings:

A week's shopping in minutes! And you haven't moved from your car. It's that simple at the Drive-In Market of tomorrow. Just select your items from the monitor screen; electronic impulses select, assemble, deliver your order, total your bill and return your change. It's just a dream away! And when it takes shape, look for New Departure to provide the proper bearings to keep all moving parts functioning smoothly. New Departure ball bearings keep parts in perfect alignment, support loads from any angle and require little or no maintenance.

Commenting on this ad, Matt Novak writes wryly: "General Motors, like so many advertisers that would come before and after them, loved to position themselves firmly at the future's door. An association with the sleek, techno-utopian ideas that were just around the corner meant that even a product as boring as ball bearings could look as bright and sexy as a rocket to the moon."[35]

What we elegize now—the promise of robot nurses, colonies on Mars and food replication machines, even the notion that once all of humanity was connected we would establish some kind of global nervous system that would make war inconceivable—were also part of a worldview, a psychological framework. This was the future as a major thing, a giant project to be undertaken by us, but also for us. In this time, future was a kind of inevitable destiny, and the makers of future laid claim to overall social benefits that dwarfed even the rhetoric of a Google or Amazon. Consider, writes David Edgerton, "the extraordinary litany of technologies which promised peace to the world."[36] New modes of transportation and communication, from the steamship to the airplane, from the telegraph to the radio to the television, were going to unite the planet as never before, bringing "people together, ensuring a perpetual peace."[37] Meanwhile, the rhetoric swirling around the new technologies of warfare held that they would be so powerful that they would have the paradoxical effect of actually ending war—the risk of being on the wrong end of a machine gun, and then a bombing raid and then a nuclear warhead would be just too great. Again, the message was clear—sit back and let these problems get worked out by the technology. We're on the case and pretty soon you'll be farming from your living room while watching an educational show about Laplanders—who are way more like you than you realized!

We watch the future arrive and are intrigued by it, but we don't see (and are not invited to see) our role in it as active; we don't imagine that our role is to start a killer app for the locomotive or offer a hefty sum for whoever can build a more efficient musket to help out on the battlefield. We still see ourselves as in thrall to the fortunes and vagaries of a predestined future we primarily imagine as both being mostly similar to our present, and as being beyond our *individual* capacity to alter.

At the World Fair held in the borough of Queens in New York City in 1939, David Sarnoff, the powerful head of radio giant RCA, unveiled a massive pavilion formed in the shape of a giant vacuum tube. Those who entered it were welcomed to the "Radio Living Room of Tomorrow."[38] It's not hard to guess what the room was showcasing. It was the modern miracle that would change everything. It was television. At a press conference ten days before the fair and this exhibit were to officially open, Sarnoff stood before a row of veiled sets. "It is with a feeling of humbleness," he said, "that I come to this moment of announcing the birth in this country of a new art so important in its implications that it is bound to affect all society. Television is an art which shines like a torch of hope to a troubled world. It is a creative force which we must learn to utilize for the benefit of mankind. . . . Now, ladies and gentlemen, we add sight to sound!"[39] The curtain was pulled back and the press corps were treated to the line of televisions all broadcasting David Sarnoff standing triumphantly on the stage before them. "It was," writes author and technological historian Tim Wu, "an image of such power as to overwhelm facts."[40]

The facts became these: Once again, a great corporation had harnessed the latest technologies to turn the mundane into the marvelous. As with the telegraph and the telephone, the doings of humanity could now be instantly projected. Once again, the present could now be said to be available simultaneously and instantaneously. For most of the short history of television, this meant millions of people instantly connected to the same broadcast, living as one in the present that unfurled with such rapidity it felt more like the future than images of things that had already happened or were just then happening. What was television? It was radio with pictures, it was a "torch of hope to a troubled world," it was a fait accompli, something you acquiesced to and accepted into your living room as an unquestioned good.

This was the age of unmitigated belief in the promise of technological progress on a cohesive and collective level. For a time, it even had a name, the Progressive Era. It had an early spokesperson in President Theodore Roosevelt who exhorted civil servants and elected politicians "to look ahead and plan out the right kind of civilization."[41] Here change was embraced, yes, but only the right kind of change leading to the right kind of civilization—Fordlandia meets Tomorrowland. Here, unceasing change came with the guarantee that essentially everything would still be the same—just better. Writes one scholar about the progressive era in the US, "The term *progressive* connoted a steady, teleological, restrained pace of improvement. . . . This peculiarly American paradox of kinetic change made stable appears to have contributed to the ubiquity of efficiency claims in this era."[42]

This was a kind of transitional era of future thinking: one in which the rhetoric of society positioned change as very much under the control of those beneficent institutions who knew precisely how to look after us. Yes, much was changing, but it was all good, there was nothing to worry about. I'm reminded, here, of the 1920s discovery by Edwin Hubble that far from being static, galaxies were (and of course still are) actually drifting away from each other. The universe was on the move. Before Hubble, it was a given that the planets and stars stayed where they were put, beacons of eternal light. "This idea," notes a historian, "had settled into the brains of men as deeply as an ingrained universal truth can settle."[43] The new unsettling realization that the perpetually shifting universe was probably the result of a giant helium explosion fifteen billion years ago required some fair degree of grappling with. Enter the notion of the Progressive Era: stability, would, paradoxically, be brought about by ongoing change. In a 1929 speech to the United States Chamber of Commerce, famous General Motors inventor Charles F. Kettering warned of "advancing waves of other people's progress" and instructed the corporate powers in attendance that they needed to "organize departments of systematic change-making."[44] And for a time, this seemed to be true. After all, this was also the period of the long boom—a historical epoch of unprecedented economic growth spurred by cheap oil which in turn allowed such innovations as the widespread use of chemical fertilizer and pesticides on crops. Technology as liberally dispensed by the great overseers. The world is richer, fatter and more comfortable than ever before. The universe is smoothly coasting along toward the-almost-here future, so sit back and relax.

o o o o o o

One of the points that Matt Novak makes to me is that we are vastly overstating the role of the private sector in space exploration, because although the work is being done by private companies, a large percentage of the funding is coming from NASA and other government institutions—you can't make much money on space missions that aren't ultimately funded by the government/taxpayer. I hear what Novak is saying, and I have to ask: Why are we so keen to emphasize the fact that space is now a territory dominated by profit-oriented corporations even when that statement is not necessarily true? But truth isn't the point here. The point is that perception around "future" has changed. There is a rupture in the rhetoric. The commons, the group, the collective—they will not get to the future. The individual and the individual's feral proxy—the new future-first (anti)institution—they are the future, they are what will get you there.

As Matt Novak points out to me during the course of our conversation, Obama evokes the future in a very similar way to how Nixon—and before him, Kennedy—evoked the future: America has long been concerned with being on the technological upswing. But, again, there's the change in perception, in rhetoric, that brings about the change in substance. Once, the specter of the Soviets being first to launch a manned spaceship into orbit was a galvanizing force. It was equivalent to Pearl Harbor. The blow had been struck and we all had to pull together. Today, when we ask people to join together and support institutional efforts to seize the future, we are evoking a competition with the rest of the world that few of us seem profoundly invested in. What threat are we desperately competing with? And what are we pulling together to achieve? The popular fantasies of today revolve around creating global name brands, conquering the world by offering greater ease of connection or shopping convenience. Aside from occasional presidential pronouncements, or newspaper columnists raising the threat of profound moral struggle to preserve our way of life supposedly under shadow of the (Chinese, Indian, Israeli, Brazilian) hordes on the cusp of techno-overtake, nobody at gatherings like SXSWi is talking about what they can do for their country. They're talking about what their country can do for them—get the hell out of their way as they bulldoze a new path straight to the future.

In Yale computer scientist David Gelernter's novel *1939: The Lost World of the Fair*, an homage to the great era of institutional futurism, the author recreates a time when we believed we could shape the future in amazing ways collectively through our institutions.[45] But here's the thing: he wrote the book while recovering from a package bomb sent to his office by the Unabomber, Ted Kaczynski. The bomb blew off most of his right hand and left him almost blind in one eye. Ironically, by then, like Kaczynski himself, he had become disillusioned with technological change. But unlike Kaczynski, who sought to kill scientists in order to bring a halt to technological change, Gelernter believed in the opposite problem: that we had lost our fervor, our collective faith in the revolutionary possibilities of technology to build a better world for all. Where Kaczynski saw only destruction at the hands of, as he wrote in a letter to Gelernter two years after the attack and still in the midst of his murderous campaign, "techno-nerds like you [who] are changing the world,"[46] Gelernter saw a time when we had stopped believing as a society in technology as a uniting force that makes the entire world better.

In many ways, both men were right: a whole new epoch of techno-futurism was about to emerge with far-reaching and unexplored consequences for individuals and the planet. This would be the era we currently live in, the era of chasing future. This era would achieve the feat of at once making technology more pervasive and powerful and potentially more destructive than ever before, while also making it far less cohesive, far less meaningful, far less likely to bring us together to work toward common goals for the betterment of all living things on the earth. The full-fledged unhindered embrace of technology continues, but without the promise of progress anchored to ongoing stability, without the sense of working toward and for something greater than ourselves.

o o o o o o

Now, let's get back to the Tricorder Challenge. The details of this device, how it is envisioned, and why there is a specific challenge for it are very telling. Mark Winter, XPrize senior director of the challenge, and I start talking about the tricorder generally and what we'll be able to do with it. "If we get it all right we have a great chance to transform health care for the better, lower the cost of care and help improve millions of lives." How will all this be achieved? The tricorder will alter the entire health care system by "empowering" people. Winter uses that word—empower—several times. People will be given the responsibility to not just take care of themselves but to perform the kinds of tests and analysis that were previously left up to medical professionals. Any technology that shifts power from the institution to the individual is liberating. "The big theme that we are talking about today," Mark Winter tells me, "is that it is a personalized medical health care strategy that is really relying on individuals taking charge of their health." It's no accident that the XPrize Foundation has pushed forward projects that seek to emphasize the role of the individual over the collective. This is a deliberate choice. Why should hospitals and accredited health care professionals have access to knowledge about my health that I don't have? Why should governments control access to outer space? As Winter explains to me, it's a philosophy that's all about giving individuals the tools they need to chase and own the future. "I think that's true and that as a trend that we're seeing all around the world, people are relying less on government and institutions to do things for them, we're seeing an emergence of more of this with the DIY movement and the Maker movement—more and more people taking their future into their hands and being innovative."

Today, innovation and individualism go hand-in-hand. The notion of the tricorder isn't just appealing to the XPrize Foundation because it's an exciting device that has been floating around pop culture for the last fifty years. It isn't just appealing because it will be disruptive to the present-day model of health care delivery. It isn't just appealing because a major company was willing to back it (Qualcomm, a telecommunications company, has no specific interest in tricorders but clearly a vested interest in generally increasing our reliance on a wide range of wireless devices). In talking to Mark Winter it emerges that the appeal of the tricorder runs deeper, tapping into the same subterranean currents that are reshaping our mental landscape and bringing us to the age of future. The appeal beneath the hype and rhetoric is for a device that shifts responsibility for controlling and owning the future to the individual. Any such device or technology is an automatic upgrade, an inherent net positive; breaking down institutions is a by-product of that, since institutions, whether they are educational, governmental or even corporate, slow down the individual, slow down the race to future. So we cut through the fat, empower the individual and create new anti-institution institutions capable of bringing about even faster cycles of tech upgrade. As Peter Thiel puts it: "There's this alternate virtual world in which there's no stuff, it's all zeros and ones on a computer, you can reprogram it, you can make the computer do anything you want it to. Maybe that is the best way you can actually help things in this country."[47]

Will the Tricorder work? Will it really solve a wide range of health care problems ranging from lack of access to doctors to the ordering of unnecessary tests? Well, we have no idea. But the bigger question is: Does the contest model really work better to advance technological solutions to the world's problems? I ask Winter if the XPrize or anybody else had done a study or any kind of analysis on the efficacy of incentive-driven challenges versus traditional research. He told me he didn't know of any research of that ilk. So how, I asked him, do we know that the XPrize model is actually the better way to stimulate research into applied technology? "Is there any other way?" Mark Winter asks me. "What are the other paths in front of us, show me an alternative path that would work as well. Give us a viable option. I have not seen it yet."

This is more than just impatience—it's ideology. When Peter Thiel founded PayPal, he envisioned it as a way to disrupt, as George Packer writes in his book *The Unwinding*, "the ancient technology of paper money" and "create an alternate currency online that would circumvent government controls." At PayPal meetings, Thiel revved up the troops by telling them that "PayPal will give citizens worldwide more direct control over their currencies than they ever had before." He told his staff, "It will be nearly impossible for corrupt governments to steal wealth from people through their old means because if they try, the people will switch to dollars or pounds or yen, in effect dumping the worthless local currency for something more secure."[48] What do Peter Thiel and many of the suddenly rich dot-com gurus of the '90s want to achieve? As George Packer writes, Thiel and many of his cohorts are pushing for "an America in which people [. . .] no longer rely on old institutions."[49]

CHAPTER 4

Data Harvest

Owning the Future and Everyone In It

I get lost looking for the ESRI compound. For some reason, my GPS can't find the address I have for the company's headquarters, which is ironic—ESRI, a mapping company, doesn't seem to be on the map. I drive around Redlands, California, a small city of 70,000, trying to get my bearings. Redlands is sixty miles or so east of Los Angeles. It sits below a modest mountain range, and occasional glimpses of cloud-clinging peaks distract me from my mission: finding the head-quarters of the world's market leader in Geographic Information Systems (GIS). I end up on a small road running between two orange groves. I can see the fruit dangling from the trees. I pull over. For a life-long East Coaster, it's a great California moment—alone in the perfect sunny morning smelling the tang of the orchard. I linger for as long as I can justify before resuming my mission, finding the compound of the biggest company in Redlands and one of the least known but most influential software purveyors in the world.

Having given up on my GPS, I eventually manage to return to the main road running through town. I pull into a mini-mall and ask an elderly gentleman if he knows where the company is. Of course he does. ESRI's been based in Redlands since CEO and owner Jack Dangermond started it in 1969. Founded to apply new technology to land use management, ESRI has grown exponentially over the last forty years. The kind gentleman tells me to keep on going up the main road and I pretty much won't be able to miss it. As it turns out, I'm no more than a three-minute drive from the ESRI compound. I thank the gods of tech for letting me get lost—which gave me the opportunity to get at least a sniff of what this area once looked like when orange groves, not high-tech hubs, dominated the landscape. I pull into the compound with a few minutes to spare.

When I write that we are obsessed with, and increasingly organizing our society around, shaping and owning future, I mean that literally. Our pursuit of the future is not metaphorical or hypothetical, it is actual. I'm visiting ESRI because it is one of the primary places where people go to figure out how they can know what is going to happen before it happens; ESRI is in the business of predicting the future.

ESRI (originally Environmental Systems Research Institute) is attached to many widely diverse projects, but its core product is a multidimensional, interactive map that allows for the buffet-style combination of super-detailed 3-D mapping with all the data you can eat. Think of it as Google Maps hooked up to live feeds of data that might include things like constantly updated traffic, weather, crime reports, and credit card activity. Sounds pretty cool, right? But minor start-ups with pie-in-the-sky business plans get more press than ESRI. ESRI operates under the radar, working almost exclusively with other companies and governments. Still it's what ESRI, its collaborators, and its handful of competitors are doing that shows just how dramatically we are changing our approach to the future.

ESRI's geographic information system (GIS) mapping software is used in almost every country on the planet. The company's clients include major oil outfits around the world, scores of federal agencies ranging from the Environmental Protection Agency to the Department of Defense, the cities of Los Angeles and Beijing, the state of Maryland, police departments across the world including law enforcement in major cities like New York City, Washington DC, and Vancouver, and companies ranging from Starbucks to major banks and telecoms. And unlike a lot of much better-known tech darlings, ESRI consistently makes a lot of money. According to *Forbes*, Jack Dangermond is the 554th richest man on the planet and ESRI (which is still privately owned), brings in about a billion dollars a year in revenue.[1]

ESRI's Redlands campus is, unsurprisingly, beautiful. Tropical flora spill out onto paths that twist around unassuming low-slung buildings. It reminds me of Google's headquarters campus only less groomed and significantly smaller. Inside ESRI's buildings, things look a bit more—well—business-oriented than what you'd see at Google. Here there are no arcade games and bowls of candy and interns zipping past on Segways. ESRI gives off more of the sense of *important activity being conducted*. But despite the aura of substance, it is remarkably open for a tech corporation—for, really, any corporation. When I request meetings with ESRI executives, I am eventually set up with an entire day of interviews featuring no fewer than seven different ESRI higher-ups.

I start out talking with Peter Eredics, a steady, solid guy who manages ESRI's forestry operations. It's a good place to start, since, as Eredics tells me, "the forest industry is one of the first industries that ESRI built its business on."[2] Eredics tells me how ESRI goes about converting a forest into a three-dimensional treasure trove of data. It starts with the scan. In the same way we scan documents in an office, ESRI scans landscapes. "Forests are the most important base layers, and then you would have streams, lakes, roads, ownership, who are your neighbors—all this data has to go into the system." Once ESRI has scanned the land via remote sensing and aerial photography, and all the borders and delineations are identified, including the types of trees in different areas, then the real fun can begin. Say your forest is an area subject to severe windstorms. "We can look at slope or terrain, and analyze wind patterns to determine where you are having the biggest challenges. We can mash the data together with soils, with tree species information, to determine . . . the best species to plant, and that would be used by the foresters to go out and replant, as well as [by] harvesting teams to log and salvage any of the trees that were blown down. If you map out where the windthrow may be occurring, you can change your practices based on what you're seeing and then design plans that mitigate the potential of this kind of disaster."

What's the end game here? I ask Eredics. "It's to develop short and long term plans, where you are going to harvest, where you are going to replant, it could be wild forests or plantation forests. It's to do predictions or calculations, predict future yield, determine optimal rotations, cutting times, harvesting times, trying to predict risks and future vulnerabilities, forest fire or pine beetle or wind or other influences from weather like tornadoes."

Software for trees isn't exactly teleportation, but the language Eredics uses is our way into a bold new era. Predict, calculate, plan, determine, and, of course, future. Weather isn't outside of your control any more than the question of what tree species will grow best in mildly acidic soil bordered by a creek and a highway. Working with ESRI and their partners, foresters can develop a map of the land with data going back several hundred years on everything from rainfall in your area to growth rates of specific types of trees in your specific soil to the frequency of tornadoes. All of this can then be used to do the really important thing: decide what to plant, where to plant, how to plant, and when to plant, all based on what the data predicts is going to happen in the next ten, twenty or even a hundred years (some of those trees take a while to grow). Peter Eredics tells me that when he first started out in forestry, long-term planning maps included using pencil crayons to shade in the different kinds of trees. To bring in other data, they "used acetate overlays, inventory on top of our soils map, water map, [to] build up the layers." It would take four days to generate a map to show what you were planning, and when it was done, it was done, you weren't going to rip it up and start the process all over again using entirely different sets of assumptions. Today you can try hundreds of different land use scenarios, including moving roads and streams and swamps with the click of a mouse.

But ESRI isn't making a billion dollars a year helping people to decide how many Christmas trees America's going to need in 2050. As I discover, a whirlwind of major companies and institutions are using the exact same technology that helps the foresters with the exact same underlying intentions—to figure out what's going to happen before it happens.

So let's move on to my meeting with Simon Thompson, director of Commercial Solutions at ESRI. Thompson gives me a quick overview of what other kinds of commercial entities are now using ESRI GIS mapping. "It's an incredibly diverse area," he says, "people like agro businesses, Monsanto, then people like McDonald's, or a retailer receiving McCain French fries, there's a whole range of ways that this connects."[3] Agriculture I get—it's not that much different from forestry; there's land and data, and ESRI can bring those things together for better management. But what's a McDonald's or a grocery store chain got to do with all of this? Thompson explains that they come to ESRI for help divining the future, or, as he puts it, to get answers to the question: "What's the pattern?"

Let's unpack this a bit using examples Simon Thompson gives me. More and more, retailers ranging from Starbucks to Target want to do specific location-based marketing and promotion. They don't just want to dump a truckload of coupons into the world. They want to know precisely where to put those coupons—what areas will reach what kinds of people. Then they want to know how it went, how many people used the coupon, who they were, where they were, etc., so they can apply that data to their next promotion. "They offer a coupon through e-mail. People immediately want to see how effective that is, and location is becoming a huge part of that." And not only that, but as Thompson explains to me, many retailers want to connect all of this to their supply chain—they don't want you to show up with your coupon and find that the product is sold out or not in yet; they also don't want to have a tower of items in one store that aren't selling while the customer stares longingly at an empty shelf in another store. This goes way beyond tracking page impressions on a website. It's about taking that tracking and extending it out of the virtual and into real places and spaces. ESRI's location-based services can help with all that by bringing the data together in one interactive map that can tell companies who is buying what, where, when, and even how. Data about how people pay, where they live, if they are using a coupon or discount code, what time they are making their purchases—all of that can be integrated into an ever-widening picture that includes traffic patterns (garnered from cell phone and GPS use), weather, time of year and day, and so on and so on. All this amalgamated data pulled into real time can show a retailer what is happening as it happens and, perhaps more importantly, capture that data forever so that what happened before can be used to understand what is very likely to happen next. As Thompson explains: "So we can look at the intensity of search by product and brand and category, and then overlay the behavior afterwards." I'm struck by that phrase: *overlay the behavior afterwards.* Someone searches online for the nearest Starbucks. What happens next? Do they go there? Are they encouraged to go there by a coupon that pops up? If they don't go, where do they go (perhaps a competitor)? Before, much of this was unknowable. Now, behaviors can be plotted, studied, predicted. Indeed, a study out of Carnegie Mellon University found that smartphone users had their locations captured "hundreds of times a day, as many as 5,000 times in two weeks."[4] If we offer this coupon to this kind of customer driving in this direction at this time of day, it will be 20 percent more effective than offering the coupon to a different kind of person at a different time of day in a different location. The future is coming into focus.

"It's about what people are doing at different times of day," explains Thompson. "If you look at a particular city center, you can see that people leave an area for a lunch, and then all go to a certain area, and then go back. All of a sudden these people are leaving, moving around— that type of insight becomes incredibly important." On sunny days in spring, you can literally watch the cell signals of people pouring out of office towers and marching over to the nearby park. Where should you place your next coffee shop? Or maybe because on cold days they go in an entirely different direction, you should figure out some kind of pop-up coffee stand? Knowing the future (whether it's an hour from now, a day from now, or a year from now) suddenly becomes not a fanciful notion but a science, or at least an equation that can be applied to the problem, an equation based on granular tracking of data points cross-referenced and combined with geography.

The rise of real-time granular data sets is absolutely crucial for the application of ESRI's technology to more and more organizations from police departments to retail establishments. It is, ultimately, what liberates ESRI from the forest. As Thompson explains it, "The change in the second decade of the twenty-first century is from page impressions to place impressions. What am I doing when I'm in a place? That is the thing that's going to get monetized or data-ized, where they are coming from and where are they going. Understanding where people go when, and understanding that by time of the day and time of year." Thompson cites the ever-increasing trail of data we leave behind while we go about our lives as the great shift that makes all this possible: "Cell phone, CRM [customer relationship management] systems, point of sale," but also, he notes, "check in on places like Foursquare or searches on Yelp, some of it is social media, tweets, some of it is really in the stream—all these devices are monitored in real time so your presence and location can be captured."

The much-touted and vaunted move to mobile technologies—primarily phones that operate via cellular signal but also an evolving array of eyeglasses, watches, and other objects gradually joining the Internet of things—are used to triangulate position (collectively or individually). With the position of just about everybody moving through a metropolis now reliably charted for the first time in human history, patterns and trends can be discerned. "Geography delivers context and understanding," says Thompson. "Who are the people and where do they come from? How do different things interconnect?"

The same approach is increasingly being used in the rise of what has come to be called predictive policing. Predictive policing is essentially the ESRI big-data-meets-mapping idea adjusted to meet the needs of law and order. Chris Ovens, a leader in ESRI's Location Analytics Department, joins me to explain how it works: "We did work with IBM and the NYPD Real Time Crime Center. We took historical data and predictive information through their SPSS [statistical analysis] capabilities and presented both of those on a side-by-side map. Now you can see what crimes have taken place, and what crimes might take place, so you are able to visualize key information spatially, allow the user to interact with information spatially, draw a circle around an area of interest, what crimes actually take place in this specific region, detailed reports on the crimes and their status."[5]

The police department (PD) in Richmond, Virginia, is a pioneer in this kind of predictive policing approach. They've been applying the BI or business intelligence approach to policing since the early 2000s. By

2007, they were able to report, "Using predictive analysis and BI technology, we are applying information-based policy to predict the likelihood of crime and prevent future crimes from occurring. . . . Already, our officers have arrested 16 fugitives and confiscated 18 guns based on this system's guidance. In the first week of May last year, Richmond had no homicides compared with three homicides in the same week the prior year. We attribute this success rate, in part, to moving officers around based on the calculated probability of shooting incidents."[6] The book *Big Data* cites another Richmond PD discovery: "Richmond police long sensed that there was a jump in violent crime following gun shows; the big-data analysis proved them right but with a wrinkle: the spike happened two weeks afterwards, not immediately following the event."[7]

In Vancouver, Canada's third biggest city by population sitting 140 miles north of Seattle, a similar system was adopted by the city's police department in 2009. A report that begins with a quote from hockey legend Wayne Gretzky—"A good hockey player plays where the puck is. A great hockey player plays where the puck is going to be"—states that "the Vancouver PD has been able to spot where crime is headed, and, in many cases, help stop it before it otherwise would occur." The report notes that, from 2007 to 2011, property crime rates dropped citywide per 1,000 residents by 24 percent and violent crime rates have decreased by 9 percent. These goals were achieved by developing a "sophisticated crime and intelligence analysis system called the Consolidated Records Intelligence Mining Environment (CRIME). The system created the capacity to view and analyze crime-related data, to uncover trends, and to accurately predict when and where crimes were likely to occur." More specifically, Vancouver PD cites the ability to track offenders and map criminal activities over time. In this way, they can predict "crimes that occur at specific times of the day, or crimes associated with target variables such as open, unmonitored parking structures that potentially attract criminals." They are then able to dispatch officers to areas where crime is likely to take place and, in their words, "deter and prevent crime rather than merely respond to it." The Vancouver PD is making their data and analysis available to police departments across British Columbia and the continent, and "are hopeful that many locales will take advantage."[8]

See what crimes have taken place where and when, so you can see *what crimes might take place*. This isn't *Minority Report*. This is real life in which police departments can tailor their resources to reflect what happened in the past and what they predict will happen in the future. If crime has spiked five years in a row in the downtown night club district on all nights when a full moon falls on a payday and the temperature is over eighty degrees, then it's almost for sure that it will happen again. That's a good night, then, to send extra patrols to the area. Their presence may stop what's going to happen before it happens—presto, you predicted the future, you altered the future. (Of course, this kind of "prediction" can also be used as a justification for all kinds of racial profiling and stop-and-frisk tactics. Among the many ways data-based prediction is problematic is that it very easily can be used a tool to further entrench prejudices.) Back at ESRI, Chris Ovens explains the evolution so far: "A few years ago they put together predictive with spatial, so now it is two systems with weather and so on. Then the New York Police Department put historic and predictive through GIS analysis and started putting all of these together. Each one presents a shift. The next steps are to take the information to the point of action so this information is now available to the officers on the streets and on patrol." Turning predictive into preventative: pushing us in the direction of science fiction paradox after all.

In the end, everything ESRI offers comes down to a series of questions that, suddenly, for the first time in human history, can be credibly answered. As Chris Ovens puts it: "What happened, what's this data telling us? Why did it happen, what's going to happen next?"

o o o o o o

Taking their cue from ESRI, there are an increasing number of companies whose business plan is to harvest cast-off data and turn that bumper crop of weeds into cash. These companies rely on using our now almost endless computing power to near-instantaneously store and process what we have come to call *big data*. Big data underpins almost everything that happens at ESRI and in the fields of analytics, BI, and, increasingly, IT in general. It is emerging as the essential technological framework. Both a philosophy and an application, big data is the fuel that powers the ESRIs and other engines of our future-first era.

Consider the definition found in the book *Big Data*, subtitled, *A Revolution That Will Transform How We Live, Work, and Think*. "At its core," write the authors, Professor Viktor Mayer-Schönberger and *Economist* magazine editor Kenneth Cukier, "big data is about predictions."9 It's a frank, useful admission. As they write: "The possession of knowledge, which once meant an understanding of the past, is coming to mean an ability to predict the future."10 And how does big data make predictions? The authors explain, by "applying math to huge quantities of data in order to infer probabilities."11 Big data isn't some parlor trick. This is a fundamental reallocation of our resources and priorities. Getting to the future first requires "huge quantities of data" and these quantities require systemic implementation of data collection on just about every facet of daily life. The *Big Data* authors write about "systems" as in, "systems perform well because they are fed with lots of data on which to base their predictions."12 This is the implementation of an overall resetting of priorities around, "the ability of society to harness information in novel ways."13

The *Big Data* authors talk about data as the "raw material of business, a vital economic input, used to create a new form of economic value." They talk about how "data can be cleverly reused to become a fountain of innovation and new services." They assure us that big data will "produce useful insights or goods and services of significant value."14 In 2011, the World Economic Forum announced that big data would henceforth "be considered a new class of economic asset," a thing you can own and profit from, the fuel that will finally power us to the future.15 So it is that more and more companies are signing up with ESRI. Collecting, accessing and parsing huge quantities of data, paying fees for systemic access to the future, is becoming just another cost of doing business. "Technology is not really about hardware and software anymore," Eric Schmidt, Google's executive chairman, tells an audience of MIT students. "It's really about the mining and use of this enormous data to make the world a better place."16 It's a world made better by default deference to a system that knows what is going to happen before it happens.

According to the new purveyors of big data, our systems are only as good as the information they can collect. As such, everyone can and should be getting into the game of turning the throwaway moments of the present into future gold. The more we adjust how our systems function to accommodate the harnessing of information to what can only be useful insights or valuable new products, the better off our systems will be. The structure—the system—is recalibrating to embrace the big data approach in which the everyday is viewed as fodder for the future. Both because of what it is and how it works, big data should be seen as the first technological application unique to the era of future. It's the first truly twenty-first–century technological application and it has only one purpose; wherever and however it is applied, the goal is to know the future. The more big data enters into our every interaction, the more its ubiquity helps to usher in the ideology of treating the present as nothing more than a portal to tomorrow.

As such, the big data gold rush is on. You've got to have the data, if you want to own the future. In 2006, Microsoft bought big data commercial pioneer Oren Etzioni's Farecast (which used data to predict airfare oscillations) for $110 million. "Two years later Google paid $700 million to acquire Farecast's data supplier, ITA Software."[17] But that was just the beginning. Google has continued to acquire tech companies at a frantic pace and seems to be showing a particular interest in robotics—they have bought at least seven robotics companies so far and have put the man behind the development of their Android mobile operating system in charge of their robot division. But, argues one tech commentator, the goal isn't really robotics and driverless cars, it's data: "it's all about gaining a dominant position in markets where data is about to explode. . . . Whoever provides the software that controls and manages these robots not only stands to make a fortune by selling that software; they will have access to a vast new repository of data about how we live and work."[18] Another article, about the big-data–enabled race—currently being led by Google—to map every road, river, and even footpath in the world makes the same point: "Tomorrow's map, integrally connected to everything that moves (the keys, the tools, the car), will be so fundamental to their operation that the map will, in effect, be their operating system. . . . So the competition to make the best maps, the thinking goes, is more than a struggle over who dominates the trillion-dollar smartphone market; it's a contest over the future itself."[19]

Let's delve into this a bit more, since it's crucial to understanding where the big-data-future-first model is taking us. In the almost-here future, everything will be mapped in real time to such an extent that our entire world will be automatically converted to reflexive data as things happen. This will allow for computers (in the shape of cars, robots, drones, and lawn mowers) to work alongside and as efficiently as humans. Humans operate in the world by feeling and experience. Computers operate (in the human world) through prediction. Thus, Google's driverless car project works by creating "a virtual track" out of the roadways where the cars drive. This means "ultra-precise digitizations of the physical world, all the way down to tiny details like the position and height of every single curb." All this big-data map tracking creates a prediction algorithm of immense speed and complexity. Google preloads "the data for the route into the car's memory before it sets off, so that as it drives, the software knows what to expect." The more data Google has access to and owns, the more the system can tell its connected machines what to expect, extending the territory its cars and robots will be able to operate in. The more territory they operate in, the more data they'll be able to collect and offer up to an ever-churning prediction engine so that "the software knows what to expect."[20] In effect, we're creating virtual realities that exist simultaneously and parallel to the real world. The virtual reality we create out of millions of points of data can be analyzed, manipulated, and broken down the way the real world just can't. From a data-crunching, owning-the-future perspective, converting the real into the virtual is becoming more and more desirable. Knowing what is going to happen is far more efficient than responding to events after the fact. And systematically controlling what is going to happen is most efficient of all.

o o o o o o

In the first phase of big data and information technology, Walmart deduced that before big storms, sales of Pop-Tarts skyrocket. Google analyzed millions of search terms and correlated searches for products and symptoms related to flu with actual flu outbreaks coming in the days and weeks ahead, ultimately providing faster and more accurate information about what areas were going to be ravaged by flu than the Centers for Disease Control and Prevention were able to achieve at the time. (Alas, this no longer seems to work as well as it first did.) Amazon figured out algorithms for recommending your next book purchase that were far more effective at predicting what you were going to read next (or at least selling you a next read) than actual people making recommendations on your behalf. The department store Target, famously, was able to use their baby registry plus loyalty program to isolate two dozen products that pregnant women buy, ranging from unscented lotion to vitamins, leading them to be able to predict pregnancy and send out appropriate coupons for the appropriate trimester. This led to the now classic story, recounted by *New York Times* business reporter Charles Duhigg, of the furious Minnesota dad outraged that his teenage daughter had been sent coupons for baby clothes and cribs only to discover that his daughter was, indeed, pregnant.[21] (Since then, there has been a steady trickle of reports of people who have lost their babies mid-term but who have continued to be targeted by fliers and ads peddling diapers and cribs and sporting messages to the baby-to-be like "You're Almost Here!")[22]

Now we are moving into the next, even more granulose phase of big data future prediction. In this phase, the lessons Google, Walmart, and Target have applied to big data are being adopted by almost every conceivable field from medicine to insurance to traffic. Pacemakers and other medical implants are transmitting data to their manufacturers about how they are functioning, and data to doctors and patients about the health of the biosystem they are functioning in. An Australian academic working in Ontario has collected billions of data points monitoring the vital signs of preterm babies, ultimately detecting a change in heart rate before life-threatening infection sets in, and which happens hours and even days before the infection could otherwise be detected.[23] FICO, the corporation that invented the concept of your credit score in the 1950s, has come up with something called the "Medication Adherence Score" that determines "how likely people are to take their medication" based on data points like "how long people have lived at the same address, if they are married, how long they've been in the same job, and whether they own a car." The correlates between these seemingly random data sets and the likelihood of your following the prescribed course of your medicine is so precise that FICO's chief executive proudly announced, "We know what you're going to do tomorrow."[24] Follow the footsteps—they'll tell you where we're going next. The company Experian is peddling an "Income Insight" algorithm that will give customers a cheap and near-instant way to "estimate people's income level" based on analyzing its own massive store of credit histories and anonymous tax data available from the IRS. Experian has also purchased Hitwise, "which struck deals with Internet service providers to collect their clickstream data in return for some extra income."[25] This data was then sold to advertisers and marketers interested in knowing where people go on the Internet in order to influence their future behavior. Meanwhile, a similar credit bureau called Equifax is now selling the "Ability to Pay Index" and "Discretionary Spending Index"—services that, again, use data sets to analyze how much cash and credit someone might have to make purchases.[26]

But wait, there's more. One could easily fill multiple volumes with all the ways that people are harnessing data—where we click and go, what we buy, what we think—to predict future outcomes. The possibilities seem endless, because they are endless. Every action we take can be harnessed to generate probabilities about the next action we will take. The more data are accumulated, the more it can be cross-referenced to specific outcomes. The overall data set can expand in scope and accuracy. Data, like technology in general, seems to spread, occupy territory, spring out of unnoticed nooks and crannies. For instance, data about how many cars are on the road and where their drivers are going can also be used to predict things like the future state of the economy; fewer cars at rush hour means fewer people going to work, which means layoffs and decline detected long before official employment numbers are released. Inrix, a company that collects traffic data, also sells information to an investment fund that analyzes traffic around major shopping outlets, "which the fund uses to trade the company's shares before its quarterly earnings announcements."[27] Cars circling the Target lot looking for an empty spot means people inside shopping. The company LocoMobi has developed an application that takes a picture of all the license plates of cars entering and leaving a parking lot. When you leave the lot, your license plate pictures are matched up, the computer figures out how long you were in there, and a charge is automatically applied. But of course that's just the beginning: "We can have so much fun with this," the cofounder and chairman of LocoMobi, Barney Pell, tells a reporter. "Imagine knowing that people who park here also park there—you've found the nearby stores, their affinities. You could advertise to them, offer personalized services, provide 'passive loyalty' points that welcome them back to an area."[28] There are so many ways to monetize the predictive power of harnessing ubiquitous daily activity it's mind-boggling. Providing several different services to various stakeholders, often with competing interests, is what makes big data such a wonderful treasure trove of possibility.

o o o o o o

My final meeting with ESRI is the most fascinating and most revealing in terms of harnessing granular data to location in order to predict and alter the future. I spend my last hour at ESRI with Wolfgang Hall, a transplanted German national whose specialty at ESRI is logistics. Logistics is corporatese for coordinating all the different elements of shipping parts and merchandise from one place to another, a huge field in the age of global manufacturing, as products often start as parts made in several different countries. These parts are then sent to another country, where the final product is assembled before being shipped to a whole bunch of other countries, where they are warehoused and eventually put on store shelves or sent directly to customers. This is what Wolfgang Hall means by logistics, which, again, seems about as far away from the forest as you can get.

Hall starts out by telling me how ESRI revolutionized Sears service calls and deliveries by incorporating the service calls and routes taken by the technicians and drivers into GIS mapping. The routes were not nearly as efficient as they could have been, and ESRI's technology was able to help tighten things up considerably. Big deal, you might say, but this optimization saved Sears fifty million dollars a year. Weather, traffic conditions, volume of calls, time needed to do the repair, all this stuff was once left open to the fates, but with GPS and cell tracking and other data streams, it was now possible to not just know where your employees were as they did your shipping or delivering or fixing, but also where they should be based on where they were yesterday, where they were in a very similar set of parameters two years ago, and where the optimized route spit out by the new logistics software says they could be. The goal isn't to know the past. It's to know—and improve upon—what is going to happen next.

Wolfgang Hall has a wide range of examples of how this kind of logistics optimization helps companies and, indeed, consumers. He tells me about a city in Texas where road crews were able to use GIS to accomplish what they usually did in eight hours in six hours. He talks about the networking multinational Cisco, which openly explains "how they use our technology to provide better services to their customers."[29] Basically, Cisco used GIS to build service areas. "You take a position on the map and ask, 'What can I reach within two hours from that point? What's the street travel time by time of day?' You can see the coverage area that you can reach, the islands of reachability, and you can see the gaps in between." Using GIS with various data sets allowed Cisco to make service guarantees to their customers that were actually based on what they could really deliver.

Other companies took note of the success of Sears and implemented similar systems. At UPS, vehicles emit a steady stream of data so that head office knows where its trucks are, why they're there, and even if they are running hot and likely to have engine trouble. Naturally the drivers are directed to the most efficient routes calculated on maps enabled by a stream of live data. In 2011 UPS was able to optimize routes to the tune of thirty million fewer miles driven, which saved three million gallons of fuel. "Prediction gave us knowledge," said Jack Levis, UPS's director of process management. "But after knowledge is something more: wisdom and clairvoyance. At some point in time, the system will be so smart that it will predict problems and correct them before the user realizes that there was something wrong."[30]

Gradually, Wolfgang Hall switches gears and starts talking about the new logistics frontiers opening up, the many areas where tracking and mapping will soon be helping a company or institution or even society at large do more and better. He talks, for instance, about tracking convicts now on parole. The problem, he notes, is that when you are "tracking with very fine granularity, data accumulates and nobody can make sense of it." But what if, he suggests, the tracking could be merged with mapping and set up to only "see the relevant"? For instance, it wouldn't be relevant if a parolee stopped into a coffee shop, but it would be relevant if "two parolees were tracked meeting up at the same place for a certain amount of time."

What are they planning? Are they even aware that they are both in the same coffee shop? It doesn't really matter. What matters is that there is a data set that triggers consequences—consequences which allow those overseeing the data to better shape the future—a future in which two criminals can be cheaply and easily prevented from associating, thereby preventing them from putting any form of plan in motion, whether it's a plan to get together, drink a few espressos and talk about their prison past, or a plan to put their mastermind criminal abilities together and pull off the perfect bank heist. In fact, as I learned more about ESRI's services I realized something very important to understanding the whole process of future prediction: the "why" is much less important than the "what." Why these two people have come together isn't important. Why a group of people might congregate in a particular park or plaza or take a particular route on their way to work or responding to a service call doesn't matter either. What is is what matters. What is the pattern? Regardless of why, there's always a pattern. Once the pattern is determined, it can be exploited, even if we don't necessarily know what's causing it.

Wolfgang's example of the two convicts being specifically tracked is the first time I hear anyone at ESRI talk about individual tracking. Before it was all just signals and searches, electronic pulses associated with anonymous people who broadcast their lifestyles through their

patterns of communication, movement, and consumption. But now
Hall is taking it to a different level. And come to think of it, the tracking of service calls and road crews also necessarily involves tracking
specific, identifiable people, not amalgamated masses of nameless
credit ratings. Most of ESRI's work happens in the background—people don't know their data is being used to predict where they will go
next (as types in a group). But the workers at Sears and elsewhere must
have been very much aware that they were being tracked and timed.
Hall admits that workers at various companies have been less than
enthusiastic about some of the optimizations that ESRI have brought
to the table. He talks about workers trying to subvert the system by
putting cans over antennas blocking GPS signals. But, he tells me,
"those times are over—it doesn't seem to be as scary anymore." And
anyway, as Hall sees it, it is in everyone's best interest to participate.
Demands by employees that the GPS be turned on and off at various
times impinge on the data. And why shouldn't the company know what
is going on? "How reasonable is it, if you use company assets and company time? I'm working for this organization. I may as well help the
organization be more efficient."

This brings us to where Wolfgang Hall sees all of this going and
where ESRI as a company sees possible expansion. Hall tells me
that he has lately been working on new projects around what he calls
"indoor logistics" a term that he modestly admits, "may be something I
coined." This new kind of logistics will look at "the asset management,
routing, and navigation of us inside." As Hall notes, "over 80 percent
of our day is spent indoors" including workers at offices, shoppers in
stores, kids in school, and so on. What if we were tracking on GIS not
just how people got to the office or the store, but what they did once
they were in there? Could it work? Hall describes how they built an
app for Android devices that routed users through a conference ESRI
organized. Attendees opted in. They received route optimization—
the fastest way to get from point A to point B as they made their way
through the massive conference building searching for any particular
seminar or showcase. ESRI, in exchange, received data about where
every user went when.

Moving forward, Hall sees this as being something you could do with malls, big-box stores, and grocery stores—opt in on your mobile device, on an "application to tell me how to move through the stores to efficiently pick up groceries." Here Wolfgang Hall starts to visibly show his enthusiasm: "You build heat maps based on that: this area is highly frequented, this area is cold." In doing so, you can solve two problems: the customer has a better experience, and the retailer gets real-time data about where the customer is going in their store. "I know retailers are looking for more information, more data, the movement of people inside of store, and information you get through WiFi—it is megabytes and gigabytes of data." Of course there are privacy concerns. But Hall doesn't see that as a problem. It will be in the best interest of the retailers and their customers for the collected data to be stripped from specific identity. Nobody will know how long you lingered in front of the Trojans or the candy bars. They will just know that someone—a type, perhaps cross-referenced to a postal code and a credit rating category—was there, paused for 8.43 seconds, and then moved on. This, in turn, will allow them to know what you as a type are liable to do the next time, and the next time.

Wolfgang Hall's enthusiastic embrace of this "new frontier" of tracking people seems to have almost infinite applications. Already, Hall notes, ESRI is working with a German company to provide these kinds of services in airports including "tracking people inside the airport and routing them to the gate." We're on the cusp of a brave new world of tracking and data analysis. And ESRI aren't the only ones setting their sights on conquering uncertainty. At MIT, Sandy Pentland, the director of the Human Dynamics Laboratory, has been experimenting with badges that transmit data about employees' interactions as they go about their days. After analyzing data from badges, Pentland was able to predict "which teams would win a business-plan contest, and which workers would (rightly) say they'd had a 'productive' or 'creative' day." Pentland also says that his team discovered through these experiments the "data signature" of "natural leaders" whom he has dubbed "charismatic connectors." In 2010, Pentland and his partners spun this research off into a private company called Sociometric Solutions, which is now working on making the badge technology part of the everyday workplace.[31]

The modern workplace is already jam-packed with newly implemented data collection and monitoring schemes. The global financial
data firm Bloomberg "logs every keystroke of every employee, along
with their comings and goings in the office."[32] Over in Vegas, Harrah's
casino "tracks the smiles of the card dealers and waitstaff on the floor
(its analytics team has quantified the impact of smiling on customer
satisfaction)."[33] More and more companies are not just storing but also
analyzing e-mail, looking for "insights about our productivity, our treatment of co-workers, our willingness to collaborate or lend a hand, our
patterns of written language, and what those patterns reveal about our
intelligence, social skills, and behavior."[34]

The trend with much of this "indoor logistics" is to generate data
to predict the future. For instance, there's Knack, a clever Silicon Valley start-up that makes games for mobile devices. The games include
Dungeon Scrawl, in which players have to move through quest-themed
mazes and puzzles, and Wasabi Waiter, which, as you might imagine, is
a game in which players have to match up sushi to an ever-growing number of customers. But here's the rub. The games are carefully "designed
by a team of neuroscientists, psychologists, and data scientists to suss
out human potential."[35] According to Guy Halfteck, Knack's founder,
when you play any of the games, you generate massive amounts of data
about how quickly you are able to solve problems and make the right
decisions while multitasking and learning on the go. "The end result,"
Halfteck says, "is a high-resolution portrait of your psyche and intellect,
and an assessment of your potential as a leader or an innovator."[36] Hans
Haringa, leader of petroleum giant Royal Dutch Shell's GameChanger
unit, asked about 1,400 people who had contributed ideas and proposals
to the division to play Dungeon Scrawl and Wasabi Waiter. "Ultimately,
without ever seeing the ideas, without meeting or interviewing the people who'd proposed them, without knowing their title or background or
academic pedigree, Knack's algorithm had identified the people whose
ideas had panned out. The top 10 percent of the idea generators as predicted by Knack were in fact those who'd gone furthest in the process."
Haringa is now trying to get the Royal Dutch Shell human resources
executives to make the games part of the regular evaluation process in
the hiring of "all professional workers."[37]

San Francisco's Evolv makes online tests that companies can give prospective workers. Their services are used by the Xerox company, among others, to help hire workers for its 150 US-based customer care centers, employing roughly 45,000 people. Evolv's tests incorporate a range of psychological measures including "personality testing, cognitive-skill assessment, and multiple-choice questions about how the applicant would handle specific scenarios that he or she might encounter on the job."[38] With a fast-growing data set of almost half a million employees who have taken various tests, Evolv is getting better and better at predicting the future of various applicants—how long they will stay at the job, how good they will be at it, how far they might rise in the company. Using Evolv's approach, Xerox was able to lower the attrition rate of new hires by 20 percent. Similarly, Transcom, a company that provides outsourced customer support, sales, and debt-collection services, with around 29,000 workers all over the globe, worked with Evolv to lower the three-month employee attrition rate by almost 30 percent. Xerox still interviews job applicants, but, as Teri Morse, the vice president for recruiting at Xerox Services, says, "We're getting to the point where some of our hiring managers don't even want to interview anymore."[39]

Forget tracking employees and mapping the world to know the future. Why not just track every single *thing*? GreenGoose is a San Francisco–based tech start-up that is developing tiny sticker-like motion detector sensors that can be deployed across a range of objects. The sensors then send data to a GreenGoose base station, which then can publish or otherwise record the activity online and elsewhere. The user could get rewards for good activity (like tooth brushing) and other incentives while the company acquires billions of data points about all manner of behaviors that they can then use to predict everything from when you are going to run out of toothpaste to whether or not you are visiting the dentist to, one imagines, how likely it is that you will take your medication as prescribed. At one tech start-up pitch conference—the Launch Festival started by "serial entrepreneur and angel investor" Jason Calacanis—judges were so impressed they each invested $100,000 on the spot. The third judge had, apparently, already put money in the company.[40]

I ask Wolfgang Hall if he sees anything problematic about the escalation of tracking of employees in order to provide fodder for data-driven prediction. He tells me that it will be up to the government to set policies to keep these things, as he puts it, "reasonable." "When I get paid for a certain job," he tells me, "it is reasonable that the company knows how long I spend here on the job. But if I go to the bathroom I don't want to be tracked, or if I'm on a break, I don't want to be tracked."

We are slowly getting better and better at not just knowing, but even influencing and shaping, the future. And this amazing capacity, despite its many possible drawbacks, is so far proving far too enticing for society writ large to resist. Accidents are avoided. Lives are saved. More lattés are sold, more conspiring ex-cons are caught, crime goes down, the time we need to spend in the grocery store searching for vanilla and marjoram goes down, and productivity goes up up up. "I predict," announces Wolfgang Hall as our interview draws to a close, "that in a few years it will be normal to track people and route people inside and you won't even think about it anymore."

o o o o o o

When we use our GPS, flash our debit card, visit a website, download an app, we generate data to be potentially sold to thousands of entities, which then use it to predict what people like us will do next. A lot of people and corporations are now making a lot of money off of our data, but we are not making a cent. We are not paid or otherwise compensated for our data. Astonishingly, many of us don't seem to really care who collects our data, or why. Because it's an invisible, ceaseless flow captured, increasingly, by default and ostensibly for our benefit, we neither notice nor complain.[41] It is common practice to take all our data, all these seemingly tiny inconsequential details, and apply them to whatever scheme you can think of, without asking the individuals producing the data for specific permission. If somebody went around and took a few pennies from every household in America every single day, there would be a massive outcry, a congressional inquiry, heads would roll. But because big data is categorized as a benevolent off-shoot of our will to arrive at the future, we are not just accepting of it, we are lining up to contribute to the project. With only the weakest infrastructure as protection for the consumer, big data is expanding in all directions much faster than any person could ever keep up with. Even if you wanted to opt out of big data, it would be impossible. Jaron Lanier makes this point at length in his book *Who Owns the Future*, arguing that what is stifling opportunity in the twenty-first century is the steadily rising disparity between those with access to—and the ability to profit from—the future in its data form, and the rest of us, who are increasingly being treated primarily as inexhaustible mines, giant open pits feeding the tomorrow machine.[42]

A seismic and potentially dangerous shift in a short time, and all without any real opposition or even debate. A technology that feels utterly reflexive and natural, that seems to be all about our innate, tribal need for meaningful, ongoing, interpersonal connection—look, someone noticed me!—just as urban anonymity is starting to chip away at our very souls. I first noticed this phenomenon when I was writing my previous book *The Peep Diaries*, about the rise of self-surveillance as a new kind of pop culture. In that book, I met representatives of the millions around the world who are deliberately broadcasting the intimate details of their lives online in return for everything from community to notoriety to sexual titillation. What I saw as a transaction in which people generally gave away something of immense value and received, in most cases, not very much in return, those letting others peep their lives saw as an exciting portal into the technologically enabled future. It was very difficult for them to see that they were giving away tons of valuable product (the short and long tail (or should it be tale?) of their lives), which was then eagerly bundled up and resold at a profit. For them, the whole process was deeply imbued with mystery and excitement. It was all about possibility—extending the reach of the human, becoming more than they were. They felt like they were participating in the future, and that had to be a good thing.

Since I wrote *The Peep Dairies*, we've seen this phenomenon extend its reach considerably. You no longer have to opt in by blogging or uploading photos and videos or obsessively tweeting and updating your way through life to generate free data for massively profitable companies. Now all you have to do is get in your car with your cell phone and your GPS and your credit card.

The tracking of every person and every object runs counter to the collective project of individual emancipation that humanity has generally aspired to since the Enlightenment era. This is particularly true in a country like the United States, founded in fire and rebellion in part by the desire to cast off the shackles of the oppressive old world of predetermined caste. Nevertheless, in our eagerness to know the future, to own the future, we are moving speedily away from once core values. Why is this? The idea of knowing the future exerts a power over us we can't seem to resist.

PART II

Our Minds in the Future

CHAPTER 5

After

Why Our Minds are Vulnerable to the Pull of Future

In the preliterate era that lasted from the time of *Homo erectus* two million years ago to, generally speaking, the time just before the dawn of the first organized civilizations of Mesopotamia some six thousand years ago, people did not live in the segmented flow of time as we conceive it today. They—or we, depending on how much connection one feels to our metaphysically disparate predecessors—saw the world in a different way. There was no line drawn between then and now and what was to come. Neither past nor future had been conceived of yet. We lived in the moment, in one big now, a past-present-future instant sharpened to a razor's edge by the demands of survival.

Still today the Amondawa tribe of the Amazon lack a word for time. They also have no word for month or year, no calendar, and use no clocks or watches.[1] Time keeping by the native peoples from what is now Pennsylvania amounted to noting that "when the leaf of the white oak reached the dimensions of the mouse's ear" it was time "to plant the maize." In Southeastern Australia Bigambul bush tribes continue to mark the passage of the year by the timing of different types of tree blossoms.[2] People primarily noted the passage of time by the natural reoccurrences of the seasons. Time didn't pass, it was cyclical—a repetitive constant. And, just to show you how long this kind of understanding of time held its grip, in 1821 "a group of peasants from the Yorkshire village of Thurone attempted to wall in a cuckoo in order, they hoped, to enjoy an eternal spring."[3] Few thought in terms of ten years or fifty years or a hundred years from now. The notion of broadly measuring epochs in decades and centuries didn't take root until the 1890s.[4] Most people, scrabbling to survive, barely even bothered to track the passing of the days as the sun relentlessly set and rose on the circadian rhythms of their lives.

Thus, for the Amondawa and the majority who have walked the earth since the beginning of humanity, there was only the now and the realization that the now was, in some hazy way, related to what had happened and what was almost-about-to happen which were, nevertheless, all the same thing. We lived within and for and through the present day—allowing the reality of its known unknown into our everyday lives the same way we integrated the rituals and patterns of gathering food or mourning the dead into the story we told each other, the ongoing story that made sense of how the tribe lived and survived. In this way, "people," theorized Marshall McLuhan, "were drawn together into a tribal mesh" and partook of "the collective unconscious." Before past and future abstraction, McLuhan saw us as "audio-tactile," living "in a magical integral world patterned by myth and ritual, its values divine."[5] By "audio-tactile" he meant that people understood what was happening around them by feel and sense, rather than by some arbitrary divide of days into years, months, weeks, minutes, and seconds. Thomas Hobbes wrote from the point of view of someone far less removed from, and thus far less generous about, the preliterate age of myth and ritual, but his conclusion was the same: "Men lived upon gross experience. There was no method; that is to say, no sowing nor planting of knowledge by itself, apart from the weeds and common plants of error and conjecture."[6]

Lacking any meaningful conception of past, present, and future, people lived in a kind of eternal flow, which, despite all the rigors and hardships of pre-Starbucks life, was inherently comforting on a deep, primal level. In other words, the worldviews of various tribal collectives were all about continuity and predictability. One didn't have to know the future, because there was no future to know—the very notion of perpetual upgrade that we envision and frantically work toward today simply did not exist. All that existed was the never-ending present of tree blossoms and cuckoos, a present that would go on in the same way forward and forever, with or without us. As Spanish philosopher Daniel Innerarity notes, traditional societies achieved predictability by "transforming cycles into circles and continuing along the original path." In other words, when we thought about the future, we thought about it "as a simple continuation of the present."[7] We did not seek disruption; we sought to maintain continuity. We found comfort in knowing that we would continue to do what we'd always done.

The arrival of complex nation-states powered by the industrial revolution signaled the end of the tribal order. Today we no longer enjoy the comfort of the contiguous, never-ending present. Daniel Innerarity writes about our "need to find a scientific means to confront the loss of social certainty about the future."[8] I'm struck by that phrase "loss of social certainty." It's an elegant way of putting it. Compared to today, people in the tribal era didn't have much. They did, however, have the collective conviction of the inevitable present. Tribal existence manufactured certainty to the point that even the uncertain—accidental death, or death in battle, or periodic food shortages—were part of the inevitable and natural. Today, we live very differently. We live in immensely complex interwoven societies removed from singular experience and judgment based on sensory perception. The industrial order increased our life spans and produced consumer goods and food in heretofore unimaginable abundance. It also severed us from the tribal belief system that imbued people with the certain knowledge of origin and destiny—where they came from and where they were going.

Daniel Innerarity writes that "we have no choice but to attempt to overcome" our loss of social certainty "with some special approach." What is this "special approach?" Innerarity singles out the burgeoning discipline of future studies. But more broadly he seems to be referring to the overall enterprise of "owning future" that is now coming to define our times. Where once social certainty assured us of our part in the endless present, today, as he writes, we operate "not in the knowledge of, but in the structural ignorance of, the future." This ignorance looms over everything the industrial and digital eras have put in place, shadowing us with anxiety and presentiment of collapse. And so the "special approach" is, essentially, our repeated and ever more elaborate attempts to, as Innerarity puts it, "compensate" for our lack of social certainty by "scientific means."[9]

Our obsession with knowing and owning the future—reflected in everything from the rise of big data to the frenzy around technological entrepreneurship—finds its roots in our unconscious desire to return to a time when we didn't have to know what happened next because, quite simply, there was no next. We will never know what it was like to live in the time of the eternal now. But I think we can imagine just how compelling such a worldview would have been. A belief system constantly reaffirmed by the rhythms and repetitions of daily life would be ever-present, ever reassuring. Our current capability to control, own, and even know the future pales in comparison. But the overall scheme of using science and technology to reclaim social certainty by knowing and owning the future appeals to us on the same unconscious, even primal, level. From an evolutionary and developmental perspective, the possibility of knowing everything that has happened and will happen is the possibility of return to the endless tribal present. What would we do to return to a time when the specter of our mortality didn't hang over us, an inescapable chilling shadow, a cruel reminder of the way we seem to have lost more and more control over our destiny, even as our dominion over the earth has extended? When we found future, we lost the certainty of the never-ending present and, consequently, we've been trying to fill the void ever since. Our current approach—in the form of high-tech, quasi-scientific attempts to create new totalities—is incredibly powerful and appealing to us because it promises to fill the void. Still reeling from the loss of collective worldview that implicitly provided us with answers to questions we didn't ever think to ask, we turn to future and the potential of its ownership with the kind of zest and fascination we can imagine the first cave people must have applied to the mind-changing arrival of fire. After all, we've been waiting a long time, at least a thousand years, for something to replace tribal collective certainty. God, as Nietzsche proclaimed, is dead; and the steady decline of organized religion as the cultural explainer in society represents the inability of those various cosmologies to provide us with the meaningful totality we've sought ever since. But at least now we have something else to have faith in: the future of the future—a new system subconsciously aping the rhythms of the past while harvesting our present to feed to the technologically and scientifically endorsed time to come. A promise looms: we can return to the certainty of the past by owning the future. Magic is banished, but we can still be magicians.

o o o o o o

Most of us contemplate what we are going to do next, or what is going to happen next, an average of fifty-nine times a day. That's once every sixteen minutes during waking hours.[10] At Harvard, psychologists used an iPhone application to monitor the thoughts of five thousand people living in eighty-three different countries. The phone randomly paged them at different times during the day to ask what they were doing and what they were thinking about. A third of the time, as it turned out, people were thinking about something other than what they were doing at the moment—their minds pulled inexorably to the *next* thing they were going to do.[11] As British science journalist Claudia Hammond writes in her book *Time Warped*, about the psychology of time perception, "contemplating the future could be the brain's default mode of operation."[12]

This doesn't mean we sit around at work dreaming of Star Trek replicators and Mad Max war zones. When we mind time-travel, usually we stay in the very near future, picturing the conversation we're going to have with our coworker or what we're going to make for lunch. When we check in with the future every sixteen minutes or so, we're envisioning actions we're unconsciously planning out before we actually perform them. We use precious brainpower constantly running through mostly mundane scenarios: pushing our grocery cart down the aisle, calling our moms, tidying our desks.

Harvard Medical School researcher Moshe Bar has advanced the theory that when we daydream into the future, we are actually storing up
memories we can then rely on for automatic actions. This is why ath-
letes hire psychologists to help them visualize: so that in the moment,
they aren't really thinking—they've got all their thinking done, they can
react instantaneously, tap into memories they've rehearsed of things
that haven't even happened yet. Students who were asked to picture
themselves preparing for a test—finding a nice quiet place to sit down
and study—got better results on the test than students who were asked
to focus on a future memory of them getting their A+ test papers back.[13]
We succeed by imagining every footfall and panted breath of the race,
not by reenacting the moment we lunge across the line, arms raised in
triumph.

We often hear about patients with amnesia. We're fascinated with
the blank-slate nature of their predicament. Imagine not knowing who
you've been, what you've done. We rarely hear about the other aspect of
this rare occurrence. Doctors report that not only are amnesiacs without memories, but they lack the ability to imagine the future. They
can't form a mental image of the next day or the next year.[14] Brain scans
done while a person is imagining something yet to happen show that
this kind of thinking lights up the hippocampus—known to be a site in
the brain crucial to the formation of new memories—like a Christmas
tree. "In fact the regions of the brain used to recall the past largely over-
lap with those used to imagine the future."[15] When researchers gave
people a key word and asked them to conjure up different scenarios
for that word in the past and the future, they found that the "neural"
signatures of remembering the past and future looked pretty much the
same. "All three of the chief areas of the brain involved in imagining
the future are part of the default network," Claudia Hammond states.
"It is almost as though our brain is programmed to contemplate the
future whenever it finds itself unoccupied."[16]

The general assumption is that when we're not actively engaging
our brains, our minds are drifting backward into memory. But what's
really happening much of the time is that our minds are dipping in and
out of past and stitching together mental tapestries of what is going to
happen next. "The predominant theory of memory," writes a science

journalist, "is that it is an adaptive process, continually updating itself according to what knowledge may be important in the future."[17] Memory, it seems, is set up specifically to serve the goal of futuring. Notes Hammond: "The flexibility of our memories makes it relatively easy because we can meld all these different memories together seamlessly to invent a new imaginary scene, one which we have never even contemplated before, let alone witnessed. The flexibility of memory seems to be the key to imagining a future."[18]

Most likely, the surprising amount of time we spend imagining the future stems from the development of our innate, universal skills as the ultimate scrappy survivors of the animal kingdom. We developed mental structures to help us survive in the eras before grocery stores, cell phones, and rides home from dad. We developed the ability to conjure up the potentially precarious path to the watering hole, the fraught journey to the berry bushes. What dangers awaited you and how could you be ready for them? We think of memory as being about the past, but there's mounting evidence to suggest that memory developed as a kind of Spidey Sense, an early warning system urging us to consider our options before we ran out of them. A study out of New York University found that people who received an uncomfortable electric shock while viewing pictures divided into two categories "recalled about 7 percent more items from the "shocked" category. For example, they remembered more tools if they had been zapped seeing tools." The caveat: the shock effect only took hold when tested six hours or a day later. The conclusion: our brain isn't sure what might be important tomorrow, and so privileges those memories that are, for instance, associated with pain or some other emotional reaction. Joseph Dunsmoor, primary author of the study and a postdoctoral fellow in cognitive neuroscience at New York University, explains it this way: "The emotional experience of the shocks strengthened or preserved the memories of things that, at the time they were encoded, seemed mundane."[19] Writes John Coates, Cambridge research fellow and author of a book about the relationship between risk and mind: "Many neuroscientists now believe our brain is designed primarily to plan and execute movement."[20] It makes sense. Our ability to plan and execute, to mentally time travel to an upcoming event, was the thing that soft-skinned, fragile, not particularly fast or strong humanoids developed in order to get a leg up on the many predators who wanted us for breakfast, lunch, and dinner. We don't just do, act on instinct, follow old patterns; we envision, picture, predict, and plan on a whole other level than any other creature on earth. Birds build nests, squirrels put up acorns for the winter. They go about their business, but they don't picture these things happening in minute detail before they happen, imagining all the things that could go wrong or right or better or worse. "With future thinking," writes Claudia Hammond, "you project yourself forward mentally to imagine the actual experience. This is different from actively planning, and it is this skill that seems to set us apart from other animals."[21] An example of this is depicted by the anthropologist Jared Diamond who writes of going on a bird watching expedition accompanied by a group of New Guinean tribesmen. Arriving at a perfect camping spot that afforded excellent views of unplundered vistas teeming with birds, Diamond wanted to pitch camp. But his companions refused to camp there, as the clearing was overshadowed by a large dead tree. They explained to Diamond that they wouldn't camp under the tree, which could fall over and kill them. He argued with them, noting that the tree was very large and stable and hadn't begun to rot and the chances of it falling on them were practically nil. But still, they refused. Afterward, reflecting on the incident, he concluded that they were making their decisions based less on the evidence before them and more on their collective memory. They, unlike him, had spent a lot of time camping in the forest and had known people to be unexpectedly crushed by falling trees. They were tapping into memory to imagine a possible future and head it off before it happened. Diamond calls this kind of decision making about the future "constructive paranoia".[22]

Today, though we can mostly walk down the sidewalks unencumbered by concerns about falling trees, rival tribes, or poisonous flora and fauna, we still go through even the smallest journey (unconsciously) in our minds—the house where the creepy dude lives, the gap in the concrete, the place with the pretty bushes that flower in the spring. Close your eyes and imagine your daily route. You probably do, every day, without even realizing it. Harnessing memory to imagine and reimagine future turned out to be such a successful survival strategy, it's now an inherent, unconscious process at the core of how we think and are, one of those fundamental aspects that shapes us without our even noticing. What is your brain trying to do? Take care of you. Extend your likelihood of survival. Give you the edge you need to propagate the species and make more little humans who can also survive and grow up and live a long time and make a lot more little humans.

The future impulse at the core of human cognitive process is very different from the future-first rhetoric of the techno-industrial complex. Human beings pursue future primarily to know what is happening next so that they can stave off dangerous and destabilizing change. The ideological system of future first has the opposite goal: to implant destabilizing so-called "disruption" at the heart of everything that happens. On a deep, unconscious, reflexive level, future means something very different to us—not change for change's sake; not disruption under the rubric of innovation. We're envisioning the paths we will take to accomplish our goals, we are thinking about the constancy that we need to survive, within and despite what surprises and changes might come. And yet, in our minds the two things become easily conflated. They seem as one. We are, as a result, irrationally excited to be doing anything related to preparing for the future, securing the future, shaping the future, and owning the future. The human mind, often operating on a kind of unconscious auto-pilot (remember the Florida study!), is easily pulled into the orbit of anything and anyone who promises to reward it with the future knowledge we collectively and by default deem necessary for survival.

The result is a psychologically irresistible brew. Future, in the context of the unconscious rhythms of our minds, seems irresistible. Who doesn't want to increase their odds of surviving and even regaining some modicum of reassuring social certainty while they're at it? We're psychologically drawn—even addicted—to all things future, but not because we want to disrupt and change and can't resist chasing every shiny new thing. The real psychological appeal to us of future is knowing what is going to happen next so we can keep doing exactly what we've always done. Deep in our operating systems, the idea isn't to disrupt and alter everything and anything as fast as possible. The idea is to see the danger, skirt the pitfalls, and pretty much maintain our core patterns and ways of being no matter how much surface change might be adopted. We don't want to change. Not unless we absolutely have to. "Human beings, cultures, and institutions," notes Daniel Innerarity, "have always equipped themselves with procedures to assure predictability to the greatest possible degree. It is one of humankind's most rudimentary goals."[23]

o   o   o   o   o

The increasingly vocalized goal of many of the super-wealthy tech set is to live long enough to be embedded forever in a kind of virtual consciousness. This phenomenon is generally referred to as 'the Singularity.' Russian billionaire venture capitalist Yuri Milner, for one, told world leaders and influential thinkers gathered at an elite annual conference in the Ukraine that "the emergence of the global brain, which consists of all the humans connected to each other and to the machine and interacting in a very unique and profound way [is] creating an intelligence that does not belong to any single human being or computer."[24]

No doubt Yuri Milner is aware of the increasing popularity of futurist Ray Kurzweil's ideas put forward in his 2005 book *The Singularity Is Near*. According to Kurzweil, "as we gradually learn to harness the optimal computing capacity of matter, our intelligence will spread through the universe at (or exceeding) the speed of light, eventually leading to a sublime, universe wide awakening."[25] Or as the description on the back of his book puts it, "our intelligence will become increasingly nonbiological and trillions of times more powerful than it is today."[26]

For Kurzweil and like-minded spin-off thinkers and followers, the future is going to be comprised of unlimited lifespan lived out in virtual realms where we will be liberated from all physical and mental constraints. In this potential technological Singularity, computers become so smart they essentially form one giant massive intelligence (a singular intelligence) that human beings are drawn into. We merge with our hyper-intelligent technology, transcend mortality, and live the vast majority of our lives in virtual worlds.

Like Patrick Tucker's enthusiastic advocacy of futurism in general, Kurzweil's ideas have gone, over the last fifteen years or so, from fringe to practically mainstream. Kurzweil is a sought-after speaker. He's been the subject of a feature-length documentary. He's regularly interviewed by the most august media organizations in the world ranging from NPR to BBC to the *New York Times*, and literally hundreds more outlets. Many of the richest and most influential denizens of Silicon Valley unabashedly endorse his vision of the singularity, both attending and funding the Kurzweil-branded Singularity University. At the same time a (non–Kurzweil-affiliated) website called 2045.com has 30,000 members and runs conferences plus regular educational and advocacy activities all promoting the notion that we can and will reach the singularity by, you guessed it, 2045. The site is backed by Dmitry Itskov, another extremely wealthy Russian tech-investor clearly heavily influenced by Kurzweil, whose stated goal, explains a reporter, is to figure out a way to put "a digital copy of your mind in a nonbiological carrier, a version of a fully sentient person that could live for hundreds or thousands of years."[27] Not that long ago, we would have dismissed Itskov and his ilk as dreamers at best, and crazy people at worst. But, as the *New York Times* attests in a notably lengthy profile, "he has the attention, and in some cases the avid support, of august figures at Harvard, M.I.T. and Berkeley and leaders in fields like molecular genetics, neuroprosthetics and other realms that you've probably never heard of."[28] Money talks, particularly when it is combined with psychologically irresistible ideology.

I've put two ideas in play that I believe are crucial to understanding the way the doctrine of future has arrived and swept through society so quickly. The first is that we are adopting a techno-scientific notion of owning future as a replacement for the social certainty we crave and have now irretrievably lost. The second is that we are, psychologically, predisposed to future, which we see as a default survival mechanism. Both of these psychological takes on why the future is so irresistible to us nicely culminate in the idea of singularity. At first glance, the singularity might seem like the opposite of what I'm arguing is the intrinsic attraction of future for us—to reclaim continuity and extend survival by perceiving danger before it happens. But when we look more closely at it, particularly the claimed end point of all this disruptive turmoil, we see how the singularity is the future era's take on our familiar longing for social certainty, a high-tech way to return us to the times when we were assured of the perpetual repetition of what is and will always be. Not only does the singularity offer social certainty, albeit wrapped up in the mantle of hyper-individualistic technologies of permanent personalized connectivity, it also promises extended survival, perhaps even immortality. And so with the singularity—as with the general ideology of the future-first techno tomorrow—we live in complete comfort, doing as we please, and never ever having to change. Is it any wonder that in the future era there are an expanding number of real-world entities actively pursuing scenarios in which the quest for future ends in a kind of timeless stasis, an eternal sunshine for the spotless, digitally transformed consciousness?

Ray Kurzweil and others perpetuating various iterations of the singularity have the avid support of corporations and institutions that matter. In 2013, Kurzweil went to work for the world's biggest and most profitable tech company. He's now full time at Google, working flat out on his quest to build an "artificial brain." This isn't surprising since, as an article puts it, "Google's founders are involved in Singularity University, part of the belief system that humans and machines will at some point merge, making old age and death meaningless."[29] In fact, Google is more than just "involved" in the notion that innovation will eventually lead us down the path of immortality. Late in 2013, the company announced that it was creating a new venture, Calico, "a new biotechnology company to fight the aging process and the diseases that accompany it."[30] This is part of the Kurzweil ideology too. Kurzweil takes around one hundred vitamins and supplements a day as he seeks to forestall death long enough to get to the singularity. Other technologists and Silicon Valley entities are also betting on life extension to get us there. Peter Thiel invested in and sat on the board of Halcyon Molecular, a company with the goal of eventually curing, or at least forestalling, aging. It closed down in 2012 after receiving roughly $20 million in investment funding. Thiel also gave $3.5 million to the Methuselah Foundation, an organization aiming to "reverse human aging" and he has supported a nonprofit called Humanity Plus, "dedicated to transhumanism—the transformation of the human condition through technology."[31] Like Kurzweil and so many others, he is spreading his ample supply of chips on both odd and even, black and red, figuring that at least one of those bets will pay off eventually. In the meantime, keep betting, keep fighting against what he calls "the ideology of the inevitability of the death of every individual."[32] In our future era, death isn't the ultimate institutional certainty, the penultimate collective truth—it's an ideology that needs disruption; it's a problem to be solved. Billions of dollars are now being spent on the parallel tracks of figuring out how to "conquer aging" and extend life indefinitely and, because there is probably a limit to that process, learning how to transfer our brains into machines so we can live forever in a virtual, interconnected world of our making—a heaven that can exist right here on Earth.

All of this is going on despite the fact that 1) the general consensus in the scientific world is that we remain thousands of years away from "nonbiological intelligence," if it's even possible at all, and 2) it's in no way clear that making such transhumanism possible would be in the best interests of humankind. I'll note that this latter point is not even on the radar of Singularity proponents who take the beneficent nature of their project as a given. The popularity of the singularity epitomizes the way an individualized future of endless (virtual) bounty has become dominant in our society. It also shows just how powerful the idea of future is in our psychology. We don't intrinsically desire eternal life or our minds downloaded into virtual realities. What we've always wanted and needed, however, is the kind of assurance of repetition generated by tribal certainty. In the absence of this, in the wake of the collapse of social certainty, outlandish promises of the post-human era are, increasingly, filling the void. Which is to say that this whole process has more to do with belief than it is has to do with science or engineering. Even in the age of big data, instead of actual, meaningful knowledge of the future, we have for the most part the promise of that knowledge. We have the *sense* that schemes involving things like mapping every aspect of the physical and interior worlds of humanity to create a parallel virtual world of infinitely malleable and ever-expanding data sets will allow us to ultimately return to a state of absolute certainty regarding the ebb and flow of humanity. These schemes seem so appealing—despite the fact that in many instances they require us to give up our hard-fought civil liberties, particularly the right to be unmonitored in what we say and do—because of the assurances they seem to offer. In this roundabout, quietly exponential way, we enter a new kind of belief system devoted to getting to the future where these hazy promises can actually be fulfilled. In this way, the future-first project has become a psychologically irresistible belief system, though it is no more grounded in an inevitability born out of the unbreakable laws of nature than it is a path chosen by society through discussion, debate, and elections.

Out of the ashes of the old emerges the new. In this case, perhaps we need an entirely new religion that can accommodate the way our desire for social certainty is increasingly masquerading as our buy-in to the quest for personalized techno-immortality. One candidate is Terasem, a faith organized around four core tenets—"life is purposeful, death is optional, God is technological, and love is essential."[33] Founded by Martine Rothblatt (who started the satellite radio network Sirius XM) along with her wife Bina, Terasem followers are devoted to "personal cyberconciousness," which manifests itself in the quest to make "mindfiles." Mindfiles are basically recordings of yourself—your most detailed thoughts and feelings. Terasem stores those mindfiles on servers in Vermont and Florida and promises to keep them safe until they can be organized and uploaded into not-yet-invented singularity-like technology that will recreate your consciousness. "For us God is in-the-making by our collective efforts to make technology ever more omnipresent, omnipotent and ethical," Martine says. "When we can joyfully all experience techno immortality, then God is complete."[34] Terasem also gives you the option of beaming the mindfile out into space via satellite just in case there's some other race of aliens out there who have already figured out all this stuff and feel like reincarnating some humans. Around 32,000 people have created free mindfile accounts to date. "Einstein said science without religion is lame. Religion without science is blind," Martine Rothblatt tells *Time* magazine. "Bina and I were inspired to find a way for people to believe in God consistent with science and technology so people would have faith in the future."[35]

The *Time* report, along with all the rest of the coverage, is respect-
fully incredulous: these people are nice, but nuts. But, in fact, Terasem
is only seen as being on the lunatic fringe because they are putting a
spiritual spin on what is an otherwise increasingly mainstream technological goal—virtual life extension via mind-machine meld. In 2013,
Martine Rothblatt, who is also the founder of the biotechnology company United Therapeutics, was one of the speakers at Dmitry Itskov's
2045 Global Future Congress in New York City. Clearly, her spiritual
beliefs fit right into the tenor of the times. In fact, they neatly dovetail
with the overall techno-utopian belief system revolving around "faith in
the (technological) future." In this extreme but also now mainstream
belief system the goal of technological upgrade, of speeding up the process of change, isn't the perfect iPhone; it isn't a device downloaded
into your brain, amplified and accessed via Google Glass; it isn't even
an army of robots we control with our minds who do our bidding and
create unimaginable wealth and luxury for all. The goal is to arrive at
the perfect end—the end of institution, the end of collective humanity, the end of death, and even the end of future itself, which emerges
triumphantly re-engineered as the endless present moment. For our
minds on future, this last point is the one we fixate on. It's the return to
certainty, the reclamation of pattern. In this way, the promise of social
certainty will finally be fully realized. Unconsciously, we feel that the
more we believe in future, the more we invest in pursuing the future,
the more likely it will be that no one has to die and everything and
everyone can go on just as it once did—uninterrupted and forever. This
is the future as an endlessly arriving second coming. In the future we
will be infinitely intelligent. We will solve all of humanity's problems
by merging with our machines, downloading our brains, and living
forever in a virtual reality where there is no poison air, no extreme
weather, no hordes of angry poor people wondering what happened to
their share of the trickle down. And guess what? This future isn't thousands of years away. According to a growing number of technologists
telling us exactly what we want to hear, it's just around the corner.

CHAPTER 6

Put a Spell on Me
When the Magic Became the Information

In the age of social certainty, trying to control or intervene in the future was considered highly uncertain, even extraordinarily dangerous. Those who laid claim to the knowledge that took one down the path of magical cures, portents from the spirits, and even eternal life were a small subset of people whom the tribe set apart. We called them elders, or shamans, or, eventually, priests, and we looked to them to maintain our sense of continuity by explaining the actions of the divine and assuring us that all was as it should and would be—the famine would end, the sickness would lift, the new would be born to replace the old. Our magicians were invested with special powers, but were expected to use those powers to reassure us and maintain cohesion and the sense of continuity. They were our intermediaries with the deities, but often also our historians and encyclopaedias, passing on herbal remedies and memories of the great flood or the time the earth shook.

Occasionally, when they were seen to have gained too much power, when they were perceived as controlling the future in ways unnatural and outside the human scope—in ways that increased our anxiety,

rather than diminished it—we rose up against them. Whose side were
they really on? Outbursts of anxiety toward the shaman intermediaries
who professed to move between this world and the murky unknown
were infrequent but violent. These outbursts became more intense as
we inched toward the rupture of modernity. Witches burned, medicine
men found themselves run out of town, and professed visionaries from
Jesus onward were persecuted for their presumptions. We sensed,
though we did not always verbalize, the inherent contradiction: accessing the magic might inevitably lead to just the sort of disruption of
continuity we sought to avoid by accessing the magic. There's something about messing with the future, about the act of trying to pull the
unknown into the known that we were (once) intensely wary of. Knowing too much seemed somehow counter to survival, to the simultaneity
of the tribal permanent present. After all, the role of the magic was to
assure us that everything would and could stay the same.

But today, what was seen as dangerous intervention into the realm
of the gods is now commonplace. We have an impressive variety of
shamans and intermediaries projecting into the unknown and profess-
ing to own the magic. I'm not talking about strip-mall palm readers,
1-900-number fortune-tellers, or even the slowly fading tradition of
anointed priests, rabbis, imans, monks, and nuns called to duty by
God. I'm talking about our new intermediaries, people who seem to
be able to own the future and conjure up millions of dollars out of thin
air. We clamor to be among those who can intervene, magic-like, in the
future. We race to be among or near the elite who can demand their
price in money and status and the power that comes with having the
right amount of both. That we can and should mess with the time to
come is now taken as a given; it's the basis for our future era. Those
who worry that messing with the future is somehow tempting fate or
going against the plan of God are considered retrograde reactionaries.

In the future era, we are mesmerized not by the pattern of divine
magic, unattainable yet predictable, but by the idea that we, personally,
can control the magic; we can control change and own the future; we
can be gods and magicians, one and the same. It's tempting to char-
acterize this shift as a kind of perversion of social certainty. Instead of
generating social certainty through the collective actions inherent in

caring for each other and the world we live in, we are looking for the quick fix. We are trying to find the pill we can pop that will take away our anxiety and sense of futility and replace it with our individual ability to master each and every situation. This is true, but it's also reductive. It turns the complexity of this issue into a series of retrograde moral judgments. The truth is far more nuanced. For when we look at how humanity has changed over the last 500 or so years, we see that the crucial transformation lies in the very process of remembering/futuring. The more we learned to project the past into the future, the farther we got from a permanent present of social certainty maintained by our collective belief in the magic of eternal repetition.

What changed us from creatures who feared to mess with the future into the only beings on the planet who assert dominion over it? As we'll see, it's what has been changing us all along. The development of humanity is rooted in the development of our capacity for abstraction, our ability to infer things based on what has already happened. This is the story of how the magic turned into the information, which also happens to be a big part of the story of how we came to believe in and order our lives around the future.

o o o o o o

If the numeral 2 represented two items yesterday, then it is reasonable to assume that it will again represent two items today. If a photograph yesterday could be understood to be a picture of my three-year-old daughter, then ten years from now, it will still be a picture of my three-year-old daughter, even though she no longer exists in that form. This is the kind of abstract thinking that human beings developed (and that animals never have) and that we've been steadily developing ever since.

Let me give you a quick example of how the rise of abstracted knowledge changed our perceptions of what could and could not be known. In the 1930s, the Russian psychologist Aleksandr Romanovich Luria studied illiterate peoples in far-flung regions of Uzbekistan and Kyrgyzstan. Writes James Gleick: "Luria found striking differences between illiterate and even slightly literate subjects, not in what they knew, but in how they thought." Quite simply, those without reading and writing struggled to think symbolically. Written words are stand-ins for real things in the real world. They operate in the realm of abstraction and necessarily follow rules derived from logic. "Oral people," Gleick noted, "lacked the categories that become second nature even to illiterate individuals in literate cultures: for example, for geometrical shapes. Shown drawings of circles and squares, they named them as 'plate, sieve, bucket, watch, or moon' and 'mirror, door, house, apricot drying board.'"[1]

They could not grasp abstraction. They lived in a pre-historical world of "audio-tactility." All things were present and real. There were no symbols, no stand-ins. Here's a question Luria posed to the illiterate tribal peoples he was studying: "In the Far North, where there is snow, all bears are white. Novaya Zembla is in the Far North and there is always snow there. What color are the bears?" A typical response, notes Gleick, is: "I don't know. I've seen a black bear. I've never seen any others. . . . Each locality has its own animals." But, writes Gleick, a man who recently learned to read and write answered the question very differently: "To go by your words, they should all be white."[2]

The development of the written word—something no other living creature has come close to replicating—changed our minds (physically and psychologically) and hence our worldview. Having learned to write things down, we learned to symbolize, we learned to think abstractly. We were ready to invent time, history, progress—future.

This is the kind of thought process that has been leading us away from magical ways of understanding the world, and toward what James Gleick calls "the information." What is "the information"? Well, in my interpretation of Gleick's book on the subject, "the information" is the progression—the expansion—of the notion that all things are knowable and, once made known, can be quantified and ultimately controlled. The notion of information is what makes us believe, today, that even unknown heretofore magical realms as seemingly ungraspable as the future can be somehow known, if only we can convert them to information or, even better, to data. And so philosopher Daniel Innerarity writes of "modern societies, which no longer acquire their knowledge of the future through the interpretation of dreams and no longer act vicariously through a person who wields both vision and power." Instead, we attempt to derive our knowledge of future from, as he puts it, "the corresponding processes of investigation and collective deliberation."[3]

o   o   o   o   o   o

Philip Tetlock is Annenberg University Professor of Psychology and Management at the University of Pennsylvania's School of Arts and Sciences and Wharton School. He has joined forces with the United States government to figure out how to cultivate the skillsets necessary to know the future. In fall of 2011, he began collaborating with the Intelligence Advanced Research Projects Activity (IARPA), which is the research arm of the intelligence branches of the government. IARPA was founded in 2006 and is pretty open about its goals. When I visit their website I am immediately confronted with the telling tagline, "Be the future." There's also a want ad right there on the homepage: "Are you a scientist or engineer with a creative idea that you think could provide the nation with an overwhelming intelligence advantage? If so, consider joining IARPA." How does IARPA think of the future? They'll tell you: "IARPA invests in high-risk, high-payoff research that has the potential to provide our nation with an overwhelming intelligence advantage over future adversaries."[4] In other words, it's a race, a competition pitting our braincases against their brainiacs. It's the start-up mentality—own the future before the future owns you—applied to the shadowy world of spying and stealth.

Fittingly enough, Philip Tetlock's collaboration with IARPA takes the shape of an online competition. Officially called the Good Judgment Project, it's led by Tetlock in collaboration with a dozen or more researchers from universities across the US. "The idea," writes *Washington Post* columnist David Ignatius, "is to use forecasting competitions to test the factors that lead analysts to make good predictions."[5]Volunteers and recruits to the study are divided into teams and asked a variety of questions focusing on the short-term future (events to come in the next two to twelve months). The questions are about the political future of elected officials, the possibility of armed conflict in an unstable country, what might happen to a certain sector of the economy in a certain part of the world—hard questions, but ones firmly rooted in the here and now.

From his office in Philadelphia, Philip Tetlock tells me that in the first phase, the competition has been trying to identify the people who are actually good at predicting the short term future. Once the people who are able to score highest based on being most right about future events are identified, the really useful stuff can start. What aspects of a person's thinking make them good at predication? Can those attributes be taught and enhanced? In other words, by identifying the attributes that make a person good at predicting the future, can we then, literally, teach people how to predict the future with a higher degree of accuracy? Can we get to the part where we really can "know" the future with a measurable degree of certainty? The goal isn't to know what will happen in the future, it's to know what kinds of things we have to know to turn what will happen in the future into fact and information.

"There's been interest," Philip Tetlock tells me, "among thoughtful people in the intelligence community about quantifying uncertainty and keeping track records."[6] Tetlock tells me that he was on a committee commissioned by the National Academy of Science that released a report in 2011 on "intelligence analysis." The report recommended that intelligence-based agencies should learn, as Tetlock explains to me, to be "more evidence based; don't just buy products, test things; don't just rely on word of mouth and anecdotes, test them the way the FDA does with drugs."

Out of that report emerged the IARPA experiment. (For the record, I requested an interview with IARPA through Professor Tetlock, and he passed the message back that they had declined to talk to me about the project.) At the time I spoke to Tetlock, the project had already involved "over 5,000 forecasters" who had made "more than 1 million forecasts on more than 250 questions, from euro-zone exits to the Syrian civil war."[7] So is it working? I ask Tetlock. Are the predictive trials isolating the attributes that will turn prediction from a blustery showman's game into the information?

What the trials do first off, Tetlock tells me, is essentially force people to be quick thinkers who don't get stuck on ideology or groupthink. "Falsification is imminent, you can very quickly be shown to be wrong, and people learn to be more circumspect and thoughtful in that kind of environment. I think that helps to explain why we are observing such superior levels of performance." Naturally, I'm immediately captivated by the end of that sentence: "superior levels of performance." So it is working. They're raising a generation of super forecasters who are going to be able to tell me what the German chancellor is going to have for breakfast while she's still happily snoozing away. And you're going to be able to do this without looking at the National Security Agency's apparently voluminous data on Angela Merkel including years of phone calls and e-mails. Alas, Professor Tetlock declines to be specific about what he means by "superior levels of performance." "I can't say too much more about that right now, but I will say they've done better than I thought they could do and there is a group of them whom we have dubbed 'super forecasters' who really have just blown past the performance expectations both inside the government and outside the government." Tetlock tells me that all the results will be made public in due course, when he and his colleagues have finished working on various academic papers. A few months after our interview, he provides more specifics in a short column in the *Economist* magazine. "Results are pouring in and they are revealing. . . . The big surprise has been the support for the unabashedly elitist 'super-forecaster' hypothesis. . . . When we randomly assigned 'supers' into elite teams, they blew the lid off IARPA's performance goals. They beat the unweighted average (wisdom-of-overall-crowd) by 65 percent; beat the best algorithms of four competitor institutions by 35-60 percent; and beat two prediction markets by 20-35 percent."[8] Around the same time, Ignatius of the *Washington Post* made the (unattributed) claim that "the top forecasters, drawn from universities and elsewhere, performed about 30 percent better than the average for intelligence community analysts who could read intercepts and other secret data."[9] In other words, according to Ignatius, intelligence analysts with security clearance to read every secret report and see every drone image were still considerably worse at prediction than Tetlock's best performers.

So, yes, it seems to be working, not only for Tetlock and his forecasters but for a wide array of researchers and social experimenters who want to find ways to know what is going to happen before it happens, who want to turn what was formerly an abstract unknowable into controllable data. IARPA and Philip Tetlock's network of collaborators aren't the only group trying to incorporate big data and psychology and crowdsourcing to get us to the point where we can actually turn future into information. In January 2014, George Mason University in Virginia launched SciCast, billed as the "largest and most advanced science and technology prediction market in the world." I'm not going to get into all the technical details of how SciCast works, but basically the idea is that anyone in the world can join up and start answering questions about what will happen in the realms of science and technology in the next six months to two years. The more questions you answer correctly as time goes by, the higher your score. "The more correct forecasts a participant makes, the more influence they'll have in other forecasts."[10] Eventually, the board should be dominated by a crowd of people with a proven track record in knowing the future. Five years down the road, SciCast should be able to throw a question out there and know with a very specific degree of certainty to what extent the answer they are getting back might actually represent what is going to happen in the near future.

Similarly, back at Patrick Tucker's World Future Conference I sit in a packed room and listen to a presentation on the construction of a global knowledge hub called the Millennium Project. This project features "a coherent and cumulative process that collects and assesses judgments from over 3,500 people" who are invited into the project via "U.N. Organizations, governments, corporations, NGOs, universities, and individuals from around the world."[11] Their goal, too, is the building of a kind of massive hive mind of crowdsourced pundits—a postmodern oracle to soothe the fragmentation of our age by converting the mystery of future into information.

Sensing that interest in the psychology of prediction and future perception has never been greater, I again check in with social psychologist Cheryl Wakslak, who teaches and researches at the University of Southern California Marshall School of Business in Los Angeles and has a PhD in psychology from New York University. "It's something of a hot topic now in psychology," Wakslak tells me.[12] Wakslak notes that around the turn of the millennium, psychology started shifting focus away from trying to understand memory, and toward trying to understand how people think about the future. "People," she says, "have looked at time from a historical perspective, how people's sense of time is different, how people process time passing. Now a lot of people are looking at the future."

Why the new focus on the future? Well for starters, it's a case of supply and demand. As we saw visiting ESRI and with the rise of big data, there's huge demand. Philip Tetlock puts it to me this way: "There's such an insatiable demand for forecasting and we have such a pathetic supply it's very, very dissonant to think how little we know about our future." This dissonance is even more disconcerting at a time when we are making ownership of the future the central weapon in our arsenal. We're counting on our ability to harness the magic, to shape the future and solve the major problems of humanity including the now ongoing disaster of climate change and the always looming specter of global epidemics of disease, hunger, and terror. But on a deeper, granular level, we are counting on our ownership and control of future as a bulwark against our fear of the unknown. Ever plagued by the ominous awareness of our mortality and deprived of the spiritual solace of living in the pre-historical era of past-present continuum, we aren't just interested in kinda maybe knowing the future. We are interested in conquering the future, banishing the unknown and arriving at a new era of total dominion over the time to come. "We are increasingly conceptualizing the future in terms of now," says Cheryl Wakslak. "We want to control the future; we want to create a sense of proximity with the future. The more ways in which we see connections, the less the future is the future." In other words, we are literally restating the future as something we can break down, control, and own—the future isn't the future any more, it's the next present, it's the new now.

All of this neatly confirms the notion advanced by Daniel Innerarity that we have moved from a time when what we didn't know reassured us, to a time when we are reassured only by what we think we can know—everything. Having lost the magic and magicians who once were able to reassure us by saying that, yes, everything will go on as it always has, even after you're gone—we now seek the same balm through the quest to turn what we remain afraid of into information. Can we ever really know the future? In some crucial way, that's missing the point. It's the story we tell about the future that is important here, as opposed to any actual knowledge of the future. Just the feeling of control over future is enough. I don't know if Innerarity has heard of Philip Tetlock and is following the work of IARPA, but I suspect he would not be surprised by the example of Professor Tetlock and his quest to develop systematic knowledge of best practices to predict the future. Tetlock's work provides a great illustration of how we moved from the magic to the information and where this transition is taking us. The witches congregate in the boardroom. The warlocks don suits and project spreadsheets.

o   o   o   o   o   o

The transition we've undergone can be expressed in this way: death=known mystery is now death=unknown solution. In the time of magic, death was known, assured, and inevitable; it had a purpose. People had to die to continue magical cycles of life beyond our understanding. But it was okay: what was would continue without us; death did not mean obliteration, it was part of the natural process of life. But in the age of future, the apogee of the rise of the information, death is a problem to be solved and dying is a kind of failure; the dead failed to hang on long enough to arrive at the future where no one will have to die. We don't want to fail and so our new soothsayers, the new magicians who promise they can know the future and end death, are multiplying exponentially. We don't know which exact "scientific" approach to curing death will succeed. But we do know that once converted into information, everything is knowable, thus everything is possible. Whether it's gene therapies or DNA manipulations or good old brain transfers to lifelike robots, the new projects and products of the future seem to be offering a whole new way to understand our ongoing struggle for continuity: the murky workings of the brain is our future just waiting to be captured, converted into code and ushered into being—darkness awaiting light.

If I had told you a hundred years ago that it would be mainstream to believe that death could be forestalled, even rendered obsolete, you would have questioned my sanity. But today, as we saw in the last chapter, death is being recast as something in which we can intervene in. And the price to be paid is no mythological Gilgameshian quest for eternal life or a day coma in a coffin awaiting midnight feedings on the blood of unsuspecting comely virgins. The ghouls wear lab coats now, their bosses jet-setting not to Transylvania via batwings but to Davos via private jet. Death is no longer part of the fabric of magic that glimmers in the seams of the otherwise plain weave of life. Death is something we can quantify, examine, study, and deal with. Death, like so many other things, is the future. And the future is just chaos waiting to be shaped into the information. In the big-data age, the future, far more than the past and the present, is open to quantification, manipulation, alteration and disruption. This—not technological progress or the rise of the computing age—is the great story of the postmodern era.

Am I exaggerating our faith in the power of abstraction—that ruptured awareness that abruptly separated us from the rest of the living creatures on Earth—to allow us to know and then control all things? Well we've already established that under the auspices of future our largest most powerful corporations are investing billions in schemes to convert the world to data. And we've already established that the idea of some kind of transhuman mind-machine merge that achieves not just immortality but immortality with endless virtual possibility is also, now, considered both desirable and increasingly doable, an actually attainable goal. With the end point clearly visible, it's easier to look back into the so-called history of progress and find that all along we were moving (sometimes being pushed, sometimes pulling) in this direction. Our journey to the time of future is the journey from the certainty of materiality to the slippery ubiquity of abstraction. Whenever there is the symbolic abstraction of language, there is the disruption of time from place, there is humanity displaced from eternal limits and pushed toward the limitless eternal.

To look even briefly at the history of knowledge storage and transfer is to see the growing certainty, even faith, in what would eventually become the transcendent power of information to replace magic and banish the unknown forever.

Enlightenment thinker Denis Diderot's stated aim in editing and publishing the Encyclopédie, published in Paris beginning in 1751, was "to collect all the knowledge that now lies scattered over the face of the earth, to make known its general structure to the men with whom we live, and to transmit it to those who will come after us."[13] Then there was the Encyclopedia Britannica, first produced in Edinburgh in 1768. It arrived in installments—one hundred in total for sixpence apiece. Writes James Gleick: "It seemed finished—in every edition."[14]

With the rise of the book also came the emergence of a new faith in language and its power. There could be "a certain script of language," speculated Gottfried Wilhelm Leibniz in 1678, "that perfectly represents the relationships between our thoughts."[15] The seventeenth-century German philosopher and mathematician Leibniz put his faith in a language of pure reason—the language that would allow us to symbolize all disagreement, all controversy, all known unknowns through the pure intractable truth of logic. He spoke of using this mathematical language to "work out by an infallible calculus, the doctrines most useful for life, that is, those of morality and metaphysics."[16] Leibniz invented calculus and even, in 1679, "imagined a digital computer in which binary numbers were represented by spherical tokens, governed by gates under mechanical control."[17] He laid the groundwork for the information-based computer revolution to come. But first, there would be Charles Babbage, who never did quite manage to bend the steam technologies of nineteenth-century England into his difference engine—the massive calculating machine he believed he could build. But that didn't stop his supporters from trumpeting what the thing would and could eventually do. In particular, Ada Lovelace, daughter of the poet Lord Byron and Babbage's mathematically gifted muse, enthused that Babbage's analytical engine would not just calculate numbers, it would perform operations on "any process which alters the mutual relation of two or more things." She went on: "This is the most general definition, and would include all subjects in the universe."[18] Lovelace, dubbed everything from "the prophet of the computer age" to "the enchantress of numbers," had that rare combination of mathematical genius and inherited gift for language; as a result she had a vision for what a language of pure information could make possible—just about anything. She writes with beauty and scope about the information landscape to come: "A new, a vast, and a powerful language is developed . . . in which to wield its truths so that these may become of more speedy and accurate practical application for the purposes of mankind than the means hitherto in our possession have rendered possible."[19]

Around the same time, Pierre-Simon Laplace, the great French astronomer and mathematician, an advocate for Newtonian principles, wrote of a new kind of "intelligence" that "would embrace in the same formula the movements of the greatest bodies of the universe and those of the lightest atom; for it, nothing would be uncertain and the future, as the past, would be present to its eyes."[20] Uncertainty banished. The future brought under our control. What was needed to achieve this goal? A formula for a new kind of all-embracing intelligence. A language, in other words, to encompass all information, known and still to come. Everything would be converted to information, represented by symbols, the functions of the world nothing more than code, hidden, awaiting discovery and translation. Wrote Charles Babbage himself of his aspirations regarding his difference engine: "We may perhaps be enabled to form a faint estimate of the magnitude of that lowest step in the chain of reasoning, which leads us up to Nature's God.[21]

Babbage works on his counting machine, and around the same time countless others compete with Samuel Morse for another way to convert what there is into information and, in the process, conquer the limitations of the physical world. The telegraph transmuted information across space faster than any other medium of transfer previously attempted. Runners, galloping horses, passenger pigeons, signals drummed from the top of hills, bonfires lit on a contiguous series of peaks—all were to be eventually made unnecessary by the introduction of the telegraph in the mid-1840s. Time and space could finally be compressed, even conquered, transformed into information and sent in an instant everywhere and anywhere. This was the rhetorical promise of the future era taking root. *The New York Times* announced the telegraph represented "a result so practical, yet so inconceivable . . . so full of hopeful prognostics for the future of mankind . . . one of the grand way-marks in the onward and upward march of the human intellect." *The Times*, notably, highlighted "the transmission of thought, the vital impulse of matter" as the telegraph's great achievement, as if the telegraph had somehow erased the alphabet and tapped directly into the simultaneity of the thought process.[22]

Now we are no more than a hundred and twenty years from the time Marshall McLuhan would write of a new global consciousness; the "village" he envisioned would be a triumphant return to the unified audio-tactile consciousness of the tribal prehistoric, only without the blinders, without the limits, without the obsfucation of magic. "Today," enthused the great 1960s philosopher, "we have extended our central nervous systems in a global embrace, abolishing both space and time as far as our planet is concerned. Rapidly, we approach the final phase of the extensions of man—the technological simulation of consciousness, when the creative process of knowing will be collectively and corporately extended to the whole of human society."[23]

As we gain momentum and hurtle into the computer age, the pronunciations become both more certain and more precise. "Tomorrow," promises Albert Einstein collaborator John Archibald Wheeler, who coined the famously cryptic phrase 'it from bit,' "we will have learned to understand and express all of physics in the language of information."[24] Wheeler sets us on a quest: to pull into information nothing less than the totality of everything that is or was or could be. "If and when we learn how to combine bits in fantastically large numbers to obtain what we call existence, we will know better what we mean both by bit and by existence."[25]

All existence can be manipulated as long as we embrace the process. What is the process? The process is the act of turning "its" into bits and bytes, ones and zeroes, logical progressions. The process is logic itself, the embrace of life as nothing more than a continuous flow of information that can and should be corralled, funnelled, dammed like a river, domesticated and controlled. Think of Wikipedia, often mocked for the way its "information" is constantly changing, subject to various whims and shifts in the opinions of its contributors. But if you look at it another way, Wikipedia represents the future-era big information project well: it changes, it grows, it never becomes stale or dated, no new edition is ever necessary; its fungible essence is the heart of its legitimacy because it, too, lays claim to the goal of one day creating through abstraction a totality of all things known and to be known. It is our ten commandments, and we are its gods. This, too, is part of the process: the shift from the guiding principle of gods and their magic to the command and control principle of information.

We have begun to see the world, notes researcher James Flynn, through "scientific spectacles." Flynn should know: the New Zealand–based scholar has been writing since the mid-1980s about what is now widely called the Flynn Effect. The Flynn Effect is essentially the phenomenon of rising IQ scores. To put it simply, after studying IQ tests given in the same place in the same way to the same kinds of people since 1930 (around the same time Russian psychologist Luria was studying increasingly smaller pockets of people who remained functionally illiterate) Flynn found that we've been consistently improving on IQ tests. How to account for this? Some, of course, are anxious to trumpet humanity's overall smarts. We're just getting smarter and smarter and smarter. But Flynn doesn't think so. He says that the pattern of rising IQ scores does not mean that we are comparing "a worse mind with a better one," but rather that we are comparing minds that "were adapted to one cognitive environment with those whose minds are adapted to another cognitive environment."[26] Seen in this light, the Flynn effect does not reflect gains in general intelligence. We aren't getting smarter; we are getting more modern. Or to put it another way—we aren't smarter, but we are more steeped in the language of abstraction, more used to the idea that everything and anything can be expressed in the prismed refraction of virtual totality—the information.

"One of the defining features of modern times," write the authors of the book *Big Data*, "is our sense of ourselves as masters of our fate; this attitude sets us apart from our ancestors, for whom determinism of some form was the norm."[27] Big data, as the fuel source for the permanent future, is the information expanding beyond anything we could have ever have hoped for or imagined. It epitomizes the arrival of the future era, an age not just of expanding information, but of hyper information, of exponentially expanding information. What do we ultimately want from the information age?—a promise: that we can arrive back (not a return, a going forward!) at the irrefutable continuity of life. Only, the big-data permanent-future promise is even more expansive than what the magicians could ever offer. Once we were assured that life as we know it would go on forever. Now we are assured that our specific lives will go on forever. Big data is another step on the journey, another incarnation of magic into the information. It's something from nothing. It's the holy grail. It's living forever at the end of the never-ending future.

o o o o o

Ariel Garten curls up on the couch in the foyer of her company's prototypical brightly lit, hardwood floored, open concept office. She tucks her bare feet under her and starts speaking to me, intensely and quietly, about the magic. "It's like doing a Jedi mind trick," the CEO of the Toronto-based InteraXon company tells me. She is describing harnessing the power of brain waves to perform simple tasks including turning on and off a light switch or pouring a beer out of the tap they have at their headquarters. "You focus on it and say in your head like 'beer, beer, beer, beer, beer, beer, beer,' and it pours." Garten is quick to point out that it's still faster and easier to just get up and pour yourself a cold one. Still, the future is bright for the magic: "If that's the functionality we have right now," Garten says, "in thirty years that functionality will be light years ahead. It will be seamless communication with the world around you, potentially seamless communication with other people as well."[28]

InteraXon was founded in 2007 by Garten, former live music entrepreneur Trevor Colemen and computer engineer Chris Aimone. They got international notice when they worked with the 2010 Vancouver Winter Olympics to allow crowds in Vancouver wearing brain wave sensors to control colored lights installed on famous Canadian landmarks like Niagara Falls and the Parliament buildings in Ottawa. But now the company is focused on a more prosaic activity—launching their first commercial product, Muse, "the brain sensing headband." When I spoke to Garten they were taking advance orders online for Muse to be delivered in 2014. The magic, coming soon to a store near you. Or not quite. Muse, which Garten describes as "slim, sleek, usable, something that would fit into people's lives," is, sadly, not the average person's admission to "the force." Muse and its brain wave–sensing technology won't give you the power to manipulate objects with your mind. So what can it do? I ask. Ariel Garten furrows her forehead. She spends quite a bit of her time in interviews explaining what Muse doesn't do to enthusiastic reporters eager to hear about psychokinesis and telepathy—all of which are coming, she assures me, again noting that this technology is just in its infancy. But for now, Muse is essentially a brain wave monitor. It comes in the form of an off-white, vaguely plastic-y looking headband. It sits on your forehead just below the hairline and communicates wirelessly to your smartphone or tablet. Its primary functionality will be through applications made both by InteraXon and third parties. In a 2013 article, Garten said that 700 hundred or so outside parties had registered with the company to make applications for the product. Among those promised was EmoType, a text editor that changes its font style based on the user's current state of mind. "In a few years," writes an enthusiastic journalist, "worries over whether someone misinterpreted the tone of your e-mail could be gone for good."[29]

But for now the primary app that ships with the $299 device is one built by InteraXon. The app is called "Calm" and Garten tells me it "lets you actually see your brain states, see what's going on in your mind at all times, and then it gives you the opportunity to actually improve your mental abilities." The app comes with "exercises to improve your attention, your working memory." But the real selling point so far is that "it can also give you the ability to decrease your stress. So it can give you beautiful and engaging experiences that actually track the state of stress and relaxation in your brain and take your brain to a relaxed state and then your body to a relaxed state."

Basically, the device transfers information about your brain waves to an app on your mobile device. The app monitors what causes spikes in your brain waves and gets you going, and what settles your mind into a flat, relaxing plane. It is primarily a meditation aid. "We are able to teach you to maintain a stable state of attention," says Garten, "and show you when your mind is distracted." A major component of the brain health system, then, is that it assists the user in mindfulness mediation, an increasingly popular method of decreasing anxiety by thinking about being in the here and now, focusing on the singular moment, one breath after the next and nothing more.

Is there a market for Muse and its current level of functionality? Garten thinks so. "Most people know that you've got to work on your body, you've got to go to the gym. And just now we're beginning to be aware that we can have the same understanding of and influence on our brain and our thought processes. There's starting to be a big dialogue around keeping your brain fit."

It's easy to see why investors might be attracted to InteraXon's plan to sell a product tailor-made to appeal to the well-off, health-focused, and tech-obsessed. But then again, the concept's current functionality is fairly narrow. Plus it's relatively untested. Garten talks to me about family doctors recommending Muse to patients suffering the physical symptoms of stress and anxiety. I ask her if there is any scientific evidence that Muse is, actually, a successful brain aid. Is it proven through any kind of study that it reduces stress? Can it really improve memory? She tells me that an independent study of Muse's potential mental health benefits has been commissioned, but at the time of my speaking with her, the results were not yet available. Nevertheless, Garten, who graduated from the University of Toronto with a bachelor's degree in psychology and neuroscience and has worked as a practicing psychotherapist, is convinced that Muse can help people with not just stress and anxiety but with a wide range of mental health issues. In fact, the second app her company is developing is designed to help children with attention deficit disorder (ADD). The app allows the kids to monitor their brain waves while completing tasks and playing games, which is meant to give them more insight into when their focus wanders and why. Again, I ask Garten if there is any evidence that this will work. "The methodology that underlies it has been clinically validated and used for probably thirty years," she tells me crisply.

In fact, what Garten offers via Muse is a variation of the brain wave monitoring-as-therapy that was first studied in the 1920s and became a more common tool in mental health treatment in the 1960s. Popularized then as the faddish Biofeedback and now more commonly called Neurofeedback, there is still quite a bit of dissent around whether or not people can use these techniques to train their brains and bodies. Indeed, though devices, treatments, and processes continue to move out of the laboratory and into the proliferating world of personalized consumer electronics, most of the claims made around biofeedback are at best considered unproven. A paper published in the *International Journal of Mental Health*, titled "Brainscams: Neuromythologies of the New Age," summarizes a wide range of product and treatment claims around biofeedback. The late Simon Fraser University professor Barry Beyerstein concluded that "there is virtually no credible scientific support for the programs."[30] On the other hand, as more and more Muse-like devices emerge, and our understanding of the brain's neuroplastic potential to reshape itself continues to develop, it might yet be proven that some of these devices and approaches do work.

Whether or not Muse can help kids with ADD or adults de-stress remains to be seen. It's also an open question as to whether or not family doctors will start prescribing the device instead of or alongside antidepressants. A scan of customer reviews online after the device became widely available shows that right now, Muse is primarily used via the Calm app as a meditation aid. So it's a device that adds a futuristic techy component to mindfulness. Since just about everyone in mental health agrees that following a daily mindfulness program is going to reduce stress and anxiety, I wonder if those who claim positive results from Muse would have had any less of a positive experience simply spending the same time every day following a program outlined in a book they took out from the library. (Though the same argument can be made for so many of the gadgets and gizmos we suddenly feel like we can't live without, I still think it's worth asking that question.)

And yet Garten has no shortage of believers and admirers. She's traveled to tech trade shows and conferences the world over demonstrating Muse. She's given the requisite TED Talk. Search her name and you find glowing articles with headlines like "Meet the Extraordinary Woman Behind InteraXon" and "Meet the woman making brainwave control look more like meditation and less like the Matrix." Most of the stories are accompanied by photos or videos of the slim, impeccably dressed Garten staring mysteriously into the ether, her long shimmering brown hair flowing behind her as her piercing blue eyes ponder what comes next.

All of this has clearly paid off. There's another category of believer that Garten's company has recently been able to attract: investors. Following on the heels of a successful Indiegogo crowdsourcing campaign that brought in $300,000, InteraXon embarked on a venture capital campaign that culminated in a major August 2013 announcement: InteraXon had raised $6 million from firms including Horizon Ventures, OMERS Ventures, and A-Grade Investments—Ashton Kutcher's investment company.[31]

I haven't seen InteraXon's business plan but it seems hard to imagine from the outside looking in how the company is going to manage to repay that investment in the short or long term. I suspect that there's another reason why six million dollars in venture capital flowed to a small Toronto start-up headed by a woman previously best known in the fashion industry (she once ran a boutique and designed her own line of clothes). The secret is Ariel Garten herself. Garten has charisma. She has mystique. She has conviction. The more I talk to her, the more I want to give her the benefit of the doubt. Garten is soft-spoken, intense, and utterly self-assured. She has the magic. She's going to give you the magic. "This isn't just a technology company," Garten tells me. "I'm not actually particularly interested in technology, to be honest. It's an opportunity for people to discover and enable themselves in new ways."

InteraXon is an emblematic future-era company. After all, it's not what Muse can do now that's interesting, it's what Garten and her crew say that Muse and related technologies will do soon. Discover. Enable. Extend. Become. Garten's skill is to envision the relatively limited capabilities of Muse as being at the heart of everything that is coming next for humanity. "When we look at the development of the technology over time, in three to five years you're going to start to see applications that let you share with one another using this kind of technology. It might be posting, tagging photos on Facebook with the emotions you had when you saw them." As Garten sees it, wireless monitoring of your brain waves will eventually allow "your technology to understand you more effectively and interact more effectively with your world on a daily basis. For example, "your phone will know that you're asleep and the fricking thing will stop ringing." And maybe, I ask Garten, we'll have the force after all? "In the far future we will," she sagely assures me. "Not in thirty years. Telepathy in the eighty- to hundred-year horizon, absolutely." For all of Ariel Garten's promises, the Muse is essentially telling the story of the journey: a device *available now* that will help us to know and own the future in the form of information about our brain processes. It's a device that tells us what just happened to our brain in order to help us control *what's going to happen next* in our brain. But for many of us, even those of us actively involved in pursuing future and transferring more and more of life into captured information, in some hidden part of the brain, a plate is still a circle and death is still the known unknown to be feared and placated. The old modes linger. We have not yet, and may never, end our longstanding relationship to the magic that once overshadowed almost everything in human life. The process is slow and confusing. "Man the food-gatherer reappears incongruously as information-gatherer," remarked Marshall McLuhan in 1967. We look at what Ariel Garten is selling and wonder: Is it magic or information? Is it story or science? (It is both and neither.) The time of the permanent future is not the triumph of knowledge over magic, of logic over feeling. It is the triumph of information.

Magic—the narrative of the perpetual unknown—lingers in the crannies of our consciousness. And so a figure like Ariel Garten succeeds on two levels: First, she is a classic intermediary, a high priestess with powers only she can control, powers that provide us with long-term spiritual reassurances that are a promise and relief—believe in me and I will lead you to a place where you won't die, or if you do die, your death won't be an erasure. Second, she appears as a scientist, someone who can help us harness information and shape it into pattern. Fused together into one irresistible package, the result is the (new) magic that brings us one step closer to knowing the future, one step closer to staving off our no longer inevitable demise. Everything up to that point is just a problem to be solved, a lack of information.

PART III

The Case Against the Future

CHAPTER 7

Consumption, Innovation, and the Truth of Change

My Sonne, feare thou the Lord, and the King, and meddle not with them that are given to change. For their calamity shall rise suddenly; and who knoweth the ruine of them both? (Proverbs, 24: 21)

In the beginning there was the unknown, the vast nothingness: "The earth was without form, and void; and darkness was over the face of the deep." (Genesis 1:2) 3.5 billion years ago the earth was host to nothing and no one. Not even the tiniest microbes stirred amongst the churning boiling seas and oozing seabed volcanoes whose cooling lava would eventually form the first masses of land. But then there was the word. "And God said, Let there be light: and there was light. And God saw the light, that it was good: and God divided the light from the darkness." (Genesis 1:3–4) God, the original innovator. The first disruptor. The Steve Jobs of the heavens. The word was innovate. Two and a half billion years ago, cyanobacteria, single-celled microbes—more plant than animal—frothing on the waves of the sea prospered under the hot sun, absorbing solar energy and oozing oxygen. Let there be life. God gave us light and the tiny micro-gods gave us atmosphere. The lesson? God—the über-human, the prototype that we have modeled ourselves after ever since, the main character of the best-known story we tell each other across the world—was an innovator. And God's creatures, from the tiniest invisible planktons to pterodactyls taking flight, growing feathers, and eventually becoming the pigeons of today, were also innovators.

So you see, we always innovated. We will always innovate. Innovation is biblical. Innovation is natural. It is inherent. It is practically elemental. "Natural selection rewards innovation," writes Stephen Johnson, author of *Where Good Ideas Come From: The Natural History of Innovation*.[1] After all, those tiny invisible bacteria and microbes were the building blocks of life on earth. And, according to Johnson, they were awfully clever little guys, constantly figuring out new ways to diversify their DNA, get bigger, stronger, more complex. As he writes later on in his book: "When the going gets tough life tends to gravitate toward more innovative reproductive strategies."[2] Even back when we were just a twinkle in a microbe's mitosis we were inherently innovative.

And guess what all those microbes innovating their evolution led to? Guess what they wrought? Us, of course, the species now standing at the pinnacle of the food chain. It hardly even needs to be said, but I'll say it anyway. If the microscopic organisms that created the atmosphere millions of year ago were innovators, then surely the *Homo sapiens* that emerged from them to rule the earth must be even more naturally innovative—must, in fact, be imbued with near-superpowers of innovation. We are creatures tethered to change, made whole by the quest to let our dissatisfaction with what is pull us toward the endless journey to the future. Writes Johnson: "Good ideas may not want to be free, but they do want to connect, fuse, recombine. They want to reinvent themselves by crossing conceptual borders. They want to complete each other as much as they want to compete."[3] We inherent creatures of the idea just want to be free to become what we were destined to be—complete! And so from the microbe to the human, we have sought to reinvent, to compete, to complete the as yet unfinished business of humanity.

That's the story we now tell each other. It's the biblical story of the beginning of our world—Made something! Made it better!—and it's the prevailing narrative thread of modern human history. As Thomas Frank notes about Johnson's book, "the creative epiphany itself becomes a kind of heroic character, helping out clueless humanity wherever necessary."[4] It's simply natural history to spin the tale of humans as the ultimate innovators. Johnson is one of many sought-after speakers and pundits appealing to our reflexive faith in future by promulgating innovation as the natural edifice for all progress; for them, the era of future is just the progression of that extraordinary, maybe even God-instilled human drive to innovate and change and challenge the status quo.

It's a great story, but is it true? There is an equally powerful counter-narrative. In this compelling but far less marketable narrative, most of human(oid) existence—the vast majority of it happening before there was such a thing as history—has been pretty static. For one thing, as I've already suggested, our primary attraction to future is counterintuitively wrapped up in a need for certainty—the desire to know what is going to happen so we can reassure ourselves that life is going to go on in more or less the same way. What innovation there has been has been the exception, not the rule. In fact, even in today's seeming maelstrom of technological change and discovery, the core pattern of human existence has not deviated much at all. Life has pretty much followed the same cycle ever since we were thrown out of Eden and left to our own devices. What did we get up to? We roamed around in smallish groups roughly the same size as the social units formed by our simian predecessors. We hunted, we gathered food, and we sought shelter. Throughout most of prehistory, the massive two-to three-million–year chunk of time before we started to plant crops, form permanent communities, and create the conditions that would lead to modernity, we would eat what there was to eat and then, when there was not much of anything left, we would move on. This was our pattern, the circle of life, *Lion King*–style. Through good times and bad, we barely changed at all. We stayed in the loop. We repeated our successes until they became our failures and then we roamed elsewhere and started the whole thing over again.

The Chumash people first settled on Southern California's Channel Islands some 13,000 years ago. Jeanne Arnold, professor of anthropology at the University of California, Los Angeles, has been studying the Chumash for over thirty years. As she tells me, "This particular population of the people that we call the Chumash today have close to 13,000 years of ancestry genealogically linkable in the same place, which is extremely remarkable for any population anywhere in the world."[5] Around the year 1100, the Chumash people were in their middle period. They had a large population and control over significant territory both on the islands and the mainland. They were, Arnold tells me, "making everything needed for daily lives. Most households were self-sufficient with regards to the things they wanted to use and extract food from." The Chumash fished, hunted, grew, and gathered. They developed simple tools to help them do what they needed to do. "They had bones and they had shells and they had stone," says Arnold, listing off the resources available to the Chumash a thousand years ago. "They had to make do, and so in order to survive they had to figure out what was going to work. And once they figured that out, there really wasn't much room to do anything dramatically different." (Remember social certainty? That's one thing the Chumash had in abundance.) For roughly 7,000-plus years, as far as the archeological record reveals, the Chumash stayed in the same area and made only minor changes to their technology, to their religious and social practices, to how they organized themselves in their culture and society.

But around 1150, change came to the Chumash. Droughts and El Niño weather conditions become more frequent. The tribe started to have trouble feeding itself. There's also evidence to suggest that the Chumash might have overused their natural environment, in part possibly because of the demands of a growing population. Anthropologists Torben C. Rick and Jon M. Erlandson found "overwhelming proof" that any number of ancient peoples "depleted or otherwise altered coastal areas" including California's Channel Islands.[6] We of course don't know the exact cause of the changes, but we do know that around this time environmental pressure was the stimulus for change. The leaders of the Chumash reorganized the division of labor within the families on the island, creating, for the first time, specialization. After thousands and thousands of years of living one way, the Chumash broke up self-sufficient family units and assigned certain people certain jobs described by Jeanne Arnold as "people specializing in deep sea fishing, in making canoes, making beads and so on."

This was a deliberate strategy of the Chumash people. They were facing drought conditions and they were going hungry. But they had a near monopoly on high-quality shells in the region and plenty of stones to make tools. So the Chumash developed a new commodity—shell beads, much in demand by other tribes on the mainland—which they were able to trade for what they needed: additional corn and seeds. Increased trading, in turn, stimulated relatively quick improvements to the plank canoes the Chumash were experts in constructing. As Arnold points out, "there was always a strong incentive to be very adept with the plank canoe technology so you didn't end up in the bottom of the channel."

Arnold doesn't see any of this, however, as evidence of a particular inherent need or, as she puts it, "desire to be innovative." Rather, she notes, this first and only major shift in how the Chumash people organized themselves over the course of 13,000 years was the result of sheer necessity. "If the population wanted to stay where they were living, we think they needed to augment their plant food supplies in order to have a healthy diet, and one way to do that was to produce something there that people can't get somewhere else." Ultimately, the relatively modest improvements the Chumash made to their technology, and what we might think of now as greater efficiency in the organization of their labor force, was, as Arnold puts it, "more of strategizing to keep up the quality of life than thinking 'we're going to advance our technology.'" Indeed, Arnold describes the entire "initial reorganization" as being done "out of something approaching necessity."

Having made the adjustment out of necessity, the Chumash saw no further need to adjust or "advance." They stayed pretty much the same from 1150 on all the way up to historic contact which occurred in the early 1700s.

What do we learn from the Chumash? We learn to question the notion of owning the future as an inevitable natural, the key to the human story. Change as the basis for human life, particularly technological change but also a whole host of other kinds of social and political changes aimed at making society supposedly more efficient and productive, is simply not found in the historical record. The Chumash support the counter-theory that when we changed, when we adapted or "innovated," it was largely out of necessity as opposed to some natural desire to endlessly upgrade. "Certainly the technologies were not static," Jeanne Arnold tells me, "but these societies also seemed to embrace and treasure their ways of life and not easily move onto other technologies if they were not demonstrably superior." That didn't mean the Chumash were intellectually deficient. It was just that, swaddled in their own sense of social certainty, they were not naturally predisposed to change. "People were just as smart then as they are now," says Arnold. "So pretty quickly they found the best solution to a technological problem and until they found a new resource they would pretty much stick with what they had. Over thousands of years, things look more or less the same. There are only so many ways that you can make fishing equipment out of shell resources or bone resources."

o   o   o   o   o   o

Wherever we've gone, we always started out by killing and eating the biggest animals. They were slow, easy to track, and abundant in meat plus all kinds of other bonus items like fat and skins; we hunted them into oblivion in the relative blink of an eye. Naturalist writer James McKinnon describes in his book, *The Once and Future World*, a time roughly 250 million years ago when "large and fierce beasts" roamed. We primates were scared creatures huddled in caves. But over a relatively short period of time, the large fierce beasts came to have reason to fear us. We learned how to hunt them down with an efficiency redolent with the suggestion of our future ruthlessness. And so, our destiny reveals itself: over the time span of a mere 10,000 years, the giant fauna that had ruled our planet for more than ten million years were dispatched by what were once their much smaller, weaker, prey.[7]

This cycle would repeat itself again and again. Over the course of our tenure on Earth, human beings have managed to eliminate just about every larger animal species we came across wherever we came across it. And then, still hungry, we hunted the medium-sized creatures next, tracking down bison and caribou and deer (hard to believe now, but deer were almost extinct at one point in North America) before grabbing up the plentiful little beasts that used to scamper around us while we were busy hunting, skinning, and smoking their much larger peers. Very often, we starved a bit (or a lot) before realizing that we had no choice but to move onto a new food source or a new region. And then we wandered along into new territory to start the whole process over again until, in relatively short order, there was nowhere new left to go.

Only at that point, having, as McKinnon despairingly notes, "largely eliminated the mega-fauna of our age" did we get around to showing the slightest interest in changing our way of life, in "innovating." Like Stephen Johnson's clever microbes, we sought out new energy sources, desperate to diversify. But in the counter-narrative to the story of natural human creativity, this wasn't an act of natural innovation, but an act of desperation. Writes the historian Clive Ponting:

> Human societies did not set out to invent agriculture and produce permanent settlements. Instead a series of marginal changes were made gradually in existing ways of obtaining food as a result of particular local circumstances. The cumulative effect of the various alterations was important because they acted like a ratchet. Changes in subsistence methods often allowed a larger population to be supported but this made it difficult and eventually impossible to return to a gathering and hunting way of life because the extra people could not then be fed.[8]

It wasn't our natural will to innovate that inspired many of the changes from hunter-gatherer to agrarian society—what Ponting calls "the first great transition." It was hunger. From generation to generation, we forgot to take it easy on the buffaloes and bears so we would have some left over for next year. Eventually, this took its toll on our ability to survive. We started to tinker with seeds. And even then, it took us another solid 10,000 years (a laughable pace of change when you consider that many proponents of the singularity believe we'll be downloading our consciousness into computers by the year 2024) before we finally came up with any kind of cohesive system of agriculture. But, as Clive Ponting argues, once we had agriculture, we had more people living longer—farming being a lot less dangerous than tussling with rhinos for their meat, and a lot more productive from a nutritional standpoint too. So we had to keep ratcheting up productivity. We had to learn to get better at farming. Of course, the better we got at finding new energy sources for our hungry, fledgling civilizations, the more our populations kept expanding, putting more pressure on us to harness more energy sources in order to maintain survival of an ever-growing mass. It wasn't that we were so inherently innovative that we just couldn't leave well enough alone. It was that we had no other choice—we'd exhausted resources, we had more and more hungry mouths to feed. For Ponting, this is the ratchet effect—"societies," as J. B. McKinnon summarizes it, "needing to advance their technologies and degree of organization in order to respond to environmental challenges that are often of their own making."[9]

But surely once we came up with agriculture we stopped strip mining our food supplies and then, finally, got down to what we were meant to be doing all along—innovating our way to being a kinder, gentler, smarter species living in harmony with each other and the world. Well, maybe not. In the modern age, despite the so-called agricultural revolution bringing us all the mono-crop you can eat, the killing and plundering continues apace. As historian David Edgerton notes in his book *The Shock of the Old*, we have this sense that we are more evolved today than our warring and hunting brethren of old. We imagine them as somewhat unrefined in their dedication to brutality and mayhem, both in their interpersonal and survival skills. But in truth, despite the rise of civilization and its many technologies, "the rate of killing—of all sorts of living things—increased in the twentieth century, and did so drastically. For plants, bacteria, insects, cattle, whales, fish and human beings, the twentieth century was murderous."[10]

Let's consider the case of whaling. For thousands of years, small tribes hunted whales. But catching and processing a whale was a slow, arduous process, and it didn't happen every day—it was a big moment for the whole tribe when the hunters managed to kill a whale. Gradually, as our societies grew larger and hungrier, we began to get better at hunting whales—we used lookouts to track their spouts, we sailed further and faster in their territory. By the fourteenth and fifteenth centuries, the nations of Europe were sending out whaling fleets and squabbling among each other for access to the best areas for hunting. Small refinements in the hunt were made, but the slow procedure of killing a whale and dragging it back to shore for processing remained fundamentally the same, and whales continued to be abundant. Then, in the 1930s, came the global super substance known as margarine. We needed cheap sources of oil to make this miracle spread. Whales were the solution. The Germans, hungry for fuel and energy as they ramped up their plans for world domination, invented an entire new way to process whales, "floating factories that hauled dead whales into their bellies through a ramp at their sterns."[11] Sent to the southern oceans in the mid-1930s, the first factory was able to process 1,700 whales in one season, from which was produced 18,264 tons of whale oil, 240 tons of sperm oil, 1,024 tons of meat meal, 104 tons of canned meat, 114 tons of frozen meat, 10 tons of meat extract, 5 tons of liver meal, 21.5 tons of blubber fiber and 11 tons of glands for medical experiments.[12] In fact, 30 to 50 percent of all margarine being made in Europe in the 1930s was coming from whale oil. This new floating factory method was so effective that by the end of the 1930s, the Germans had seven of these whale slaughterhouses going. Of course other countries took notice and, at the height of the whale hunting industry, there were as many as 20 of these factories hunting and processing whales at the same time. The end result? Another of J. B. McKinnon's noble giants disappearing into the charnel house of human hunger. By the 1960s, the whole industry collapsed. The whales were gone. There was nothing left to kill. No whales no problem! In the 1950s, we were developing a whole new scheme—factory fishing. The Soviets came up with ships equipped with massive freezers and proceeded to "dominate world factory fishing," leading the way in "strip-mining the fish colonies."[13] Well, we know how this went, with seemingly endless stocks of fish, like the legendary cod teeming off the Newfoundland Grand Banks disappearing over the course of a single generation. Of course, the ocean is vast—it's taken us a while to fully plunder it. Still, today we're sending out ships that can process 1,200 tons of fish a day, which means that "since the total global catch is now 100 million tons per annum, this suggests that, say, 300 of these ships could catch all the fish now caught worldwide."[14] Is it any wonder that the 2010 census of marine life found that 90 percent of all large fish in the oceans—including Atlantic salmon, tuna, halibut, and swordfish—were gone, and that these and other species were on the brink of extinction?[15]

Speaking of moving on, with factory fishing quickly depleting the oceans, it was time to switch to another source of plentiful protein. The second half of the twentieth century oversaw an almost unfathomable expansion of the mass killing of animals for meat. Factory fishing meet factory farming. Where meat was concerned, "annual global production increased from 71 million tonnes in 1960, rising to nearly 240 million at the end of the century. Per head of population meat consumption nearly doubled over the period."[16] At the end of the twentieth century, the United Kingdom alone was feeding its roughly 63 million residents with 792 million chickens, 35 million turkeys, 18 million ducks, 18.7 million sheep, 16.3 million pigs, around 3 million cattle, 1 million geese, 10,000 deer and 9,000 goats every year.[17] Sounds like a lot, but, hey, the United States killed 8 *billion* chickens in 2014.[18] In order to sustain this meat production, vast territories of land and water have to be befouled, and the animals have to be pumped full of ever-increasing doses of various drugs ranging from antibiotics to sedatives. We are in a constant battle to keep "innovating" new ways to make factory farming—and now factory farm fishing or so-called aquaculture—more productive long term, since everything about it is destructive, including the fact that the food emerging from these factories is so cheap that most rich global north countries are now struggling with epidemics of heart disease and obesity, our instinctive hunger preyed upon by an ultra-efficient food production system calculated to maximize addiction and minimize inhibition.

So is all of this advancement? Have we innovated ourselves into better people living longer and healthier and happier in peace with each other? The counterargument here is that what seems like advancement and innovation is actually the same pattern repeating over and over again. What we've done in many cases is not advance, just speed up. We've exponentially increased our consumptive patterns, changing almost nothing as we tore through vast swathes of the world plundering everything in our paths. You can call this innovation, or you can call this the trap of progress—the ratcheting up of the process of doing what we've always done, killing and moving on. Writes virtual reality inventor turned technology pundit Jaron Lanier: "We have been obliged to invent our way out of the mess caused by our last inventions since we became human. It is our identity. . . . It is hard to be comfortable accepting the degree of responsibility our species will have to assume in order to survive into the future. The game was entered into long ago and we have no choice but to play."[19]

It would seem that the Chumash, by staying relatively stable, by not evolving or adapting or innovating too much, were able to weather the storms and even the environmental depletions they brought on themselves. Their remarkable survival as a coherent people for 13,000 years may very well have been due to the fact that they didn't change much at all. They didn't play the game. They didn't get too big. They didn't become too successful. They (mostly) avoided the ratchet effect in which societies, constantly growing and consuming resources, must constantly find new ways to extract more resources. Other societies, of course, didn't manage the stability that even the Chumash couldn't quite perfect. Canadian thinker and novelist Ronald Wright calls the ratchet effect the "progress trap" and notes that it made a significant contribution to the collapse of empires as iconic and powerful as those of the Romans and the Mayans. In Wright's A Short History of Progress, he describes civilization as basically a Ponzi scheme. He argues that we've built our incredible wealth and comfort by borrowing on the future. He talks about native people coming up with the buffalo run, the idea of driving an entire herd off a cliff rather than hunting them one by one.[20] It seemed like a great idea at the time and it gave the tribes almost unimaginable wealth and security. It allowed them to comfortably develop their culture and economy. It was all working great. Until they killed all the buffalo.

More efficient means of hunting and gathering led to larger and larger populations which eventually led to bigger and bigger problems. Whoops! Maybe we were a bit too efficient there. We've stripped the place bare. No worries. We've figured out how to plant crops and domesticate animals. But, see, the animals are eating an awful lot and our fields are generating smaller and smaller yields. No worries. We'll cut down trees and plant bigger fields. We'll tap into new resources like coal and rushing rivers. We'll cut down more trees to dig big holes in the earth in order to produce fertilizer and fossil fuels. Uh-oh. We're running out of trees to absorb all the methane and other greenhouse gases we're producing. Which means the earth is getting hotter. Which means we're running out of water.

It's the buffalo run all over again. Each level of "progress" propped up by another finite resource we didn't know how much we would miss until it disappeared. Wright's argument resonates today because it seems to many like we might be reaching the end of the game. We're standing on top of all those shaky buffalo skeletons desperately reaching for the next rung. But the bones are old and desiccated. They are disintegrating. We are in danger, for the first time in Wright's "history of progress," of falling backward: in this alternative narrative, we were never so much innovators as we were people relentlessly dedicated to replicating the original pattern no matter what.

The history of life begins with the accidental appearance of molecules complex enough to serve as building blocks. These were most likely RNA replicators. The replicator is an information carrier. It survives and spreads by copying itself. The copies must be coherent and reliable but need not be exact; on the contrary, for evolution to proceed, flaws in the copy appeared, which eventually turned out to be beneficial. Replicators existed long before DNA, even before proteins. They copied and developed such innovations as cell membranes—a protective skin—and gradually gave rise to more and more complicated molecules which in turn continued to develop via natural selection.

So what's the pattern here? It is to be found in the core of our programming, as innovation pundit Steven Johnson claims, but it's not innovation that pushes us onward, it is, as our psychological fundamentals have already suggested, survival. "We are survival machines," writes Oxford zoologist Richard Dawkins in his groundbreaking 1976 book *The Selfish Gene*. We are, he famously proclaims, "robot vehicles blindly programmed to preserve the selfish molecules known as genes."[21] When we adapt it's not because we love to innovate and just can't stop changing. It's because like all the other creatures of the Earth we have by and large bested, we are programmed to do one thing and one thing only: survive and replicate. Genes encourage us, drive us on and do so with, writes James Gleick, "no foresight, no intention, no knowledge."[22] Genes do not chose the future, they do not relentlessly seek innovation. "They do not plan ahead," writes Dawkins. "Genes just are, some genes more so than others, and that is all there is to it."[23]

Genes don't plan ahead but, as we've seen, people do. We think about the future, as we now know, as much as every sixteen minutes. And much of the time, we're only thinking sixteen minutes ahead. We're not really thinking about the future. We're thinking about survival. We're thinking about staying alive another day longer, long enough to replicate our genes, or to help the genes we've already replicated replicate their genes. In this story of human development, we are not busy beaver innovators endlessly gnawing on the trees to keep making our pond better. We are more like rats, doomed to Sisyphean gnawing, trapped by a "progress" that's really just our built-in need to survive gone amok. Led by our genes, we've developed a relentless ability to keep extracting resources and keep expanding—but at an increasingly more evident cost.

There have been three significant, dramatic, periods of technological change in the history of humanity, and, tellingly, all three of them have occurred in the relatively short time frame of the fully agrarian era of the last four to five hundred years. To provide context to just how fast these shifts occurred, my grandfather, who was born in a shtetl in Poland before World War I and died at the ripe old age of ninety-two in Montreal in 2010, managed to live at a time when all three of these technological shifts were overlapping each other.

The first change was the invention of steam harnessed to all manners of engines. This age begins in the middle of the eighteenth century, around the same time the Chumash would make the fateful contact with European colonists that would end their thirteen-thousand-year

dominion over their coastal territories. The second change was the harnessing of electricity, which begins in earnest in the late nineteenth
century. And the third big change was the rise of the computing age
beginning in the 1970s. Each new technological period led to what
seemed like a massive overhaul of the way we lived our lives. We
moved from the farm to the factory and from the factory to the office.
We ate differently, raised our children differently, spent our free time
differently, got from place to place differently, and even thought about
the world around us differently. And all of this happened very, very
quickly in the span of five or six generations, a wink in the history of
humanity which begins around four to five million years ago, a blink
in the span of the planet, which first started showing signs of life 3.5
billion years ago. So fast were these changes that in one single twenty-year span from 1890 to 1910 more planet-altering technologies were
developed than are likely to emerge over the next hundred years. The
time span generated, among other things, "X-rays, the motor car, flight,
the cinema and radio."[24] Everything we do today builds off these technologies. The twenty-first century with its unceasing obsession with
innovation and technological future has not even come close to giving
us the entirely new ways to communicate, move, and see that were the
legacy of the nineteenth century.

We don't have a history or tradition of living and desiring constant
change. Even our own era of supposed disruption is far less innovative
than it seems—mostly building on the ideas we came up with a hundred or so years ago—television, now on your phone! The telegram,
now on your phone! Three phases of massive technological change
have not really altered our essential pattern of plunder and move on,
plunder and move on. In fact, the big changes to our lives have largely
come about because the waves of tech change have accelerated and
intensified our core pattern. We are able to plunder much more and
much faster than we ever could before, and there are fewer and fewer
places we can move onto. As a result, each so-called change we have
introduced has come with significant, and generally either ignored
or unrecognized, costs that are now becoming a massive burden on
all of humanity. The price of accelerating consumption through technology, and of organizing human life almost entirely around that

consumption, is so high it may ultimately claim our entire species. It's already claimed tens of thousands of species of other kinds of living creatures as the planet inextricably moves into what scientists are calling "a mass extinction event." The consuming urge to survive and replicate is a wolf in sheep's clothing. Hiding in plain sight, we pretend that new ways to consume are future innovations, ignoring the way we're repeating ourselves over and over again, the only change being the speed at which we perform our dizzying excisions.

James McKinnon tells us the story of the great auk, a flightless bird resembling a small penguin. Once plentiful and found in both the old and new worlds, the auk was hunted for meat, eggs, feathers, and its oil (animal oil being very much in demand before the age of fossil fuels). McKinnon notes that it took "a thousand years for European hunters to eradicate the auk from their home continent." When the Europeans got to the much vaster continent of North America, the same process was put in place—only this time, with "better technology," the auk was eradicated from North America in a mere three hundred years. A few years after the last auks were killed in Iceland in 1844, a commentator wrote that "in all probability, the so-called great auk of history was a mythical creature invented by unlettered sailors and fisherfolk."[25] The tools we used to do the deed developed apace during the time frame that it took to eradicate the great auk in the old and new worlds. But my counter-narrative says it's what we *do* with the tools that matters. A 1,300-year time span goes by complete with all kinds of technological upgrades, but the result is exactly the same for the great auk—hunted down to nothing and then conveniently forgotten about. We tell the story of innovation, but somehow forget the story of the great auk, innovated into extinction not once, but twice. This is humanity, resource extractors par excellence. No mystery of magical creativity found in this story. Driven by our genes to do what we do, we keep doing it until there's nothing left to be done.

o o o o o o

As I've said before in this book: words matter. How people talk about the world around them is a portal into the belief structure of any given society or culture. To that end, when we look at how the idea and even the specific word *innovation* developed, we get a very interesting and revealing picture of just how dramatically our thinking around change in general, and technological change in particular, has developed. To properly tell the fascinating history of the ideologically fraught term innovation, I first need to introduce you to Professor Benoit Godin, author of the December 2014 scholarly book *Innovation Contested: The Idea of Innovation Over the Centuries*.

You are forgiven if you haven't heard of him. His work isn't much in favor in today's cultural climate. Godin, a Québec academic, has been studying the concept of innovation. He's been asking where the idea of innovation came from, and how and when innovation became the unquestioned good that we know it to be today. At a time when everyone from academics to psychologists to CEOs and senators are trying to figure out how to innovate faster and better, Godin is trying to figure out when and why we became so concerned about innovating in the first place. Godin sticks out like a pacifist at a boxing match. Still he persists, slowly and carefully crafting an invaluable biography of the word innovation.

And what a life story Godin tells. The story of "innovate" has all the trappings of a Hollywood blockbuster biopic. Murder, power struggle, imprisonment, the quest for knowledge and truth and, then, finally— triumph. Malcolm Gladwell, eat your heart out. Here comes the real story of the outlier in from the cold. At the very least, Godin's research deserves a snappy title. Let's call it "Innovation: The Little Word that Took Over Our World."

The first thing I ask Professor Godin when I reach him in his Montréal office at the Institut national de la recherche scientifique, the research-oriented branch of Université du Québec, is why he studies something so seemingly obscure as the etymological history and development of the word innovation. "Everyone is talking about innovation today," Godin tells me. "But no one has looked at what the history of it is, what it means, where it comes from, how innovation got so fashionable, how this happens, and why." Godin came to innovation through prior work studying how statistics are used in science. The more he explored the social and cultural biases that accompany supposedly unprejudiced numbers, the more the word innovation cropped up. So he took a closer look. "And I was amazed that no one had ever studied this concept this way. There are hundreds of books published every year [on innovation], but not one researcher on earth has ever asked about the origins of this. I'm the only one doing this kind of research."[26]

I ask Godin where the term innovation came from and how it was first understood. I find out that, like many abstract concepts, the notion of innovation was introduced in the golden age of the Greek city-states. And it was considered, generally speaking, a bad idea. As Godin tells me: "Innovation meant introducing change to the established order, particularly the political order. So this is negatively understood, and for most of Greek history it has a pejorative meaning." Indeed, many of the noted philosophers of the day seemed very wary of the way small changes could cause unexpectedly large alterations in the political and social fabric. Aristotle explores the origins and consequences of political uprisings in his treatise *Politics*, noting that "the revolution may be facilitated by the slightness of the change; I mean that a great change may sometimes slip into the constitution through neglect of a small matter." Artistotle goes on to implore us to beware of the little changes, for "transgression creeps in unperceived and at last ruins the state, just as the constant recurrence of small expenses in time eats up a fortune." Lest there should be any confusion, he reiterates later on, "In the first place, then, men should guard against the beginning of change."[27]

So the Greeks, it would seem, introduced the concept of innovation as a kind of warning. Beware creeping change for change's sake. Remember the story of Prometheus the Titan? He was chained to a rock for all eternity by Zeus, boss of the gods. By day, birds were to eat his liver and by night it was to grow back again so the whole thing could start over. What had Prometheus done to deserve such a horrible punishment? He gave the mortals the gift of fire. From fire came progress; technological advancement; inevitable, constant change. The Greeks seemed to have an ambivalent take on this tale, which comes in the form of a warning as much as it celebrates a junior immortal's sacrifice for humanity. As Plato writes in the *Protagoras*, Prometheus essentially acts out of pity for the plight of the hapless humans: "Prometheus arrived to examine his distribution [of gifts to animals and men], and saw that whereas the other creatures were fully and suitably provided, man was naked, unshod, unbedded, unarmed."[28] We not only lacked the innovative spirit, we lacked, well, just about everything. But in coming along and providing us with a power no other creature possessed, a technology we could harness to countless schemes, we became somehow corrupted, no longer those naked hapless creatures to be pitied, but the now all-too-familiar, endlessly dissatisfied beings perpetually questing for bigger, brighter fires. The Greeks, it would seem, weren't so sure Prometheus was the good guy in all of this. What he sowed, we now must reap.

But let's fast-forward to the more familiar world of Christian Western Europe, particularly post-Reformation England, where we find a steady increase in the use of terms like innovate and innovation, primarily as a way to more effectively lob invective against those who seem to be proselytizing for change. "The Puritans accused the kings and the high bishops of the time of trying to bring back England to the popish doctrine," Godin explains. "So from this time on, innovation acquired a really definite negative meaning."

It's the sixteenth century, an age of strict doctrine, prevalent illiteracy, and systemic misconception of everything from disease to physics. This is an age of magic—of prayer, of witchcraft, of devilry. It's an age so devoid of general scientific understanding that we look back on it with a kind of bemused horror. It's the age in which Copernicus and Galileo Galilei found themselves persecuted for defending ideas that, today, we simply can't even comprehend ever being in question. We live on a round earth that revolves around one of many suns? Heresy! Let's haul the best minds before the church, find them guilty of violating religious doctrine, and sentence them to death or, as in Galileo's case, lifetime house arrest. How's that for innovation?

But those in charge were not necessarily ignorant fools. Their fear of science and what it represented was rooted, as it always seems to be in the end, in politics. Like the Greeks, they knew that a little change could be far more dangerous than anybody imagined. After all, it was a slippery slope. God and king are inextricably woven at this time.

Kings ruled by divine right, not by the semantics of hanging chads and how they looked on TV pretending to drive a tank. To question God and faith, then, was to question the king. As Benoit Godin put it in a scholarly paper: "Innovation was forbidden. Church and state were interwoven, and innovation in one threatens authority in the other."[29] Or as preacher and scholar Peter Heylins stated back in the fifteenth century: "If every man had leave to cast his cruple, the balance of authority would soone weighed downe" and bring "Anarchie."[30] Innovation, then, is not in the best interest of the powers that be, which is why regular proclamations against popery, religious innovation, and even tiny political changes were issued with the kind of verve world leaders today reserve for speechifying about getting to the future first. These people were seriously committed to preserving the status quo. Consider a 1548 announcement by Edward VI, King of England (1547–53) entitled "A Proclamation against Those that Doeth Innovate":

> Considereing nothing so muche, to tende to the disquieting of his realme, as diversitie of opinions, and varietie of Rites and Ceremonies, concerning Religion and worshippyng of almightie God (. . .); [considering] certain private Curates, Preachers, and other laye men, contrary to their bounden duties of obedience, both rashely attempte of their owne and singulet witte and mynde, in some Parishe Churches not onely to persuage the people, from the olde and customed Rites and Ceremonies, but also bryngeth in newe and strange orders (. . .) according to their fantasies (. . .) is an evident token of pride and arrogance, so it tendeth bothe to confusion and disorder (. . .): Wherefore his Majestie straightly chargeth and commandeth, than no maner persone, of what estate, order, or degree soever he be, of his private mynde, will or phantasie, do omitte, leave doune, change, alter or innovate any order, Rite or Ceremonie, commonly used and frequented in the Church of Englande (. . .). Whosoever shall offende, contrary to this Proclamation, shall incure his highness indig-

nation, and suffer imprisonment, and other grievous punishementes.[31]

Quite simply put, there's "nothing" as "disquieting" to the realm as "diversitie" and "varietie." Ideas lead to change, and the official mantra on change is that it is pretty much all bad. Not to be outdone, in 1626, only one year into his reign, Charles I, King of England, Scotland, and Ireland (1625–49) issued a "Proclamation for the Establishing of the Peace and Quiet of the Church of England: Suppressing Dissent, Innovation, and Controversy":

> In all ages great disturbances, both to Church and State, have ensued out of small beginnings (. . .). Because of "the professed enemies of our Religion, the Romish Catholics, the professours of our Religion may bee drawen first to Schism, and after to plaine Popery (. . .). His Majestie therefore (. . .) hath thought fit, by the advice of his reverend Bishops, to declare and publish, not onely to his owne people, but also to the whole world, his utter dislike to all those, who to shew the subtility of their wits, or to please their owne passions, doe, or shall adventure to stirre or move any new Opinions, not only contrary, but differing from the sound and Orthodox all grounds of the true Religion, sincerely professed, and happily established in the Church of England; And also to declare his full and constant resolution, that neither in matter of Doctrine, or Discipline of the Church, nor in the government of the State, he will admit of the least innovation (. . .).[32]

Two years later, Charles even went so far as to dissolve Parliament, to "tie and restrain all Opinions that nothing might be left for private Fancies and Innovations (. . .)."[33]

Innovation as understood at that time, writes Benoit Godin, "had nothing to do with originality or creativity—not yet. Innovation has nothing to do with progress either: it is rather subversive."[34]

The subversive element of innovation is made clear in the following obscure bit of English history. In the time of Charles I, a full-fledged innovation controversy developed, pitting lowly English minister Henry Burton against none other than the Archbishop of Canterbury, chief primate of England, one William Laud. The controversy, bizarre as it might seem today, involved each of the men attempting to brand the other with the damning label of innovator. Burton, aflame with righteous indignation, produces a pamphlet in which he accuses the archbishop of introducing innovation to the religion, by which he means small changes that ever so subtly and slightly shifted the religion toward the menacing specter of "pope-ism" and the evils of the Roman Catholic Church. Burton, channeling and quoting Aristotle, spouts the by now familiar argument that small changes in religious practice can lead to big consequences, including, for him, the possible arrival of the Antichrist and the overthrow or even assassination of the king. To Burton, men given to change "are always notorious detractors, and sycophants, derogating from those things, which they goe about to innovate or abrogate, that so they may establish their owne novelties, whither in Church, or State, or both."[35] The archbishop, not to be outdone, shoots back at Burton by accusing *him* of engaging in the terror of innovation in order to "misinterpret his Majesties most pious Act, in an undutiful and scandalous manner (. . .) to serve your owne turne"[36] The archbishop notes that any changes introduced were meant to return the church to older, purer ways of worship and that by opposing them Burton is actually supporting those same creeping innovations he rails against.

At first, Archbishop Laud seems to have the upper hand. Burton is sentenced to life in prison. But he's released only three years later when public sentiment turns. He finds himself adopted by the English people as a hero in the fight against creeping innovation. With the tide of public opinion clearly in Burton's favor, the king quickly shuts up the archbishop in the Tower of London before, finally, beheading him, putting a definitive end to the great innovation controversy.

When we consider the interwoven totality of God and country that people lived under at the time, just about any innovation—scientific, religious, or political—would have struck at people's entire worldview, disturbing a sense of social certainty so fused with daily life that we can only imagine how upsetting seemingly minor changes could be. These are the dying days of the tribal order. This is a society desperate to preserve social certainty under assault from almost every direction. The people, and, eventually, the power structure, side with Burton against any perception of innovation. This is in keeping with the general tendency of almost all cultures and societies from the Greeks to the Chumash to many contemporary cultures still clinging to the remnants of tribal order. Despite, or perhaps even because of, ongoing technological change, human beings at their core are essentially conservative, distrustful of even the smallest alterations in the quotidian of daily life.

Mainstream, official, cultural, and social distrust of innovation remains generally in place in Western Europe for at least several hundred more years, years of ongoing and tumultuous change represented by near-constant warfare generated by the schisms created out of the rise of Protestantism. The era is marked by the regular parade to the jail and the hangman of anyone daring to think thoughts that contradicted the orthodoxies of Christianity. The suspicion of innovation was a deep and constant stream. When, in 1670, the Quaker William Penn (who had already gotten himself in trouble for distributing a pamphlet questioning the Trinity) found himself arrested for "preaching in the street" after the Quaker meeting house was padlocked by authorities, he pled not guilty. The jury agreed, sending a verdict of not guilty. Upon hearing the verdict, the court immediately ordered the jury imprisoned too—for contempt of court. "You shall not be dismist till we have a Verdict, that the Court will accept; and you shall be lock'd up, without Meat, Drink, Fire, and Tobacco; you shall not think thus to abuse the Court; we shall have a Verdict, by the help of God, or you shall starve for it."[37] (Incidentally, Penn would eventually move to the colonies where his Quakers would be instrumental in establishing Prince-Town, later Princeton, eventual site of MANIAC and the birth of the digital era.) A hundred years after Burton, an anonymous British Baptist could be found bemoaning the "innovation of singing" in the church. Singing in itself is not "a matter of the greatest moment," says the author, but if similar innovations multiply, in forms of praying for example, "it might tend to the utter ruine of Primitive Christianity."[38] Another hundred

years later in 1785, amid the age of Enlightenment, the scientific revolution, and populist turmoil in America and France, the English divine
George Berkeley would pronounce a sermon in which he suggested:
"At first [innovation] runs in a gentle rill, but, by degrees, the rill swells
into a mighty torrent that sweeps away every thing before it."[39] Similar
convictions can be found responding to all manner of changes and
innovations. Here, for instance, is an eighteenth-century Anglican
archbishop's over-the-top take on the newly introduced procedure we
now call vaccination: an "abominable mixture of corruption, the lees of
human vice, and dregs of venial appetites, that in after life may foam
up on the spirit, and develop hell within, and overwhelm the soul."[40]

Just like vaccination, innovation was (and in some cases still is)
viewed with suspicion not so much for what it was but for what it
represented—something hidden, something suggestive, a whispered
reminder of the enduring presence of that thing nobody really wanted:
change. We don't like to change. Change threatens our replication. In
the counter-narrative to the human being as fundamentally an agent
of perpetual transformation, change means that we are growing weak;
we've run out of resources, we are losing faith in our creed, we are
besieged by outside forces and ideas. The prouder we are, the more
fiercely we resist the potential corrosions and corruptions of change.
There must be a way, we say to ourselves, for us to keep doing what
we've always done.

o o o o o o

In our brains, knowing the future means survival, and survival basically means the ability to keep doing the same things humanity has
been doing over and over again for more than half a million or so years.
So why change? We keep getting better at it, and we keep getting the
same results: expanding populations, longer life spans, and expanded
technological know-how in order to deal with the destruction our primal replication strategy inevitably brings about. So far these results
have been great for our genes and have meant more people overall

living longer and further from the knife edge of sheer survival than ever before. Our genes are happy knowing that sometime around the hypothetical arrival of the singularity in 2045 or 2048 there will be, on the low estimate, around eight billion people on Earth (nicely up from a 2010 total of 6.9 billion) living, on average, longer than ever.[41]

But on the other hand, the consequences of having more people programmed to live as long as possible in circumstances as comfortable as possible is becoming increasingly problematic for our long-term survival. This is a dangerous blind spot for our genes, programmed only to pass on the message of consumption and survival and reproduction in any and all conditions. A great example of this is the development of the nuclear bomb and the electronic calculating machines that would become our first computers. The creation of the atomic bomb was an amazing effort. It tasked the best minds in the free world to come together to create weapons of mass destruction lest the Nazis and their allies get there first. This was technological development of astonishing speed prompted, quite literally, by our embodied will to survive—embedded in us, as Richard Dawkins theorizes, on the molecular level. The loser is wiped out, after all; a poor result from a genetic perspective.

At any rate, in the lead-up to America's entering World War II and throughout that epic conflict, a ragtag group led by Jewish Hungarian John von Neumann worked feverishly to build the bomb and, at the same time, build one of the world's first multiuse electronic calculating machines, the ENIAC machine housed at the Princeton University–based Institute for Advanced Study. The military provided substantial funding for ENIAC, having already seen what these fellows could do when unleashed on a problem. But there was a catch: These computers were, first and foremost, to be set to the task of performing the complicated reckonings necessary for the development of bigger, better nuclear bombs. Indeed, on the very same day that the bomb was dropped on Nagasaki, the military was hard at work using ENIAC to perform the necessary mathematical calculations for the H-bomb. "The military wanted computers," is how one scientist connected to the project remembers it. "The military had the need and they had the money but they didn't have genius. And Johnny von Neumann was the genius. As soon as he recognized that we needed a computer do the calculations for the H-bomb, I think Johnny had all of this in his mind."[42] "*This*" was nothing less than, as George Dyson, technological historian, puts it in the subtitle of his book *Turing's Cathedral*, "the origins of the digital universe." In 1951, a new, more powerful machine, also funded by the military and based on von Neumann's ideas, came online at the Institute and was given the appropriately apocryphal name MANIAC (Mathematical and Numerical Integrator and Computer). Immediately it was "put to its first test," a "thermonuclear calculation that ran for sixty days nonstop." The results of that calculation were used to conduct experiments in the South Pacific, particularly the detonation of the first hydrogen bomb, Ivy Mike, "yielding the equivalent of 10.4 million tons of TNT" (the equivalent of 750 Hiroshimas) in 1952, and the detonation of Castle Bravo, "15 megatons" in 1954.[43]

In the counter-narrative, that other far less popular story about humanity and its inherent urges, we tell the tale of how the simple genetic urge to replicate over and over again, while avoiding the nasty business of change as much as possible, morphed into something else altogether. Nuclear begets digital which begets bigger better nuclear which begets more precise digital to be put into more effective devices of mass destruction. Writes George Dyson: "First-generation electronic computers fostered first-generation nuclear weapons, and next-generation computers fostered next-generation nuclear weapons, a cycle that culminated in the Internet, the microprocessor, and the multiple-warhead ICBM."[44] Even von Neumann, the mathematical genius, architect, and relentless enthusiast, had his private reservations. He returned to his home in Princeton from Los Alamos in 1945 and, after an uncharacteristically long twelve hours of sleep, woke up in the middle of the night and "started talking at a speed which, even for him, was extraordinarily fast." The gist of what he said to his wife Klári that night, as she recollects it, was this: "What we are creating now is a monster whose influence is going to change history, provided there is any history left."[45] Was von Neumann envisioning the evolution George Dyson describes? Was he imagining drones controlled from computer terminals in Kansas delivering fatal payloads to enemies in far-flung countries? Pure need has become

an unruly driving force that we are unable to curb. We've created a
monster, and the monster is you and me.

o o o o o o

For most of human life there is little tradition of embracing chaos,
of fostering the new, of empowering people to be change agents. The
ancient Greek philosopher Heraclitus was quoted by Plato as saying
that "everything moves on and that nothing is at rest; and, comparing
existing things to the flow of a river, he says that you could not step into
the same river twice."[46] This bit of profundity is taken to be the source
of the comforting bromide that "everything changes but change itself."
It's a cliché, but a useful one. It suggests the way in which we generally
resign ourselves to the natural progression of life. Days pass, we can't
get them back, we will die no matter what we do, a new generation will
come along and forget about us and they, in turn, will grow up, live,
die and be forgotten. Everything changes. But of course this does not
mean that human beings—unique in being, as far as we know, the only
creatures fully aware of, and thus truly haunted by, their mortality—are
inherently predisposed and preconditioned to be change agents. To the
contrary. We want to live in the pattern as much as and for as long as
possible. We want to dam up the river, harness the power of change by
controlling its flow. We want to stand on the edge of our massive dam
and gaze down in satisfaction at something we've built that looks very
much like forever. Forget Heraclitus. We've got this river locked down.

CHAPTER 8

The Human Robot
Homo Economicus in Decline

It's a day's drive from Silicon Valley to the massive warehouses of Ontario, California, a nowhere zone of seemingly endless suburban sprawl an hour east of Los Angeles. But in many ways, it feels like the other side of the world. Here's where you go to find the people future left behind.

I am in the unadorned offices of Warehouse Workers United, an organization with a threadbare headquarters in a strip mall in the center of one of the largest concentrations of warehouses on the planet. Warehouse Workers United seeks to improve the living conditions of the 85,000 or so workers—mostly Latino—who are employed to load and unload, sort and ship, the hundreds of millions of tons of products that come across the ocean from Asia in shipping containers and are then trucked over to an area known as the Inland Empire, a region encompassing San Bernardino and Riverside counties.

Once known for agriculture—in the nineteenth century it was called the Orange Empire—this area is now known for its abundance of relatively cheap real estate with easy access to major highways. And so it has become a shipping and distribution hub. More than 80 percent of California's imports end up in the Inland Empire at facilities like the Whirlpool Corporation's 1,700,000-square-foot distribution center, which is larger than thirty-one football fields and one of the biggest warehouses in the country.[1] Despite the area's attraction as a warehousing and distribution hub, the Inland Empire, far, far away from the venture capitalists and software engineers of Silicon Valley, is a relatively poor region. In one study of the wages of fifty-one metropolitan areas in the US, it ranked second to last, with an annual median salary of $36,924.[2] And the unemployment rate in the Inland Empire is consistently higher than the national average: 10.4 percent of Inland Empire's roughly four million residents were unemployed in August 2012, compared to a nationwide rate of 7.3 percent.[3]

High unemployment, and poverty as a result of many people trying to make a living in a new country without formal education, creates a situation where the grueling, low-wage jobs of the logistics industry are a sought-after commodity. Every day, tens of thousands of people arrive at these walled-in sprawling enclaves to await the endless waves of tractor trailers arriving with loads of cargo from the factories of China and Bangladesh. Trucks arrive at all hours and need to be emptied and filled as quickly and efficiently as possible to meet the demands of the industry and ultimately the consumer. The warehouses are a key step in the journey from Asian factories to stores all over North America including, of course, the biggest chains like Walmart, Costco, Target, and even Amazon. Your phone might be conceived in California, but it's put together in China and has to get into your hands somehow. We take for granted that we can drive to the big-box store—or click a button on a big-box store's website—and get what we want when we want it. But that assumption involves a complicated process that most of us never see or think about. At Warehouse Workers United, I meet the people whose job it is to unload, unpack, reload, and repack the miracle devices of the future faster than anyone ever could before.

Meet Juana Ibanez. Ibanez works for Quetico, a warehouse company that operates several massive facilities in the Inland Empire. The company is contracted by big-box realtors to store and ship goods ranging from clothes to electronics to, well, just about anything that is made overseas and shipped to North America. Juana is thirty-seven , but she could easily pass for ten or fifteen years older. She has not had an easy life since moving from Oaxaca, Mexico, in 1996. With no skills and no education, she's had a hard time finding work to support her two daughters. She's been working for two-and-a-half years at a Quetico warehouse, where she packs boxes and tags clothes. It's the lowest skilled labor in the warehouse industry, and she's paid eight dollars an hour and works forty hours a week. Speaking to me through an interpreter, she tells me that "it's a good job" though it's tiring and dangerous work—she's seen many coworkers get injured by everything from falling boxes to careless forklift drivers.[4] And, of course there's the fact that despite working full time at a backbreaking pace she still doesn't make enough money to support herself and her daughters, aged twelve and seventeen. I ask Juana where the boxes she packs go, and she tells me that the boxes go to Costco, JC Penney, Sears, and Walmart. She says that she knows they "move Walmart product, but Walmart trucks never enter the warehouse. They bring in a different truck, never any truck with the Walmart logo." Juana explains that once she and a few others "started organizing, they took off the logos from the trucks." This seems like an important point for Juana, who is essentially telling me that, as she sees it, in making sure that any trucks associated with Walmart are not branded with the company's logo, Walmart is being very careful to distance itself from the conditions workers experience in the separately owned warehouses. Juana got involved with Warehouse Workers United as conditions in the factory deteriorated. The warehouses weren't air conditioned or ventilated and the heat was topping one hundred degrees in the summer. The workers weren't given breaks or access to drinking water. The bathrooms were not being cleaned and there was no toilet paper. She tells me the story of a coworker who was injured on the job: "A lot of the forklift workers were driving recklessly, and I was working on a line with another female and the guy drove by and took out her ankle. The managers pulled her into a meeting and they told her they wouldn't fire her, they would take care of her. They sent her to therapy for two weeks. . . . It didn't get better and they fired her."

I ask Juana why more people who work at the factory aren't involved in protesting the conditions. She tells me that there are only eight

workers at her factory who have joined Warehouse Workers United.
The others are too scared because the managers tell them "they are
going to close down the warehouse or call immigration on them."

Two coworkers were fired after they were part of a delegation that
went to management to talk about their rights and about making
improvements to the conditions in the warehouse. Juana is worried
she'll be next. She tells me that "once they found out they were trying
to organize they began to lash back. They send you to go do more work
and they isolate you, so you aren't in the lines with everyone else. Yes,
that has happened . . . they move you so you don't talk to other people."

I ask Juana about her relationship to technology. She has a cell
phone. She doesn't have Internet at her house. Juana does not have an
e-mail account. She says her daughters go online at the public library.
There are no sleek laptops, slim tablets, and fancy iPhones in her life.
What does Juana want for the future? She tells me she wants to keep
trying to improve conditions at the factory. "I just wish the rest of the
coworkers knew like I did about their rights." She tells me her kids are
getting good grades and she wants them to go to college. I ask Juana if
she ever shops at the stores where the boxes she packs eventually end
up. No, she tells me, she doesn't shop at any of those stores.

In early 2013, after Warehouse Workers United made a formal
complaint, the California Labor Commissioner's Office ordered the
Quetico company "to pay $1.3 million in overtime, penalties, and other
compensation." Among the findings of the commission was that the
company shorted workers of wages by forcing the workers to show
up early and stand in long lines to punch into time clocks. They also
were denied their thirty-minute lunch and rest breaks because they
had to wait in line at the same time clocks to punch in and out for
their breaks, and that waiting time was part of their break, meaning
their thirty minutes became fifteen. "Workers who complained about
the situation and the resulting unpaid wages illegally received disci-
plinary memos and suspensions," the labor commission concluded.
Quetico released a statement denying the allegations and promising to
appeal. "The notion that Quetico systematically prevented employees
from receiving the wages and benefits to which they are entitled under
California law is outrageous, misleading and false," the company said.[5]

Juana is one of six workers I spend the day with. I also meet Raul, thirty-seven going on sixty, who has been working in the warehouse industry for four years. Raul has two kids, ages thirteen and ten. He used to have a good job at a factory making parts for airplanes, but the factory closed down. Now he makes nine dollars an hour loading and unloading shipping containers. He tells me through a translator that "it's bad conditions," they yell at the workers and pressure them, they don't let him drink water, he has time constraints, he has to go faster.[6] Sometimes he works forty hours a week, but sometimes there's no work for a month, in which case he runs out of money for rent and food. When I ask him what he sees for his future, where he wants to be in ten years, he gets a sheepish look on his face. It's like he's never thought of it that way before, or at least has never been asked that before. He grimaces doubtfully. He doesn't know. I prompt him. Is he interested in technology? Does he go online? Raul shakes his head. He doesn't use a computer. He's never been online. I ask him why. "I'm not interested in that," he tells me. Finally he tells me that in ten years he wants to be living back in Mexico. With his kids. He hasn't seen his kids in a long time. They're with their mother in Santa Rosa, California.

I meet with Javier Rodríguez, thirty-three years old with three kids, the youngest just three months old. Rodríguez is from Mexicali, across the border from Calexico, California, and has been in the US since 2001. He had a solid job in a family business that sold Japanese motors, but the company fell on hard times and he was laid off. He looked for work in construction but everyone, he tells me, was looking for work in construction. Eventually he managed to get work driving a forklift at a warehouse. I ask him what kinds of items he loads and unloads. "Clothes, toys, food, electronic devices, vacuums, the smallest box that could only have hairpins, giant boxes with tools, trampolines for Sam's Club, everything you could see in a store. Everything but meat and fruit."[7] Javier became involved with Warehouse Workers United because of the poor working conditions, the low pay, the lack of regular hours. He helped organize a series of protests at his warehouse, including a two-week strike and a fifty-mile march to the company's head offices in Los Angeles. He tells me conditions improved after that. They went from not having water to getting watercoolers. Ventilation was upgraded, ramps were added and fixed. "Before," Javier tells me, "there was no opportunity to be a direct hire." In order to avoid extra costs, the warehouse workers were mostly hired through "temp" agencies. But after "you could apply to be a direct hire at a higher salary." Most important for Javier is that the workers "gained respect."

But then the company announced new, seemingly random "standards" in worker efficiency. "They developed the standards where a forklift worker like me would have to unload four trucks in a day. The trucks weren't able to be unloaded quickly, you have to have a slow pace, you have to be careful what you were doing, I could finish three in a day, but never four in a day. The people who move the boxes with their hands, the lumpers, they had a standard of 200 boxes per hour, and sometimes when they were in the trucks the boxes were all mixed up. There are really small boxes or giant heavy boxes, and they couldn't make the standards of having 200 boxes an hour. If there are two people working one truck, it's no longer 200 boxes an hour, it's 400 boxes an hour. So that's how they started to attack us at the workplace. And that's when they started bringing to [our] attention that if you weren't making production, you would get cutbacks in hours or they would let you go."

Known as a vocal organizer, eventually Javier was targeted, accused of unsafely driving his forklift, and then fired. He's fighting his dismissal and wondering where he can find another job paying him anything near the wage of $12.25 he got at the warehouse. He wants to go back even though at that salary he had to work two jobs to support his family, working from 9:00 a.m. to 4:30 p.m., then at another job from 5:00 p.m. to 1:30 a.m., also driving a forklift. "I didn't see my family till Saturday and Sunday," he noted ruefully.

I ask him what he thinks about the future. Is he interested in technology? He doesn't have Internet at home, but he does have a smartphone. His four-year-old daughter, he tells me, laughing, "uses my phone better than I do." Then he gets serious. "In ten years," he tells me, "I see being a better worker and better father." Part of being a better worker for Javier is continuing to reform the system so that people like him can work decent hours and make a decent wage. "Our work is very valuable," he tells me impassionedly. "What we do helps the company make a lot of money. The right and just thing to do is about twenty-five dollars an hour, forty hours a week. I think the people that don't use machines, at least eighteen to twenty dollars an hour. I think it would be just enough. It wouldn't make anybody rich, it would just be the bare minimum. I don't think it would affect the billionaires that much. Last year, I made $35,000 combined with both my jobs, and the Waltons had $447 billion divided by three members of the family. . . . Would [it] affect them to give the workers what they deserved—maybe one billion?"

It's not all so grim. There are some warehouses that have responded to the pressure by improving conditions and raising wages. I spoke with José Martínez, age twenty-seven, who came to the US in 2009 with his wife and who has a three-year-old daughter. He told me about coming to Warehouse Workers United desperate for help in improving working conditions at the warehouse he was working in. The issues were the same as in all the other warehouses—he cites being paid a hundred dollars to empty a container truck—a job that took two people fourteen to sixteen hours to complete. After a series of protests and complaints, the warehouse reformed its operation and things are "completely changed." Martínez now gets steady hours as an employee of the factory, making $14.40 an hour, and set to earn a twenty-five-cent raise every three months. "I think it's good work. I get good money, I actually make enough to take care of my family, and I have more time to spend with my daughter. I don't go home as tired anymore. Before I would just go home and sleep. I wouldn't even eat."[8] Martínez, younger than everyone else I speak with, has a computer at home, and uses it to go online and visit Facebook. He uses the Tango app on his phone to talk to his family back home. When I ask him if he is excited by the technological future, he pauses and thinks about the question. His answer is revealing: "Yes and no," he says, "because it helps work be easier, but at the same time they are making technologies that eventually are going to make us useless."

These workers are so close to the future, they can feel the burn as it rockets past them. They are on the frontlines, relentlessly controlled and manipulated by the new IT systems of big data now being used to track how many boxes they lump from a truck per hour. They are at the front of the line to lose their jobs to the next wave of robotic workers. Ironically, they are also the workers who literally make the future for the rest of us—it's their labor along with other folks like them in low-paying, rote jobs around the world who make it possible for us to have all the latest, greatest devices just-in-time. None of our futuristic devices would exist without the subsistence-pay miners who pull the rare metals needed to make those devices out of the ground and the factory workers in China paid a few dollars an hour to assemble phones and tablets selling for $500 each to eager phalanxes of preteens. Restated in the blunt terms of global (i)commerce, an Apple executive puts it this way: "You can either manufacture in comfortable, worker-friendly factories, or you can reinvent the product every year, and make it better and faster and cheaper, which requires factories that seem harsh by American standards."9

You can't outsource the logistics grunts, someone's got to unload the trucks. So it's China-in-America for the workers in the Inland Empire warehouses doing backbreaking labor for minimum wage and uncertain hours. They are nothing more than replaceable cogs in the on-demand supply systems that allow businesses like Walmart and Amazon to crush competitors and provide access to the latest in tech wizardry coming from Samsung, Apple, and all the rest. Behind our pursuit of future is a whole army of barely paid, partially employed workers whose place in the future era is tenuous at best. Has organizing our lives around the perpetual arrival of future made their lives better? They are paid as little as possible. In the workplace, their every move is monitored. They are treated like robots, and, as José Martínez knows all too keenly, will one day be replaced by robots. Though they use technology—to send money and stay in touch with families they had to leave behind in order to survive in the new tech-dominated global economy—it's hard to argue that their lives are made better by the arrival of the future era. Although more and more of us have reason to fear that technology will someday render our professions obsolete, these people are already nearly obsolete, reduced to nothing more than automatons soon to be replaced by even more efficient automatons (ones who don't strike, don't join unions, don't receive protection from labor rights commissions). For the warehouse workers of the Inland

Empire, ongoing disruption is incoming disaster. The future has been taken from them. They can barely imagine it.

o o o o o o

The temptation is to dismiss this cohort of largely uneducated, immigrant Latinos working in the warehouses that supply our on-demand gadgetry as just one large bunch of very unlucky people. Surely they are not representative of the way the future is trending for those of us with the good fortune to be born in the right places and circumstances. But I'd say the evidence suggests a different interpretation of the situation the warehouse workers of Ontario, California, find themselves in. The future casts a large net, and more and more of us are finding ourselves under it.

Consider the overall economic situation for the recent graduate of a college or university, those bastions of the middle class, ready to reap the rewards of the American dream. Andrew Sum is an economist at Northeastern University and lead author of a Brookings Institution paper published in March 2014 called "The Plummeting Labor Market Fortunes of Teens and Young Adults." He concluded that what he dubs "mal-employment"—"working in jobs that do not require a four-year degree or higher level cognitive skills" has been on a steady increase since 2000, leaving "young college grads in jobs that do not require college degrees" and earning much less relative to their peers in jobs requiring college educations.[10] Then there's Larry Mishel, president of the Economic Policy Institute and a coauthor of a major new study of employment patterns, who points out that an EPI report entitled "Raising America's Pay" found that "entry-level hourly wages fell on average for both female and male college graduates from 2000 to 2013 (8.1 percent among women and 6.7 percent among men)."[11] Finally, three Canadian economists, Paul Beaudry and David A. Green of the University of British Columbia, and Ben Sand of York University, give us a paper called "Inequality in the Future: The Declining Fortunes of the Young Since 2000," in which they show that from 1980 to 2000, skilled university graduates were in steady and increasing demand. But starting in 2000, the decline set in, and every year since there have been fewer jobs for skilled graduates. At this point, according to the three economists, demand is around where it was in the 1990s and continuing to shrink.[12]

Between 2007 and 2009, the height of the Great Recession, twelve million Americans lost their jobs. Many of those jobs are not coming back. Four years after the supposed end of the Great Recession, the US had two million fewer jobs.[13] What jobs did return now offer a considerably lower wage. As we saw with the warehouse workers, this is particularly true for the less educated. Only 20 percent of the 60 percent of jobs paying $15 to $20 an hour that returned after the recession offered a similar rate of pay. The rest were "replaced by those paying less than $13 an hour. Thus median income for working-age households fell more than 10 percent from 2000 to 2010."[14] It's even worse if you are a male worker without a high school education: "The median earnings of working men aged 30 to 45 without a high school diploma fell 20 percent from 1990 to 2013 when adjusted for inflation." A man making $31,900 in 1990 would be making something like $25,500 in 2013 (with both figures in 2013 dollars). Men with a high school diploma had a 13 percent decline in median earnings over the same time period. Women without a high school diploma saw a 12 percent decline, and women with a high school diploma or some college eked out a meager 3 percent gain.[15]

A 2013 Associated Press piece, written when the unemployment rate in the United States hovered around 7.5 percent, sums it up: "Four out of 5 U.S. adults struggle with joblessness, near-poverty or reliance on welfare for at least parts of their lives, a sign of deteriorating economic security and an elusive American dream."[16] The article found that America's poor are at a record number: 46.2 million, or 15 percent of the population. Among other things we can say about the era of future:

- The risks of poverty have increased, particularly among people ages thirty-five to fifty-five, coinciding with widening income inequality. For instance, people ages thirty-five to forty-five had a 17 percent risk of encountering poverty from 1969 to 1989; that risk increased to 23 percent from 1989 to 2009.

- By 2030, based on the current trend of widening income inequality, close to 85 percent of all working-age adults in the US will experience bouts of economic insecurity.

- 35.8 percent of people who are unemployed are now classified as long-term unemployed—out of work for twenty-seven weeks or more. Historically, the percentage of long-term unemployed has been at between 10 and 20 percent of total unemployment.

"Poverty is no longer an issue of 'them,' it's an issue of 'us,'" says Mark Rank, a professor at Washington University in St. Louis who worked on the numbers for the AP article. "Only when poverty is thought of as a mainstream event, rather than a fringe experience . . . can we really begin to build broader support for programs that lift people in need."[17] In his book, *The New Geography of Jobs*, economist Enrico Moretti states: "For the first time in recent American history, the average worker has not experienced an improvement in standard of living compared to the previous generation. In fact he is worse off by almost every measure. On top of this, income inequality is widening. Uncertainty about the future is now endemic."[18]

In our era of chasing future, everything is in flux and stability seems to be the most elusive commodity of all. There's greater systemic inequality between the rich and poor. There are no guarantees that getting an education and being a willing eager worker will lead to meaningful or even steady work. In the time of future, unemployment, underemployment, and declining salaries are the norm, not just for uneducated migrant workers, but for a widening swathe of the middle class.

o o o o o o

And yet, as is evident to anybody trying to buy a house or rent an apartment in Boston, Washington DC, New York, Vancouver, San Francisco, or San Jose, North America is still very wealthy, still growing, still productive. In fact, the US is on pace to be richer than ever by 2050. In the four years after the recession alone, wealth in America grew from $47 trillion to $72 trillion.[19] So if the US overall is getting richer, what's behind the decline in employment and wages? Why can't the average young person in North America count on the same stability and prospects their parents had?

To answer that question, we have to look at how, generally speaking, the economy has developed in the late stages of industrial capitalism, on the cusp of the digital/future-first era. In the three decades after World War II, humanity "saw output increases which were unprecedented in world history and have not been seen since then in the rich countries."[20] For already industrialized countries like the United States, cheap goods proliferated, jobs were plentiful, and the rising tide of affordable energy used to grow cheap food lifted all boats. For the less industrialized, poorer parts of the world, "this was the period of the first industrial revolution, as employment shifted decisively from agriculture into industry and services." No matter where you were, this "was an era when productive processes increased very rapidly in efficiency, turning out long-known products at ever lower prices." These were in many ways the best of times, a "golden era," a "long boom" when the world economy easily kept pace with "a rapidly growing population."[21]

Compare the life of a Midwestern farmer in 1900 to 2000 and it would be like they were living on two different planets. In 1900, none would have telephones, cars, tractors, electricity, or running water. By 1920, roughly half of all Midwestern farms had cars and well over half had telephones, though very few had tractors, running water, or electric lights; by 1930, 80 percent had cars, 60 percent had telephones, 30 percent had tractors, and 15 to 20 percent had electric lights and running water, though only 40 percent of farms had a radio. By 2000, needless to say, 100 percent of all Midwestern farmers in America had a telephone, a car, a tractor, running water, and electricity, not to mention dishwashers, computers, and so much more.[22]

Over the course of that hundred years, during which time just about every conceivable amenity rolled off the assembly line, we became almost inconceivably more efficient at doing just about everything. The popular Fordson tractor introduced in the 1920s allowed for the replacement of five horses and ploughed a field three times as fast. The tractors of today plough thirty times faster than a horse team. Tractors and "new regimes of intensive agriculture through irrigation, and addition of artificial fertilizer" allowed countries like Britain, Canada, and the US to double crop yields post-World War II.[23] The introduction of hybrid corn and rice that grew faster and responded better to high intensity farming also pushed yields up. At the same time, the 1950s saw the introduction of hybrid farm animals—specially bred pigs and chickens (among them the winners of a "the chicken of tomorrow" contest) that were bred for the conditions of the factory farm. World steel production trebled between 1950 and 1970, with plants becoming much larger and more efficient. Ford was building two million Model T cars a year at its peak in the 1920s—churning out a staggering fifteen million of the cars before production ended in 1927. (So affordable were these cars, so impressive was the American economic engine, that "even the richest parts of Europe would not reach 1920s levels of US motorization until the late 1950s.")[24]

Fewer workers could produce much more in far less time. Obviously, this resulted in labor market changes. After all, notes historian David Edgerton, "a key effect of the tractor was to reduce the amount of hired help on the Midwestern family-owned farm."[25] But there was so much more to produce, and plenty of money to go 'round to pay everyone enough to get in on the action of buying all that stuff. The car did not permanently displace people working in the horse and wagon industry any more than the original technical innovation of the horse-drawn plow left people with nothing to do. The car needed mechanics and assembly-line workers and dealers and designers and engineers; it needed roads and parking lots and red lights and snowplows and gas stations and hospitals to patch the people wounded in collisions back together and get them back on to the road again—a massive infrastructure that required nearly constant maintenance and upgrade. The car created far more jobs than it lost and helped make the modern long boom era of continuous, ever-growing, conspicuous consumption possible. Similarly, the lightbulb didn't leave us with destitute candlemakers, and the personal computer didn't leave the many tens of thousands of people working in the typewriter industry high and dry for long, because all these things required more workers and infrastructure, and fostered more consumption, which led to demand for more products, which led to more jobs and so on and so on. New jobs and consumption went hand in hand and everything just kept going up and up throughout the hundred years from, roughly, 1900 to 2000. Yes, there was massive technological change, but there was no systemic loss of employment. "In 1900, 41 percent of the United States work force was in agriculture. By 2000, that share had fallen to 2 percent, after the Green Revolution transformed crop yields. But the employment-to-population ratio rose over the 20th century as women moved from home to market, and the unemployment rate fluctuated cyclically, with no long-term increase."[26] Despite the automation of millions of jobs, more Americans had paychecks at the end of each decade up through the end of the twentieth century. Now, suddenly, the long boom of prosperity that we've seen for the last hundred years is coming to a definitive end. So how do we know that jobs are being lost through technological "innovation"? And how do we know this isn't just some temporary dip, like the displacement of farm workers who soon found themselves to be gas station managers, appliance salesmen, and Model T factory workers?

The answer comes through an analysis of productivity. Productivity is the measurement of how efficient we are at generating goods and services. "Labor productivity can be measured as output per worker or output per hour worked."[27] Up until very recently, it was a trusted axiom—one shown to be true by economist Robert Solow, who was awarded a Nobel Prize in 1987 for establishing it—that rising productivity leads to rising living standards. If your country's overall productivity was going up—if you could make more stuff faster and increase the gross national product produced per worker—your country's living standards were going up. The more stuff you made faster and better, the more money and jobs there were for everyone. Productivity was measured at a 4 percent increase in 2010. (It has been estimated at 1 percent annual increase throughout the 1800s.)[28] In fact, throughout the first millennial decade, productivity increased at a very good average rate of 2.5 percent, "far better than the 1970s and 1980s" and slightly better than the 1990s."[29] Overall, notes a commentator, "the productivity of American workers—those lucky enough to have jobs—has risen smartly."[30]

All these gains in productivity have been excellent for the companies that are the engines of the economy. US corporate profits reached new records in the years after the recession and continue to rise. By 2010, corporate investment in equipment and software had returned to 95 percent of its historical peak, the fastest recovery of equipment investment following a major economic downturn in a generation.[31] Surprisingly, even the manufacturing sector of the United States is doing well. A Brookings Institute analysis found that "for the past 50 years industrial production in the US has grown at the same rate or even faster than the economy as a whole."[32] The US is still making a lot of stuff, and is, in fact, doing it faster and more effectively than ever. But what about all the factories that laid off workers or shut down? Ah, there's the rub. Writes Moisés Naím in the *Atlantic*: "We perceive an industry in decline because the great strides that have been made in efficiency and productivity have not generated a proportional increase in jobs." And so even though the country is making more stuff than perhaps ever before, the United States still shed 5.7 million manufacturing jobs between 2000 and 2010.[33]

Productivity is up and people are getting very rich. In the last few decades, the amount of wealth created in the US can be measured in the trillions of dollars. But "over 100 percent of all the wealth increase in America between 1983 and 2009 accrued to the top 20 percent of households." How can the top 20 percent grab more than 100 percent of the wealth increase? They can do that because "the other four-fifths of the population saw a net *decrease* in wealth." Not only that, but "5 percent accounted for over 80 percent of the net increase in wealth and the top 1 percent for over 40 percent."[34] Now that might sound like extreme income inequality, but it's actually better than what would come next. Remember the forty trillion or so dollars in wealth the US added since 2009? The famed 1 percent captured 95 percent of post-financial crisis growth since 2009, leaving 90 percent of the population of the US poorer than they were five or ten years before.[35] The trend is the same across the globe, with almost half of the world's wealth in the hands of just 1 percent of the population, which means that the wealth of the top 1 percent richest people in the world ($110 trillion) amounts to sixty-five times the total wealth of the bottom half of the world's population.[36]

So that's the picture in the age of permanent future: plenty of profit, ever-increasing productivity, substantial corporate investment in technology and machinery, and the top 20 percent spending like it's 1985. But also an incongruous downward spiral never before seen in an era of rising productivity and profit—a chaotic spiral of chronic underemployment, declining wages, and looming obsolescence kept spinning by obscene wealth for a tiny handful.

So then we have to ask, why have rising living standards for all decoupled from advancing productivity? What changed over the last twenty years? What's different now? The answer is not technology, but specifically the development of technologies that vastly increase the speed at which we can collect, share, process and manage information. Most of technological development from the 1950s on has been primarily improvements on existing ideas. The exception is the rise of digital interconnectivity made possible by ever-smaller, cheaper, and more powerful information processers. This, alone, is something truly new to the twenty-first century.

In their book *Race Against the Machine*, MIT researchers Erik Brynjolfsson and Andrew McAfee show that in the last ten to fifteen years, infrastructure investment by corporations has been concentrated in the field of information technology or IT—defined by the Information Technology Association of America as "the study, design, development, application, implementation, support or management of computer-based information systems." IT sounds innocuous enough. Advances in "computer-based information systems" are what make possible online travel sites that can scan the price of every flight to Puerto Vallarta faster than you can take out your credit card; they're what power the increasingly more programmable robots and automated technologies being installed in cutting-edge factories to replace human workers; they're behind every innovation in big data from predictive to persuasive. IT is what allows, as the *Race Against the Machine* authors put it, "digital technologies" to execute "mental tasks that had been the exclusive domain of humans in the past."[37] An MIT Sloan School of Management study revealed that companies that had invested in some form of "data-driven decision-making" had their productivity go up by as much as 6 percent compared to similar firms.[38] The obvious conclusion was that more and more companies would be putting in place these systems. They have and continue to do so. This can be seen particularly in what has come to be called "the Internet of things," essentially the move to connect everyday devices from toothbrushes to thermostats to ovens to the Internet. Writes social theorist Jeremy Rifkin: "Cisco forecasts that by 2022, private-sector productivity gains wrought by the Internet of Things will exceed $14 trillion. A General Electric study estimates that productivity advances from the Internet of Things could affect half the global economy by 2025."[39] The systems are working. Productivity is skyrocketing. Efficiency is impressive. Money is pouring into the coffers. IT doesn't need health benefits, doesn't go on maternity leave, and doesn't get a pension. Over the next decade, it's estimated that the planet will move from two billion to seven billion Internet users.[40] The buzzword heard everywhere is "the Internet of everything" which will mean the arrival of trillions of objects moving online as we start to connect our phones, fridges, furnaces, stoves, TVs, security systems, and exercise equipment to the Net. More data will be generated, allowing for more efficiency and more productivity and analytic-based prediction.

It's upgrades in the efficiency and capacity of IT over the last decade that have enabled companies to create hyper-efficient systems in which productivity can be massively increased without the need for more hiring or increases in wages. "The historically strong relationship between changes in GDP and changes in employment appears to have weakened," note the *Race Against the Machine* authors, "as digital technology has become more pervasive and powerful."[41] "If," asks influential inventor Jaron Lanier, "network technology is supposed to be so good for everyone, why has the developed world suffered so much just as the technology has become widespread? Why was there so much economic pain at once all over the developed world just as computer networking dug in to every aspect of human activity, in the early twenty-first century?"[42]

Lest you think all of this is just Luddite rhetoric by scaredy-cats who fear change, let's look at a comprehensive study of the effect of IT on jobs. Beaudry, Green, and Sand, the same Canadian economists who wrote the paper on rising income inequality as it relates to the declining prospects for skilled university graduates, explore the issue in more detail in a study called "The Great Reversal in the Demand for Skill and Cognitive Tasks." In that study, they make several fascinating observations. Among them is the fact that information technology went through two decades of massive growth from the 1980s to the end of the 1990s. Coinciding with that growth was the increased hiring of university graduates with the skills to manage the complex investments in new software and hardware that corporations were making. But then, as the authors write, at the start of the millennial period, the IT revolution reached a "maturity stage." Now "the new capital" was in place and "cognitive task workers" were "only needed to maintain the new capital."[43] It is at this point that the demand for skilled labor begins to decline. Good jobs start to dry up. Information technology, which increases productivity through parsing billions of pieces of data including, as we've seen, data around the efficiency and whereabouts of workers, is in place. The promised future is here—instant connectivity, computers that can tell us in seconds what used to take days to figure out. Whether we're on an assembly line, delivering packages, or working at headquarters, we are much more productive at work. So productive, in fact, that it takes fewer of us to do more than we've ever done before. Around the same time that IT investment peaks and hiring starts the downward trend it's been on ever since, the economists chart another phenomenon. Not only are there fewer jobs, but the jobs that are out there are requiring less smarts to do. As the graph below shows, from 1980 to 2000, there is a steady rise in the need for employees who can reason, who can figure things out independently, who can manage complex projects. But suddenly, again around that crucial moment around 2000 when IT investment reached maturity, demand drops off.[44]

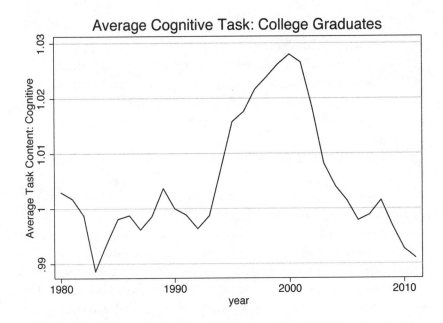

So where does this leave us? Write two economists in the *New York Times*: "Computerization has . . . fostered a polarization of employment, with job growth concentrated in both the highest- and lowest-paid occupations, while jobs in the middle have declined [. . .] This bifurcation of job opportunities has contributed to the historic rise in income inequality."[45] *Average Is Over*, thunders the title of George Mason university economist Tyler Cowen's book assessing the economic future of America. Basically he sees, as a reviewer puts it, "a future largely stripped of middling jobs and broad prosperity."[46]

Finally, there is the perfectly reasonable supposition that the pace of IT-inspired productivity is, if anything, going to increase. Every year, computer speed and capacity continues to expand in accordance with principles like good old Moore's Law, and more and more industries and occupations are learning how to get into the IT game. Soon efficiencies we haven't yet conceived of will be the new normal. Write the *Race Against the Machine* authors:

> In the 21st century, technological change is both faster
> and more pervasive. While the steam engine, electric

motor, and internal combustion engine were each impressive technologies, they were not subject to an ongoing level of continuous improvement anywhere near the pace seen in digital technologies . . . and all evidence suggests that this pace will continue for at least another decade, and probably more. Furthermore, computers are, in some sense, the "universal machine" that has applications in almost all industries and tasks.[47]

Just at the moment we've made getting to the future first our main priority, technology and so-called innovation are no longer the definitive engines of prosperity we had imagined them to be during the hundred years of unprecedented growth that shuddered to a halt at the turn of the millennium. In fact, in many ways the most lauded, widespread technologies and innovations of the last few decades have been moving us in the opposite direction—they are working against prosperity. For the first time in the history of the world, jobs are being lost—not created—by technology.

o o o o o o

Here's a quick example of how technology has helped decouple production from rising living standards. At the height of its power, the photography company Kodak employed more than 140,000 people worldwide and was worth twenty-eight billion dollars.[48, 49] They even invented the first digital camera. Eastman Kodak Co. generated good jobs and good salaries for upstate New York's Rochester area for multiple decades. But in 2012 Kodak filed for bankruptcy, and the new face of photography is found on sites like Instagram and Flickr which together process and showcase billions of photos—pixilated into digital information—every year. When Instagram was sold to Facebook for a billion dollars in 2012, it employed only thirteen people.[50] As economist and former Clinton-era Secretary of the Treasury Lawrence Summers notes in an op-ed, few of the companies that helped displace Kodak can lay claim to "a comparable impact" in terms of creating prosperous jobs in an entire region for multiple generations. Summer goes on to write that there are already now more American men on disability insurance than working in manufacturing. The jobs are gone and not coming back, and the wealth that those middle-class jobs once created is now in the hands of a much smaller pool of people who control new technologies that allow for massive productivity enhancements—billions of photos processed every year with not even 10 percent of the workforce a similar company needed in the industrial era.[51]

Despite the fact that this is happening all around us and is directly affecting us, it still seems rather abstract. So it's worth putting this in a real-world context we can understand intuitively just by looking around us. How are jobs being lost by technology in general and IT in particular? Let's look at Walmart, which dominates the twenty-first–century economy of North America and is, in fact, the largest corporation in the world as measured by annual sales and number of workers (not including the millions of workers who are indirectly employed by Walmart, making and shipping goods to the company). The family-owned, famously miserly global retail power did $285 *billion* in sales in 2005–06, employing almost two million workers around the world. In 2012 the company pulled in a not-so-inconsequential $17-billion profit.[52] What, you might ask, does a big-box chain store flogging everything from crayons to socks to flat-screen televisions have to do with IT? Well Walmart is, in fact, a pioneer in the kind of predict-the-future technology we talked about in our examination of the increasingly successful ways different actors are trying to own the future by knowing it sooner than everyone else. In fact, as the *Big Data* authors tells us, it was Walmart that revolutionized—or you might say disrupted—retailing. In the 1990s, they developed a new tracking system called Retail Link. This massive IT system enabled and required suppliers to monitor what was selling where at Walmart stores. It then became their problem to keep up. "Wal-Mart used data to become, in effect, the world's largest consignment shop."[53] Walmart's world domination came by introducing cutting-edge, disruptive IT to its systems ranging from stock to shipping to employee monitoring. The more efficient Walmart's system became, the more it could best all competitors in terms of price. Information technology allows Walmart to manage a massive outsourcing operation that wouldn't have been possible a generation ago. Thus, Walmart doesn't make anything, it doesn't own any of the warehouses it stores its goods in, it outsources as much of its logistics as possible. At its core, all Walmart does is market itself and manage information, millions and millions of tiny bits and pieces of information that give it the edge over other stores.

That information edge extends to Walmart's relationship with its employees. The company tracks everything and everybody, and is notorious for being virulently anti-union and relentlessly low wage. In fact, in 2012 the average Walmart employee earned $8.81 an hour. In 2015, the company raised their minimum wage to $9.00 an hour, a move that, notes one commentator, puts the workers being paid the least at Walmart "just a few coins ahead of the rise in the cost of living since the end of the Financial Crisis."[54] But that's only if they're working full time. A third of Walmart's employees work less than twenty-eight hours per week, hours that just happen to keep these workers below the threshold to qualify for benefits.[55] Despite protests, organizing drives, and bad press—like the media furor that arose when a store in Ohio ran a Thanksgiving food drive for its own employees—not much is changing at Walmart. Instead, Walmart keeps expanding. And when Walmart expands, it sucks money out of the community—eighty-six cents of every dollar spent at a Walmart leaves the local area for good. When a Walmart opens off the highway, downtowns are quickly gutted as local shop owners in hardware to clothing to electronics close up shop because they can't compete.

Is Walmart evil? A lot of people want to say so, but really they're just very good at doing what we're constantly being encouraged to do—innovate to own the future. As innovation booster Virginia Postrel wrote glowingly in 1999, "The expansion of Wal-Mart throughout rural America, bringing nationally branded products, represents a relatively recent example of extensive progress, one widely denounced by reactionaries."[56] When we think of the constant quest for future perfect and what it looks like in the real world, we tend to think of sleek young twenty-somethings whose every need has already been happily anticipated. We tend to think of social media entrepreneur Dave Morin's description of Silicon Valley's urban playground San Francisco—"a place where we can go downstairs and get in an Uber and go to dinner at a place that I got a restaurant reservation for halfway there. And, if not, we could go to my place, and on the way there I could order takeout food from my favorite restaurant on Postmates, and a bike messenger will go and pick it up for me. We'll watch it happen on the phone."[57] But maybe when we envision "progress" we should be picturing the cloistered aisles of the Walmart Supercenter where the real technological changes have affected billions of people—eliminating their jobs, supporting outsourcing to countries where it's normal to have entire weeks when the smog is so thick you can't see the sun, and all to give us shoppers slightly cheaper toasters and the Pop-Tarts to go with them.

But, hey, things surely aren't so very grim. For every takedown of Walmart—and really, what could be easier?—there's a fabulous new business starting in the cloud that will eventually reverse the trend and make things good again. Everyone picks on Walmart. So let's apply this same formula of information technology creating efficiencies that enhance productivity and profit but ultimately cost jobs and drop wages to a high-tech darling as far away from the Walmart aesthetic of buzzing fluorescent lights and glassy-eyed greeters as possible. Let's look, for instance, at Walmart's slick online competitor, Amazon. Despite the occasional grumbling of some disaffected worker or failing bookstore owner, the giant online retailer of everything consistently ranks in the top 5 in *Fortune* magazine's "most admired companies in the world" list, coming in at number 2 in 2014 and number 4 in 2015, alongside name brands like Apple and Google.[58] When President Obama wanted to deliver a we-have-to-own-the-future economic address in 2013, he dropped in at a Chattanooga, Tennessee, Amazon warehouse. Obama praised Amazon for its ingenuity and for creating jobs, opening his speech by saying, "Last year, during the busiest day of the Christmas rush, customers around the world ordered more than 300 items from Amazon every second, and a lot of those traveled through this building. So this is kind of like the North Pole of the South right here."[59] At Amazon, Christmas is always just a same-day delivery away.

Though Amazon has struggled to post profits, it has never struggled to find people willing to buy its stock, and the general consensus is that it is only a of matter time before Amazon starts pulling in Walmart-like money. It just seems inevitable. After all, it's simply a lot more efficient to have computers take orders and peddle products than people. It's more efficient to have a system where you can stock every book in the world without having to actually physically possess a copy of every book in the world. It's even more efficient if you can transfer all this activity to a totally ethereal system in which someone's device is directly connected to the Amazon store so that when they want a book all they have to do is tap buy and presto! the book—just about any book—is beamed into their bedroom onto their Kindle all ready to read. Of course, books were just a stepping-stone for Amazon, which now sells just about anything you could ever want and delivers it right to you, sometimes on the same day. One can even imagine that sometime in the future Amazon will be able to further extend the e-book-Kindle formula by selling patented 3-D Kindle printers on which you'll be able to download and print out your toaster. So efficient does Amazon seek to become that the company quietly patented a system for what it dubbed "anticipatory shipping," in which they will ship packages automatically to delivery hubs before a customer even makes the purchase. To do so, Amazon has come up with new ways to analyze its trillions of data points including "previous orders, product searches, wish lists, shopping-cart contents, returns and even how long an Internet user's cursor hovers over an item."[60]

This is the stuff the future will be made of. I think about getting something and there it is. If I don't want it, Amazon can always whisk it away (perhaps with one of the drones the company recently speculated would be the future of hyper-efficient delivery.) If I like it—and I probably will!—then Amazon will automatically debit my account.

This amazing level of efficiency and productivity comes with a price—just not for Amazon or consumers. Like Walmart, Amazon has gutted local businesses and sucked money out of small towns, downtowns, and entire regions. Amazon's unlimited selection, cheaper prices, and free shipping on books on orders of $35 or more has decimated bookstores and severely hurt publishers. First the small bookstores and now bigger bookstores like now defunct Borders Books and struggling Barnes and Noble. Next the big-box stores like Best Buy, which survived the initial gutting of retail by Walmart, are coming under pressure. All this means that Amazon, like Walmart, is more Scrooge than Santa.

Again like Walmart, in order to maximize discounts to shoppers and shut down the competition, Amazon has to do a lot of work in the shadows, outside of the prying eyes of customers. Occasionally, we get a glimpse of what we don't necessarily want to know, though. For instance, it's becoming apparent that the jobs Amazon does "create" aren't exactly top-notch. Amazon, unlike companies such as Google, is saddled by the need to deliver stuff, which means they have to get their hands dirty. Thus a report on *Gawker* describes a Tennessee warehouse where employees take forced overtime and work with minimal break time, while a 2011 newspaper report on Amazon's warehouse in Allentown, Pennsylvania, told of over hundred-degree temperatures and "a pace many could not sustain." During summer heat waves, Amazon arranged to have paramedics parked in ambulances outside, ready to treat any workers who dehydrated or suffered other forms of heat stress. "Those who couldn't quickly cool off and return to work were sent home or taken out in stretchers and wheelchairs and transported to area hospitals. And new applicants were ready to begin work at any time."[61]

In Simon Head's book *Mindless: Why Smarter Machines Are Making Dumber Humans,* he writes that "Amazon equals Walmart in the use of monitoring technologies to track the minute-by-minute movements and performance of employees and in settings that go beyond the assembly line to include their movement between loading and unloading docks, between packing and unpacking stations, and to and from the miles of shelving." Head notes that Amazon's system of employee monitoring is, in fact, "the most oppressive I have ever come across." This is achieved in part by a panoptical setup in which workers can be perpetually watched, combined with a sophisticated tracking system in which employees are outfitted with GPS-enabled headsets telling them "the route they must travel to shelve consignments of goods, but also set target times for their warehouse journeys and then measure whether targets are met." At Amazon, there's a three strikes you're out policy. Fail to meet your targets three times and you are quickly replaced.[62]

And then, of course, there's the pay. As the *New York Times* reported, post-Obama visit "the White House came under fire because many Amazon jobs pay only $11 an hour, and the pace of the work in these warehouses has been described as exhausting."[63] In fact, economists say that a single person living in the US "meeting the basics of housing, food, transportation, health care, personal items, plus putting aside a little for emergencies and retirement" needs to earn a bare minimum of $14 an hour. Add one child—and the cost of child care—and the calculation jumps to $23 an hour.[64] Nevertheless, since Amazon represents the future and the future's hiring, we're falling all over each other begging them to set up in our region. But even convincing Amazon to provide low paying backbreaking labor in your state will cost you. Amazon demands and receives various incentives for setting up shop. For instance, "the company got $269 million in back taxes forgiven by the State of Texas contingent upon the creation of new distribution centers and jobs." And the investment in Tennessee that Obama hailed came as the result of an agreement between the corporation and Republican Governor Bill Haslam, by which Amazon was exempt from having to collect sales tax until 2014 but has to create "at least 3,500 qualified jobs."[65] This is what it comes to—we have to pay the companies that have decimated our workforces to come create jobs for us.

Still, Amazon is awesome. Amazon delivers everything you ever wanted right to your door at prices nobody else can touch. Plus, Amazon is part of that small sector of futuristic companies that are actually expanding and hiring. The day before Obama visited the Tennessee Amazon warehouse, the company announced "the creation of 7,000 new jobs across 13 states."[66] Amazon had 149,500 full-time employees in 2014, a growth of more than one-third over the previous year. But for how long will the company keep hiring? Even though Amazon hired a lot of workers in 2014, it also put 14,000 robots into its warehouses and shipping centers, a move that reports say saved the company as much as a billion dollars in 2014, with much more savings to come. Like the warehouse workers of the Inland Empire, Amazon workers may soon find themselves being gradually replaced by a far more efficient future.[67]

o   o   o   o   o   o

The more we connect and disrupt, the more we seem to be replacing people with systems, humanism with futurism. Jaron Lanier describes it as pattern: "You get an incredible bargain up front, like super-easy mortgages, insanely cheap retail items, or free online tools or music, but in the long term you also face reduced job prospects."[68] It's finally happening, a vision foretold in the margins of the long boom and the rush to embrace the future. The end of having a full-time or even part-time job, writes commentator Ross Douthat, is "a basic reality of 21st-century American life, one that predates the financial crash and promises to continue apace even as normal economic growth returns." Douthat calls this new reality the era of "post-employment," a time period in which more and more people stop trying to find steady jobs that no longer exist.[69] As early as 1995, Jeremy Rifkin wrote in his book, *The End of Work*, that "we are entering a new phase in world history—one in which fewer and fewer workers will be needed to produce the goods and services for the global population."[70] In his 2009 book, *The Lights in the Tunnel*, speaker and Silicon Valley entrepreneur Martin Ford agreed, stating that "at some point in the future—it might be many years or decades from now—machines will be able to do the jobs of a large percentage of the 'average' people in our population, and these people will not be able to find new jobs."[71]

Industries already severely gutted and disrupted, ranging from the newspaper business to the music industry to travel agencies and mom-and-pop main street retail, are indicators of what is coming next for just about every industry. And we're not just talking about Legal Seafood, which has introduced robots that peel shrimp in its factories. You can read about devices that will replace laboratory technicians and surgeons in hospitals. You can read about data-scanning and document-reading technology that is replacing lawyers and paralegals. Truckers and bus and subway and taxi drivers will all soon come under threat by self-driving technology (and are already coming under threat by ride-sharing apps). While everyone stared open-mouthed at Google's experiments in driverless cars, companies like mining giant Rio Tinto forged

ahead, introducing "40 robot trucks operating at three Australian mining locations" in 2014.[72] Other mining companies are following suit.
Meanwhile, in Europe, they are developing automated "road trains"
on public highways and in the US, the little-known National Defense
Authorization Act of 2001 requires that by 2015 "one-third of the oper-
ational ground combat vehicles are unmanned."[73] Teachers—especially
at the higher education level—are under threat by distance learning
coupled with interactive features that allow one single Nobel laureate
to introduce ten thousand students to psychology. Bill Gates reported
that he's working on robots that can pick crops better than humans
can. Still on the farm, the new rage in dairy operations is the Astronaut A4 Robotic milking system (I am not messing with you here!).
The Astronaut A4 is a self-serve milking machine that milks cows
five times a day according to the cow's own schedule. Farmers love it
because, despite the upfront expense, it allows them to cut labor costs
and substantially reduce "health insurance, room and board, overtime,
and workers' compensation insurance."[74]

Pharmacists will be replaced by drug-dispensing computers and 3-D
printers will print many other things currently being made in factories. The pattern is intensifying, of free or low-cost services that are
great upfront but ultimately put more and more people out of work and
allow companies to ruthlessly dictate the terms of what jobs are still
available. As Keith Rabois, chief operating officer of start-up Square
(an intermediary between retailers and consumer credit cards), says
happily: "The entire cost of running this business on the human side
is incredibly low."[75] Ah, the human side. Jaron Lanier writes: "When
machines get incredibly cheap to run, people seem correspondingly
expensive."[76] The more you can do without the pesky human side of
things, the better.

At the 2014 Davos summit, where the CEOs of tech multinationals
have taken to gathering to talk to each other about how they are doing
shaping and owning the future, everyone agreed that the recession
was long over, the recovery was nicely on its way, corporations were
going great, and there was only one problem—no jobs. Eric Schmidt,
Executive Chairman of Google, talked at the conference about a jobless
recovery and the beginning of a three-decade period during which jobs

would dominate every conversation. "This is a new phenomenon that is coming on very fast," founder of Salesforce.com Marc Benioff said. Worrying about a "global epidemic of youth unemployment," Cisco's CEO John Chambers said, "We're close to losing a generation of young people."[77]

Reading this, I couldn't help thinking about how nice it was they were worried about us, since they are the ones—for the most part—who built and are refining the systems that are responsible for decoupling rising productivity from wages and living standards for the first time ever. I'll give you one final example of the way networks of optimized future owned by the CEOs at Davos are injecting themselves into real life, making the corporations who employ them richer and the people subject to them poorer. "Along with virtually every major retail and restaurant chain," writes a reporter, "Starbucks relies on software that choreographs workers in precise, intricate ballets, using sales patterns and other data to determine which of its 130,000 baristas are needed in its thousands of locations and exactly when." If the computer says, for instance, that a particular San Diego barista and twenty-two-year-old single mom earning nine dollars an hour should work until 11:00 p.m. on a Friday, return to work at 4:00 a.m. the next day, then start again at 5:00 a.m. on Sunday, then that's what the computer says. Jannette Navarro, as documented in a *New York Times* article, has a three-hour bus ride to get to work, has a hard time arranging weekend childcare for her son, and can't afford to turn down shifts since she's just a paycheck away from being homeless. The computer doesn't know and doesn't care about all that. The IT staffing system only knows that employee Navarro is available to work. It only knows that business is strong enough to bring in more staff or that in-the-moment data analysis indicates dipping sales, which means it's time to send people home early. "It's like magic," proclaims Charles DeWitt, vice president for business development at Kronos, supplier of staffing management software for Starbucks and other chains. Who's going to argue with magic? It's out of the hands of the corporation or the local franchise manager and of course the worker. After all, as the article concludes, "scheduling is now a powerful tool to bolster profits, allowing businesses to cut labor costs with a few keystrokes."[78]

The Davos set's seeming obliviousness to what is really happening under the ideology of permanent systematic disruption is vividly captured in a *New Yorker* article by George Packer. He writes of going on a hunt for someone to answer the question "why, during the decades of the personal computer and the Internet, the American economy has grown so slowly, average wages have stagnated, the middle class has been hollowed out, and inequality has surged?" He poses the question to a wide range of tech workers in the Bay Area and reports that "few of them had given the topic much consideration." But when pressed for an answer, most brushed it off, wondering "if it was really true" or saying that this was just a temporary blip. Sam Lessin, who at the time was leading Facebook's "identity product group," tells Packer that, essentially, people are going to, or perhaps already, need less money because "as communication technology gets less expensive," we'll be able to "entertain each other and interact with each other and do things for each other much more efficiently." Packer writes that Lessin, a classmate of Mark Zuckerberg's at Harvard and the son of a prominent investment banker, "found it impossible to believe that people's lives had not improved . . . because of technology."[79]

Jaron Lanier calls companies like Facebook "siren servers." A siren server, writes Lanier, makes "no specific decisions. You should do everything possible to not do anything consequential. Don't play favorites; don't have taste. You are to be the neutral facilitator, the connector, the hub, but never an agent who could be blamed for a decision."[80] Think Airbnb or Amazon or Facebook or Google or Groupon or even Walmart. Think of the management software that Starbucks uses to decide who should work when in thousands of stores. Think of the ever-expanding category of hubs that connect people who want something done with people who are willing to do that job for them. These are task brokers like Fiverr and Taskrabbit, or driver-on-demand apps like Uber and Lyft—low-wage, task-based labor hubs that take a cut of every transaction but don't take much, if any, responsibility for the estimated seventeen million or so Americans who work at least part time as "independent contributors."[81] These workers who race around walking dogs, hanging pictures, and giving rides to the airport don't know what work at what wage they'll have next day or next week.

They are hired—or connected to jobs—by companies who say they are not employees, but independent contractors, which conveniently insures that the workers "don't qualify for employee benefits like health insurance, payroll deductions for Social Security or unemployment benefits."[82] Guy Standing, a labor economist, has dubbed this rapidly expanding class of laborer "the precariat."[83] "These are not jobs, jobs that have any future, jobs that have the possibility of upgrading; this is contingent, arbitrary work," says Stanley Aronowitz, director of the Center for the Study of Culture, Technology and Work at the Graduate Center of the City University of New York. "It might as well be called wage slavery in which all the cards are held, mediated by technology, by the employer, whether it is the intermediary company or the customer."[84]

The intermediary holds all the cards. But they accept as little responsibility as possible. They are the conduit. They don't produce the products or have an opinion on the links they point to or care one way or the other if you are advocating for white power or selling white powder. But, notes Lanier, what they do do is "pattern how other people make decisions. You can get people to have less privacy or organize a business around coupons, but you never get into the middle of any specific event within the pattern template you've created for other people to use."[85] So what's the ultimate result of the rise of the siren server that acts as a near-monopolistic conduit for everything from sharing pictures with friends (Facebook) to taking credit cards (PayPal) to selling handmade crafts (Etsy) to selling just about everything (Amazon)? It's the conglomeration of the power of the network to dominate our lives in ways that could never be done before, all thanks to the rise of IT.

The end result is that we have more and more middleman for-profit systems that shape how we connect and manage relations with each other. As technology historian George Dyson puts it: "Facebook defines who we are, Amazon defines what we want, and Google defines what we think."[86] Many of these entities claim that at their core they are not in it only for the money, but that they are, in fact, fulfilling the human drive to innovate and change, that what they are doing is part of a natural process of disruption and optimization that will ultimately build a better future for you and me. But despite their rhetoric about making the world a better place, they inevitably seem to shape the world in ways that first and foremost are sure to benefit them. Writes Jaron Lanier: "The conceit of optimizing the world is self-serving and self-deceptive. The optimizations approximated in the real world as a result of Siren Servers are optimal only from the points of view of those servers."[87] Jobs are lost, local communities are hurt, and the siren servers get bigger and bigger as more and more of us seek to make up for the fact that the local store that used to sell our handmade picture frames has closed down by getting a part-time barista job and trying to continue to sell our work for diminished profits on Etsy, Amazon, and eBay. Concludes Lanier: "An amazing number of people offer an amazing amount of value over networks. But the lion's share of wealth now flows to those who aggregate and route those offerings, rather than those who provide the raw materials."[88] Kronos gets paid nicely for optimizing barista schedules. Starbucks pumps a bit more cash into its shareholders. People like Jannette Navarro are left further and further behind. Own the IT and, it would seem, you also own the future.

o   o   o   o   o   o

What can we do about systems and systematic disruption? Apparently nothing. This is the way to to the future, after all. The inevitability, the need to embrace and work with—rather than against—supposedly *inevitable* systematic change, is underscored by a panel discussion I attend back at SXSWi. The panel is called Generation Flux and it promises to explore a "velocity of change in our business world—and our culture—[that] has reached unprecedented levels." The description of the discussion goes on to note that "the ultimate lessons of Generation Flux are about adaptability. All the ways we've been taught to operate, the rules we've come to rely on, offer false comfort."[89]

The panel is moderated by Bob Safian, editor of the upbeat tech industry magazine *Fast Company*, in whose pages he first coined the term Generation Flux. The term describes, as he tells the standing-room-only crowd at the panel, those who are living and thriving in a "mobile, global, social, interconnected world where the old rules of business really don't apply anymore." Generation Flux are warriors of change, masters of the surf, riding the techno-wave straight into the sunset. Speaking of warriors, joining Safian on the panel is Padmasree Warrior, chief technology and strategy officer of global networking company Cisco Systems. Warrior follows up on Safian's introduction by immediately citing the importance of being able to embrace this flux era. "The change isn't going to slow down," she says, announcing that there will be fifty billion devices connected by 2020 and that at Cisco there are fewer and fewer rules on "how you lead, how you act, how you create opportunities." Then another self-anointed warrior of the future chimes in. It's the third member of the discussion, Troy Carter, CEO and founder of the Atom Factory, a music management company known for its embrace of data, informed cutting-edge marketing, and shepherding Lady Gaga to fame, fortune, and, apparently, deep, ongoing connection with her many fans. Carter talks about how you have to "walk the line between fear of extinction and the excitement of the future." He says, "We're creating models as we go along. You've got to take the risk." Warrior agrees: "We need to get comfortable with being uncomfortable, because the pace of change is just going to accelerate." I fidget in my seat, impatiently wondering if we will go past seemingly mandatory tributes to our new gods of change and innovation. "It's not disruption for the sake of disruption," Troy Carter says earnestly, "it's purposeful disruption." There is, he says, an entire generation—his, presumably—"looking to erase inefficiency—and that's chaos to some people."

Perhaps; though, I think to myself, the difference between purposeful disruption versus disruption for the sake of it is not always clear, particularly to those being disrupted. After several more rounds of back and forth, including the introduction of surprise in-the-audience guests ranging from other high-level tech execs to Microsoft in-house sociologist Danah Boyd, we finally get to the question and answer part of the session. I stand up and ask if there's much concern about the disrupted, if there's any thought for the disruptees, those left behind. The panel regards me like a creature from another planet. Their responses are fascinating:

Troy Carter: Not to sound insensitive or anything, but change is a way of life. There were guys who were making horseshoes before cars. In the music industry, one of the sad parts was people who'd been in it for years losing their jobs. But at the same time you have companies like Spotify and Pandora and places like that creating new jobs for people, so it's really accepting change.

Padmasree Warrior: That's where leadership comes about. You're creating something new and you're taking an existing model to a new model. There are leaders . . . that play a huge role in helping that transformation occur. It sounds trite, but it is very important how you communicate the purpose of where you're going, and how an existing mode needs to go to a new model. And yeah, will some people get left behind and other people get on the train, as you put it Troy? But I think this is where communication and leadership become very important.

Danah Boyd: I used to love just disrupting for disrupting's sake. As I've started to recognize that other people's careers are on the line, recognize my own privilege in it, a lot of it has been about finding ways of mentoring and managing people to help them understand changes that I can see coming. . . . A lot of it is helping other people find their own role. I think everybody has magic and skills in them. I think you're right, they're terrified, but there is a lot of power to be able to help people to find their place.[90]

What if there is no place for the disrupted? What if there's nothing natural or inevitable about change and disruption? These are questions no one on the panel was remotely interested in addressing; such questions aren't even admissible to their worldview. These people, as *New York Times* technology reporter Quentin Hardy writes, teach us to "treat innovation like an impersonal force, a ceaseless outcome of entrepreneurship in tech. If we displace people or distort our culture with innovations that, say, wipe out local bookstores or measure every moment in a warehouse worker's day, it is the price of a generally beneficial force."[91]

o o o o o o

Just about everyone with a disruptive idea from Ryan Konicek's Tappr app to Mara Lewis's new way to search seeks siren server status. When I was at SXSWi watching the pitches, it was pretty clear. The doctors seeking to disrupt health care by making it possible for you to instantly choose between all the different MRI providers in your region and their prices had a vision—that everyone in the world would eventually be booking their tests through their site. The woman with the idea for an app that directs business travelers to yoga classes and morning jogging tours of the downtown area wants the same—to be the only intermediary for business travelers seeking upscale fitness and mindfulness while out of town. Everything is envisioned as the next great disruption that will be so efficient it will rule, it will be dominate, it will destroy the competition. There will be only one bookstore, one search engine, one app to order a drink. It's all about singular victory. The new permanent future entrepreneur, writes Lanier, "hopes to 'dent the universe' or achieve some other heroic, Nietzschean validation."[92]

The result of this rhetorical shift, underscored by some impressive examples of those who managed to actually alter how the world works (though not necessarily make the world a better place), is the frenzy of disruptive activity that is fast becoming the acknowledged desirable outcome—disrupt, change, take a breath, and do it all over again. However, once this period of frenzied activity is over, it's not clear what we'll be left with. The case against the future comes down to our inability to care about or see the actual future. The actual future is something we can really only portend based on what is happening in the present. And in the present, we are in a prolonged, ongoing downward spiral of malemployment with no end in sight. All signs point not to a utopia just around the corner, but a near total(itarian) split between rich and poor with a shrinking middle class holding on to the crumbling edge by their fingertips. Tech entrepreneurs pat themselves on the back because they're working on something powerful enough to reshape how we read books or order drinks or talk to our friends. But in truth, most of these siren servers and wannabes convinced, as Jaron Lanier puts, that they are "analyzing and predicting events that enlighten the human world" are really "just proving" the power of IT to enable systems that maximize productivity and profit, enriching a shrinking number of people at the expense of the rest of us.[93]

CHAPTER 9

Future Shock and Awe
Anxiety Factory

One fall evening, I gather together a group of recent university graduates to talk to them about how they see the future. Their average age is twenty-seven, making them members of the so-called Generation Y. Digital Natives, Gen Y, Millennials, the Me Generation—whatever you want to call them, they were born in the '80s and '90s, they grew up with iPods and YouTube and climate change, and their lives have been more intimately connected with technology than any generation before them. They're comfortable with a world of MOOCs and ircs and LOLs in ways that many of us are not. These graduates in their mid-to-late twenties tweet and know what a torrent is. So what's their take on it? How are they responding to the new age of future?

My informal focus group consists of nine recent university graduates. I deliberately exclude anybody working directly in IT or related high-tech fields like programming or computer science. The gathering takes place in Toronto, the diverse city of 2.8 million where I've lived for the last twenty or so years. Though Toronto, and Canada in general, was not hit as hard as the US by the ongoing fallout of the 2008 economic crash, the situation here is similar to that of many cities in the Eastern United States. Over the last twenty years, manufacturing jobs have disappeared; growth is to be found primarily in high tech and the service industries, and the rate of unemployment in the Toronto area hovered around 8 percent at the time when the focus group met. (Official US unemployment at the time was in the range of 7.5 percent.) The Toronto youth unemployment rate, however, was double that number at somewhere around 16 percent. (Youth unemployment being defined as those between fifteen and twenty-four years old and actively looking for work.) This youth unemployment rate was at a rate similar to that in neighboring Michigan; was higher than in Indiana, Minnesota, Ohio, Pennsylvania, and Wisconsin; and was only slighter lower than so-called rust belt states like Illinois (18.5 per cent) and New York (18 per cent).[1]

I put out the call for participants through my online networks, asking for recent university graduates to talk to me about their "post-graduation experiences." I am surprised, though I probably shouldn't be, when over a hundred people volunteer for the task. Eventually, I whittle the list down to nine people, chosen primarily based on how chatty they seem when I reach them on the phone, how willing I think they will be to talk openly about their lives. I tell them as little as possible about my ideas and the subject of my inquiries to avoid putting any preconceived notions in their heads.

I am nervous watching them file in. What will they say? Will I see in their lives the symptoms and realities of the future era? What if I've gotten it wrong? Maybe what I perceive as a fundamental, systemic shift is really just my Gen X nostalgia for Atari, rotary phones, and steady work at an MTV that actually played music videos?

I know beforehand that I have a very diverse group on my hands. Without particularly trying, I have assembled a cluster that has degrees in subjects ranging from biology to social work to public relations. My group is made up of different races, backgrounds, disciplines, and sexualities. Some of them are first generation, born to parents who came to Canada determined to do whatever was necessary to give their children a better life. Others come from long-established families set up in the city's more affluent neighborhoods. Some want kids, houses, families, careers. Others are seeking adventure, opportunities to follow their passions.

The conversation starts off with my moderator passing around pens and pads. "I just want you to jot down," he says, "what you think of when you think of the future. Literally, just that broad, just your immediate thoughts, feelings, associations."

The focus group participants take a moment to scrawl a few words about their free-associated vision of the future, and then we start going around the room.[2]

Tameika Thomas, twenty-five, and a graduate of Toronto's York University with a Bachelor of Arts in drama and French plus a post-grad diploma in marketing and public relations: "I think about marriage, children, having a great job and loving what I'm doing. It's the next step. I've been taught that my whole life, so it's what I'm trying to do."

Kevin Lemkay, twenty-five, a politics junkie interning at a public relations firm: "I am someone who likes to have stability before I do anything else. So I'd really like that, at least, a stable career, something."

Christine Barta, twenty-nine, a recent graduate with a Master of Social Work now looking for work in her field, follows that up: "I just want a stable job so that I have the income. Travel is something that really is top of the list. It's been something I've been putting off since I graduated high school because I couldn't afford to do it. So, basically, my goal right now is get a job, make as much money as I can, take a sabbatical, and go travel for a year. And then kids."

Jacob Daniel Babad, twenty-six, with an arts background and an entry-level job in publishing: "I absolutely want a career at this point in my life. And that means, to me, benefits, job security, solid salary."

"I don't want a job, I don't want a career," shoots back Tommy Zheng, twenty-seven, who has a BA in psychology and alternates between working for a Chinese-Canadian community group as a researcher two days a week and working part-time as a massage therapist. "But I want financial freedom, which means for me, personally, right now, I'm working towards entrepreneurship, something that I can do for myself. I don't want to be controlled by a corporation or employer. I want to be able to do what I want to do and make my own hours, make my money."

How did an abstract question about the future immediately become about life goals and the obstacles to achieving them? We asked them to brainstorm about what they thought the future looked like, not where they hoped to be in two years. What happened to the billion-dollar ideas, to robots and wearable computers and bartender apps? Don't these people want to *disrupt* anything? Maybe, I'm thinking to myself, I have it all wrong; maybe getting-to-the-future-first isn't nearly as pervasive an ideology as I'd thought.

Finally, Susheela Ramachandran, twenty-five, with a BA in political science, speaks of embracing uncertainty and the positives of new possibilities. She gently chides the other participants on their conservatism and encourages them to think out of the box and even out of North America. "If you look worldwide, I see more opportunity. And there's also an emergence of a very new kind of work, that's never been before, new positions that you've never heard of." Susheela, living at home and, like most of the others, partially underemployed at a patchwork of jobs, nevertheless is convinced that she will eventually end up on the forefront of change. She cites a desire to establish herself as a consultant helping companies bring out the creativity of their employees. She ends by urging her fellow panelists to think big. "I think we are creative enough and we have enough resources compared to the rest of the world, that we can create the future that we want to."

Reema Baber, twenty-seven, with a Bachelor of Science in biophysics and the only one in the group with a full-time job, at a financial services firm, says she also sees the future differently from the other eight. She speaks haltingly at first and then with growing conviction about the way we have "access to information like never ever before. And our world is interconnected like never before." She characterizes the future "in terms of just limitless possibilities."

So two votes for the future era. Two votes for "limitless possibilities" and creating "the future we want to." And the rest? They aren't saying yea or nay. In fact, they aren't talking about the future at all. They answer the question by talking about their present-day yearning for jobs, stability, a clear path. As Harry Au, twenty-six, with an master's degree in gender studies, living with his parents and employed temporarily as a part-time research assistant puts it: "When I think of the future, it's more about right now, how do I . . . What am I supposed to do? This is what I think about it."

When I think of the future I think . . . What am I supposed to do? Reading over the transcript of the evening a few weeks later, I realize that the seven members of the group who see the future primarily in the context of their own economic security are neither immune to nor unaware of the rise of the ideology of a permanently disruptive future. There are plenty of clues throughout the conversation that show how they've absorbed the rhetoric of future and are feeling the abrupt shift.

> Jacob: You've got to work nonstop, keep your skills sharp—

> Tommy: Innovate.

> Jacob: Yeah. You got to keep . . . be the cutting edge of your industry and you have to work harder than anybody else.

> Tommy: Constantly . . . not just in terms of education but innovate yourself in terms of . . . like, for example, I take public speaking classes sometimes because I feel like I don't have confidence speaking in front of a crowd, or I take theatre so that I know how to be adaptable to an environment—

> Christine: It's more social but, at the same time . . . I mean, I was never on Twitter before last summer because when I went back to college it was made explicitly clear to me that these social media outlets are things that are very much used in the workplace . . . not only being able to use them correctly but to be able to apply that in your workplace, I think, is something that's becoming increasingly important and popular.

> Kevin: And using it to not just promote your work—

promote yourself and kind of showcase how you
think . . . like, being in PR they can kind of beat into
you that you are your own brand, and I think, speaking
of social media, in particular, you kind of have to know
how to sell yourself and know your story.

Innovate. Adapt. Brand yourself. Be the cutting edge. The language
could not be clearer. These are people who got the memo. Sell yourself,
adopt new technologies, prepare for change, be change. They understand what is expected of them in the age of future. They recognize
the new role models, the new totemic companies and devices, the new
pace. But they are, if not exactly resistant, then definitely uncertain.
Where is this future? How do I get to it? What am I supposed to do in it?
Anxious, plaintive, almost existential questions echo not only through
the evening's dialogue but through the lives of these nine very different
people. Nothing in their lives ever taught them to be part of a landscape
of constant change. Nor are they sure that they can find happiness,
satisfaction, or even a measure of economic security chasing the future
and desiring to *be change*. Their almost painful yearning for full-time
employment, job security, and the trappings of conventional domes-
ticity they grew up with is a direct and logical response to the rise of
the future doctrine: sure, we'll be change, but first can we have some
prospect of decent, meaningful work at a middle-class wage?

If anything, this millennial group is being affected more personally
by the arrival of the future than I first imagined. This is a generation
that has always enjoyed the rules, always followed the roadmap. A
survey that came out around the same time I did the focus group
provided these statistics about the average Canadian undergraduate:
a third of them reported not having had a single drink in a month and
most of them said they had never smoked a cigarette or marijuana.
"They wear their seatbelts, their bike helmets, they get vaccinations
and go to the dentist. A fifth have been tested for HIV. And half of
them are monogamous, reporting they've had one sexual partner in
the last year."[3] US undergraduates are similarly well behaved—a 2015
survey of freshmen students revealed that three-quarters of them
barely drink and only one in fifty smoke cigarettes.[4] A US study that

polled 1000 Gen Y workers and their bosses concluded that "Gen Y's have a big desire for mentoring" though only 33 percent of them reported that their bosses were actually interested in being mentors. Despite this, 59 percent of the survey participants said their managers have experience, and 41 percent said "they think their bosses have wisdom."[5] They want the assurances of the rules, they want to believe in their bosses, they want what many before them took for granted. The sudden sharp decline in their prospects leaves them bewildered and anxious. The annual UCLA survey of freshmen goes back four decades. It reveals that compared to 1966, college freshmen today are much more concerned with being financially stable. In 1966, only 42 percent reported that being financially well-off was an essential life goal. But in the present, that number has jumped to 75 percent. In the 1960s, 86 percent of the freshmen agreed with the statement that developing a meaningful philosophy of life was essential. Fast forward to the millennial age; now, less than half report developing a meaningful philosophy of life as a crucial goal.[6]

So we can see how the age of permanent future is changing these twenty-somethings. They are more worried about and focused on success and getting ahead. Beset by anxieties about the gap between what they're accomplishing and what they're told they should be accomplishing, they are less willing or perhaps less able to contemplate life in its abstract totality and come up with a set of values and beliefs. Instead, they focus on the mantra of hard work and following the rules. Only, faced with unsatisfying part-time work and diminishing opportunities, they are now being plunged into a world that doesn't make sense to them. They did their part, they followed all the rules, and just when it was all supposed to pay off, the rules changed. Time to follow new rules. But what are they? *What am I supposed to do?* If job security was more like the low-hanging fruit it had been when their parents were starting out, they would be making different and most likely more freewheeling life choices. Instead, they are struggling: struggling to escape the morass of part-time patchwork employment and sky-high youth unemployment; struggling to account for what they see as the devaluing of their degrees; struggling to figure out how to integrate the uncertainty of the slippery idea of being disruptors involved in chasing future into lives that had henceforth been shaped by the plod forward toward the predictable normal of the center.

> Harry: There's an increase in the income gap, there's increased competition, there's inflated credentials, which doesn't work in our favor, right? And then there's also, like, a streamlining of capitalism or a change of capitalism where you want to pay as little as possible for as much work done as possible. And I see it in my dad's work, where it never happened before, right? And he's telling me now that the company's making more money but they're laying people off. It makes no sense. And they're giving worse service to their clients, which makes no sense but they're looking at the short term, right? And I think we also have to look at stockholders . . . because we have such a capitalist type of economy now where stockholders want profit. And how do you get profit immediately—you lay people off. Even though you're making money, you lay people off.

> Moderator: Is there an answer for this, Harry?

> Harry: I don't know. . . . I feel like with all the credentials we're also getting, right, there's also a lot of work that we don't want to do and why would you want to . . . go back to my waiter job when I have a master's degree, right? And then there's immigrants coming in that are taking those jobs. And a lot of times . . . they have a lot of credentials. And I just feel like right now . . . everyone has so much credentials but there's just not enough jobs, that's how I feel.

> Kristen: Overeducated, underemployed.

> Harry: Yeah. There's a theme, right?

Reema: These things are the reason why I just gravitate towards entrepreneurship . . . because if the year 2008 and all of these things have taught us anything it's that your future is never secure as long as it's in someone else's hands. . . . There's no such thing as a secure job, there's no such thing as job security. I don't think that's real anymore. So that's scary for a lot of people. You don't know where to start. You know, having capital and things like that. But . . . all you really need is a great idea and, you know, some drive. . . . I think for me that, as scary as it is—and it still is for me—that's worth more in terms of taking that chance versus you're still taking a chance with your life in someone else's hands, so it might as well be in your own at least.

Christine: I'm really enjoying hearing everybody talking about this innovation and how we're . . . adapting, and we're creating these new jobs and I'm like, oh, my God, this is so outside of my head, I never even think that way because I very much will look at what's there and say, well, this is a problem. I talked about, you know, the erosion of job quality and I'm amazed at, you know, hearing people say, well, if the job's not there we'll just make it. How awesome is that. But then I think of the people that I've worked with over, you know, the last five, six years and I think there's no way that that would work for them.

There it is in a nutshell: the schism between the two who see success only by wholeheartedly embracing the ideology of permanent future, and those who are reluctant to throw away the dream of domestic stability and what little modicum of social certainty their parents and grandparents fought to attain and preserve. Is the answer to their dilemma of overeducation and underemployment (a dilemma mirrored across the global north) to throw off everything they thought they were working toward and plunge into the permanent future? Reema, like her start-up compatriots Mara and Ryan, and like their ideological companion Patrick Tucker from the World Future Society, suggests that her peers will be better off embracing an unknown in which they no longer rely on governments and corporations and even family for stability, but only their capacity to create and invent and reinvent. But her peers, who grew up believing in and being taught stability, are understandably confused by this notion. For them the answer is to do as Tameika Thomas has been doing: work hard, go to school, specialize in something that seems like it should yield a job and even a husband and family; and then intern; and when that internship fails to yield a job, intern again, and if necessary, intern again—until it all works out the way it is supposed to.

Whatever path these nine will eventually walk, the overall result is clear. They are the first generation truly confronted with the question of how to make their way in this new era. Their lives—past and present and what-is-to-come—are being shaped by the future-first doctrine that, even as they watch, is transforming the core institutions shaping their mental and physical landscape. As a result, despite their many differences, they all have one thing very much in common: a deep sense of unease, an almost schizophrenic confusion about where they should be going, and how they would get there. Their overall sensibility might be described as a combination of loss and confusion leavened somewhat by the rhetorical promises of innovation and techno-futurism. For each and every one of them, the rock-solid faith in the system that characterized their generation had been shaken. They all have different goals, but their paths intersect at the great mist-shrouded void of a future they are constantly told is very near, is coming any day now, and yet seems so frustratingly unattainable, so utterly impossible to prepare for.

"Our parents," says Reema, "were preparing for a very predictable world." "For our parents," agrees Kristen, "the future was something to look forward to." "When I say job versus career," says Jacob, "it doesn't mean my passions or my whatever, it means security and safety, the things my parents had, the things I was raised with, that's what I'm looking for, that's what I mean when I say I'm done with jobs." The group paints a picture of their parents that is actually a dramatic contrast: happy, comfortable empty-nesters relaxing in their Florida condos with secure pensions, fully owned houses, and well-stocked, hard-earned retirement savings accounts. This is their parents. They followed the rules and were rewarded. But for them, for the millennials and all who come next, no such future seems to be in the offing. Kristen put it with remarkable succinctness: "Perhaps the reason that it's hard to define the future for ourselves is because we really don't know what the future will be and we can't have those same standards. . . . We might have to work into our seventies. It might be harder in the future. And I think that that's something that's very hard to come to grips with."

Ironically, despite all the actual attempts to discern what comes next that we've encountered in this book, the thick fog obscuring the future is a heavy weight resting on the shoulders of these tech-savvy, highly educated, middle-class young people. They live in one of the most affluent countries in the world and have grown up with every possible privilege. And yet they are confused and wounded with no idea of what is coming next. The world is heaping multiple expectations on them—to be happy, to reinvent and disrupt and make new rules, to generate new sources of wealth while solving intractable problems they've inherited. As if that wasn't enough, all their lives they have followed with GPS-like accuracy a path to a destination—the defined, transparent future of their parents — that they are now coming to realize does not even exist.

o o o o o

According to the National Institute for Mental Health, in any twelve-month period, 18 percent of the population of the United States is struggling with some form of anxiety disorder. Major depressive disorder plagues up to 17 percent of the US population.[7] Marcia Angell, former editor in chief of the *New England Journal of Medicine*, noted that "the tally of those who are so disabled by mental disorders that they qualify for Supplemental Security Income (SSI) or Social Security

Disability Insurance (SSDI) increased nearly two and a half times between 1987 and 2007—from 1 in 184 Americans to 1 in 76. For children, the rise is even more startling—a thirty-five-fold increase in the same two decades."[8] The US Centers for Disease Control and Prevention report that the suicide rate among Americans aged thirty-five to sixty-four increased 28.4 percent between 1999 and 2010 (from 13.7 suicides per 100,000 population in 1999 to 17.6 per 100,000 in 2010).[9] You know how it's said that certain Arctic peoples have many, even hundreds, of different words for snow? Well perhaps one day it will noted that post-industrial future-first nations have hundreds of different manifestations of anxiety. From chronic fatigue syndrome to generalized anxiety disorder to obsessive-compulsive disorder (OCD) to panic disorder to social anxiety disorder to, of course, alcoholism, drug addiction, Internet addiction plus all the related conditions that have anxiety at their core, like hoarding, eating disorders, cutting, and the list goes on and on. The Japanese—arguably the most hyper-futuristic people on Earth—have an entire roster of these kinds of psychological disorders, culminating in the phenomenon of *hikikomori*, a mental illness in which people, usually in their early twenties, simply refuse to leave their bedrooms for periods of six or more months. Tamaki Saito, a Japanese psychiatrist who studies and treats the phenomenon, estimates that there are around one million hikikomori.[10]

A survey of roughly 100,000 public school students in grades seven to twelve in my relatively peaceful city of Toronto (with a violent crime rate a fraction of rates in similarly sized cities in the US) reveals that, as research coordinator Maria Yau puts it, "a majority of students are telling us they are nervous or anxious all the time. These are new items to us, and quite shocking." What are all these kids worrying about? High-school student Hirad Zafari says, "The Grade 11 and Grade 12 years, they can start a path for the rest of your life. We are reminded of that so often, too—if we don't make the right decision or best decision now, it's not going to work out well in the future."[11] Even if they do make the right decisions and put themselves on the path of owning future, it's unlikely that their anxiety will just disappear. The number of college freshmen entering UCLA in 2013 who reported feeling overwhelmed was 33 percent, almost double the 18 percent reporting a similar feeling in 1985.[12] Another annual poll—this one by the Cooperative Institutional Research Program—surveys 150,000 college freshman across the US annually. The 2014 survey found that 9.5 percent of respondents frequently "felt depressed" during the past year, "a significant rise over the 6.1 percent reported five years ago." Students reporting feeling "overwhelmed" by "schoolwork and other commitments" rose to 34.6 percent from 27.1 percent.[13]

What's driving these rising levels of anxiety, depression, and related mental illness? A study on suicides rates in India points to at least one important factor. In India, a country dogged by grinding poverty, the leading cause of death is suicide. But the highest rates of suicide aren't found in its poorest states as we might expect. In fact, it's the opposite. The study shows that suicide rates in the richer, faster developing states are in some cases ten times higher than rates in the much poorer northern states. The highest suicide rates in India "are found in Tamil Nadu and Kerala, the two states with the highest development indicators. The lowest is in Bihar, the state that finishes last in every measure of progress and development." How to explain an anomaly reminiscent of those happiness measures that often find that people in so-called underdeveloped countries report higher levels of life satisfaction than those in the rich northern countries? Dr. Vikram Patel of the London School of Hygiene and Tropical Medicine led the India suicide study, which was published in the medical journal the *Lancet*. Commenting on its seemingly topsy-turvy findings, he says this: "Our study doesn't answer why, and this is speculation, but it clearly points to something that is not biological. It has to point to the social environment young people are growing up in—there must be something toxic in the social environment in the rapidly developing states of India, which is not there in less developing states." He goes on to note that "the most obvious explanation" is that people have a sense of expectation that life just can't match. "Your aspirations," he says, "have been built up by opportunities that in reality don't exist." Does that sound familiar? To me it sounds like the entire edifice upon which the future era has been built. The future is coming. The future will be whatever you want it to be. Get ready to ride the crest of change! But when we try to grasp that awesome future, it melts away in our hands. Where did it go?[14]

Across the globe, we live longer, we eat more, we have more stuff, we are more educated, and we are less likely to be subjected to wars and plagues than any people who ever came before us. And we're miserable. Today, two of the top ten causes of death across all nations are heart disease (lack of exercise coupled with overconsumption) and suicide. Go back to 1900 and neither of those self-inflicted killers made the top ten. In many ways, what's killing us now isn't having too little, it's having too much—too many options, too many propulsive, consumptive urges coupled with too many pressures to jettison the past, eradicate stability, adopt perpetual change as the only possible meaning. The era of permanently chasing future is the era of permanent anxiety.

Scientists at Yale University are researching the revelation that chronic stress actually reduces the brain's ability to make an important protein called neuritin. "Neuritin produces antidepressant actions and blocks the neuronal and behavioral deficits caused by chronic stress," Ronald Duman, a neurobiologist at Yale and his team report in a study in the journal of the *Proceedings of the National Academy of Sciences*. The study found that when we get too anxious and stressed out, the brain stops making as much neuritin.[15] Once again, biology trumps ideology. Our brain's health depends on a certain level of stability, the knowledge that what happens tomorrow will be pretty similar to what happened yesterday. We don't want and never wanted constant change as the firmament of our society. No matter how much we try to accept and even profit from propulsive possibility, our minds are literally physically incapable of absorbing the shocks of the future era. We evolved to survive and perpetuate, and that process requires stability. The entire psychological framework of the human being is fundamentally about achieving and maintaining stable environments and social conditions. Without that stability, the brain gives up trying to keep up. Our minds are throwing in the towel, waving the white flag. And so the age of anxiety, exponentially expanding with each fresh push to emphasize change and future over constancy and progression. Chasing the future isn't saving us, it's killing us.

o o o o o

We're in the forty-fifth year of future shock. The book *Future Shock*, by Alvin Toffler (with contributions from his wife, Heidi), has endured since its publication in 1970, selling six million-plus copies all over the world. *Future Shock* captured the feeling and sensibility of an era in transition from the progressive shared futurism embedded in the nationalist project to the cutthroat techno-individualism we are familiar with today. The Toffler tome was widely read and quoted precisely because it tapped into the sense of a society in destabilizing flux. "Future shock is the shattering stress and disorientation that we induce in individuals by subjecting them to *too much change in too short a time*," the pair wrote.[16] (The italics are mine.)

The Tofflers had a lot of interesting things to say. In some cases, they were eerily prescient. They spoke, for instance, of technological change benefiting mainly a highly educated elite class, those who will be able to "understand the fast-emerging super-industrial social structures" while for "the majority of men . . . the options remain excruciatingly few." They wrote about "the disease of change" as a "real sickness from which increasingly large numbers already suffer."[17] The Tofflers framed the question of technological change and its speed in a way that has been largely ignored before and after: as a psychological challenge.

Articulating the stress of constant change due to propulsive technological upgrade—and, at the same time, spreading such phrases and near mythologies as "information overload"—earned the book totemic status. And, to its enduring credit, *Future Shock* may well be the first and only book exploring the relationship between technological progress and psychological stress to enter the popular consciousness. (Only McLuhan has come as close in terms of reaching a mass audience on the subject of our psychology applied to widespread technological change.)

Most people who have heard the term "future shock" assume the Toffler argument is fundamentally antitechnology. In fact, the book is not antitechnology. Nor is the book critical of the idea of living our lives in the shadow of a constantly advancing future we should be expected to both perpetuate and adapt to. Instead, the Toffler oeuvre is full of pithy aphorisms, Yoda-like epigrams to our poor, pre-postmodern, inert selves: "Change is not merely necessary to life—it is life."

"Technology feeds on itself. Technology makes more technology possible." "The illiterate of the future will not be the person who cannot read. It will be the person who does not know how to learn."[18] First, the Tofflers fetishize technology—after all, what else offers "the supreme exhilaration of riding change, cresting it, changing and growing with it"? Then they warn of its awesome danger—"future shock!" "info overload!"—then they insist that the answer, the cure to future shock, is to dive in head first. Don't fight it; embrace it.

For, as the Tofflers make clear in *Future Shock* and beyond, their solution to the problem of widespread psychological (and social) destabilization due to an ideology of permanent technological change is *more change*. What we need is to find a way to fully embrace the liberating awesome of technology freed of anxiety and fear. Or, as they put it, if you "make the necessary effort to understand the fast-emerging super-industrial social structures" and "find the 'right' life pace, the 'right' sequence of subcults to join and lifestyle models to emulate," then "the triumph" will be "exquisite."[19]

According to the Tofflers, we have future shock because we aren't properly preparing human beings to embrace the onrushing future. What we need, then, is better preparation so more people can go further faster. "To survive," write the Tofflers, "to avert what we have termed future shock, the individual must become infinitely more adaptable and capable than ever before." Forty-five years before World Future Society's Patrick Tucker, the Tofflers preached the mantra of empowering individuals to own the future; they argued that the solution to overcoming future shock was teaching people how to better navigate the turbulent, but inevitable and necessary, waters of constant change. They talked about dealing with the stress of constant technological change by employing "direct coping" and "de-stimulating tactics,"[20] basically meditation and mindfulness. They prefigured Patrick Tucker and the futurists by advancing the notion of "personal stability zones," writing that while "most people, deep down, believe that the future is a blank . . . we *can* assign probabilities to some of the changes that lie in store for us, especially certain large structural changes, and there are ways to use this knowledge in designing personal stability zones."[21]

And through it all they maintained—like the panelists at the SXSWi

Generation Flux talk I attended—that, as they write, "none of this should suggest that change can or should be stopped."[22] Society should be about helping people to understand and embrace the new reality in which everything permanent, everything that went before, is obsolete. "We must," they write, "search out totally new ways to anchor ourselves, for all the old roots—religion, nation, community, family, or profession—are now shaking under the hurricane impact of the accelerative thrust."[23] We don't question the "accelerative thrust." We open the door to it and let it sweep away the clutter of everything that once was. The old limited us. The new liberates us.

Escape from future shock won't come from lamenting the rise of a techno-industrial age and trying to push back against it through what the Tofflers describe as a "return to passivity, mysticism and irrationality" or, even worse, trying to go about "feeling" or "intuiting" our way into the future. The answer isn't to question the path we're on, it's to fully embrace the potential of the one and only path—future change all the time. We must merge with the future and go wherever that takes us. Full immersion is the solution: "Rather than lashing out, Luddite-fashion, against the machine, those who genuinely wish to break the prison-hold of the past and present would do well to hasten the controlled-selective-arrival of tomorrow's technologies." Hasten the escape. Break the "prison-hold." Don't slow down. Speed up. Open up your arms and embrace the too much happening too fast. "We need, first of all," the Tofflers advise us, "a radically new orientation toward the future."[24]

o o o o o o

In our era of future, the Toffler solution has finally and fully been implemented. Today, everyone from business school professors to newspaper columnists to CEOs to government officials promulgates the Toffler-esque prescription for humanity. We teach adaptation and endless flexibility. We teach innovation and creativity. An iPad for every kid! We take as a given that people are limited only by their capacity to withstand and harness the whiplash of "accelerative thrust." We hold that the past holds us back, that institutions are slow and in the way; that, in fact, the best institutions are the ones laying the groundwork for their own obsolescence, replaced by a fully empowered populace of individuals and corporate proxies who make change faster and better than any organization, community, or government ever could. We assert unequivocally that only change in the form of technological innovation can keep us happy, healthy and, most important, wealthy. Writes the sober economist Enrico Moretti: "Innovation is the engine that has enabled Western economies to grow at unprecedented speed ever since the onset of the industrial revolution. In essence, our material well-being hinges on the continuous creation of new ideas, new technologies, and new products."[25] Imbued with the Toffler method, we can then assume that once everyone is educated in the relentless, rootless, constantly changing tao of future, innovation will continue apace, we'll all be better off and our anxiety will be finally dispelled. Forty-five years later and it has become clear that the Toffler book, which at the time seemed like an antiestablishment screed—the *Silent Spring* of technological change—actually was dogma for the permanent future era.

Despite the myriad mental illnesses we struggle with, we continue to adopt the mantra of constant change advanced by *Future Shock*. Though we're inarguably now living in a state of permanent anxiety and stress, we are still gamely trying to make it work, trying to bring the imperative of change at all costs into our lives, trying to make our hearts beat in time to the relentless thrum of the future. If anything, as the levels of technological adoption of everything from the techniques of factory farming to smart phones to the Internet of things suggests, we have proven ourselves all too amenable to change. We eagerly bring new technologies into our lives with very little consideration for how each highly hyped, supposed innovation is going to alter our day-to-day. From traffic jams to TV dinners in front of the TV to drunk texting, the story of technology is littered with unintended consequences that we do our best to just shrug off. This is a big part of the permanent future ideology—the "assumption," writes David Edgerton, "that the new is clearly superior to what went before."[26] How many times a month does Intel cofounder Gordon E. Moore's "law" about the transcendent doubling of computer chip speed get jubilantly referenced in the media? "IBM Smashes Moore's Law, Cuts Bit Size to 12 Atoms," crows a typical headline. The article goes on to make it very clear how this is going to pan out: "Looking at this conservatively . . . instead of 1TB on a device you'd have 100TB to 150TB," explains Andreas Heinrich, IBM research staff member. "Instead of being able to store all your songs on a drive, you'd be able to have all your videos on the device."[27] We don't fear our tech and fall into future shock with each exponential leap forward. To the contrary: we're doing as we've been told to do, actively clamoring for the new, the next, the more, the better.

I was recently watching twenty-four-hour cable news in a hotel. In between segments on a Malaysian jetliner and its passengers, disappeared without trace into the Indian Ocean, a commercial caught my eye. The commercial was from a phone company advertising a new service called AT&T Next.[28] It featured shiny happy impossibly pretty twenty-somethings talking about what technology would bring them next. They mimed through a host of possibilities—sending texts with your mind!—and then we finally got to the punch line: a service that delivers you a new mobile device every year. This is clearly necessary because technology is advancing so quickly that if you don't sign up, you will risk missing out on what beautiful people like you are going to be doing next. Can you take that risk? AT&T doesn't think you can. Neither does Rogers in Canada or Telstra in Australia.

What is a good phone today will be a bad phone tomorrow. This sounds inevitable and sensible—shouldn't things change, advance, get better? But let's put it another way; as Enrico Moretti writes in *The New Geography of Jobs*, "What is a good job today will inevitably become a bad job in the future."[29] For phones it sounds optimistic and promising. Endless upgrade! For jobs, it sound like a recipe for totalizing anxiety: Am I on the chopping block too, about to be put out to pasture? Am I about to be made obsolete like phone operators, typists, travel agents, booksellers, and, soon, long-haul truckers, lawyers, factory workers, and coders?

Like the Tofflers, I believe we live in a steady state of fear and anxiety with its roots in technologically enabled social change. But our "shock" isn't about our resistance to change. We don't fear or resist change in the form of new technologies, even those technologies that radically destabilize what has gone before. What we are most anxious about, most fearful of, is *our failure to take advantage of change*. What we're most worried about is becoming dinosaurs, out of step and doomed to extinction. Though it is true that the notion of change casts a shadow over contemporary life, the foreboding we feel in the process of living life under this shadow shouldn't be called future shock, it should be called future failure. We fear not change, but that we will fail to embrace change. We fear being left behind. We fear losing out on *next*. Our desire for future is our brain seeking to know what is going to happen next so we can cling to our expectations. We seek future in the form of the pursuit of constant change in order to somehow get a handle on and be ready for what is to come. This is perhaps the deepest irony around chasing future: our intense conservatism, our innate psychological need to know what is coming before it comes, has been flipped; now we embrace constant change, and pursue it with unprecedented ardor, having been repeatedly told that such change will maximize our likelihood of replication and survival. But this flipped-around fervor for change is causing a massive mental health plague. We pursue change against our own best interests; instead of helping us to maximize our survival individually and collectively, this pursuit is now starting to actually reduce our likelihood of long-term viability. Future is killing us, but we're more desperate to get to it than ever before.

The vast majority of us approach the future with, at best, a kind of compulsory, corporate enthusiasm that occasionally gives way to fatalistic, existential dread. It's as if something inherent has been taken from us—some faith not in the future, but the constancy of the present. The more we try to know the future—the more we develop increasingly complex, supposedly scientific means to try to grasp what is coming next—the less we end up feeling like we can ever know anything. We create endless possibilities and variables and yet, writes Daniel Innerarity, "the future resists us continuously and to an increasing degree. This resistance arises from structural causes that are related to the very nature of our society. The aporia of a dynamic society is that knowledge of the future is as necessary as it is impossible."[30] Ever-elusive knowledge of the future: necessary, but impossible. This, to me, is the core of so-called future shock. A collective loss of certainty. A body blow to our ability to wake up in the morning and feel like what's going to happen that day is at least nominally under our control. Most of us have gamely attempted to at least keep up with the "accelerative thrust" of the techno-future in the Toffler-Tucker mold. But relentless pursuit of the future is making the future "more uncertain than ever." And if the future is uncertain, then daily life itself comes to feel intuitively as if it's on increasingly shaky ground. Many of us live lives of unimaginable luxury set against a backdrop of relative certainty. But we have to perpetually struggle to remind ourselves of this, largely because our all-encompassing mental environment is one of destabilizing change as the new normal; embrace the shock or you (and your middle class aspirations) will surely be left behind.

The more pills we pop, apps we download, and old ways and patterns we hasten to destroy, the further we seem to get from any kind of meaningful end point where our anxiety abates and we learn to love our era of endless change. It's not working largely because the Tofflers and their many followers had it all wrong. We don't need to learn how to ride the crest of technological change. We're so good at it, we've even found ways to normalize the anxiety and desperation we feel while trying to stay on and at the top of each and every transformation. It's normal to feel upset and unhappy. In year forty-five of future shock, it's just the price we pay for getting to the better future faster.

PART IV

The End

CHAPTER 10

Escape from the Permanent Future
The Problem of Hope

Christy Foley is going to live on Mars. Or at least, that's what she's hoping. The married, thirty-three-year-old strategic planner for the province of Alberta has a fervent desire to be part of the first-ever colony established on another planet. If all goes according to plan, in about ten years she will divorce her husband—whom she will never see again—have the last of her weekly dinners with her parents, gulp one final lungful of naturally photosynthesized air, and step into a ship bound for the red planet.

"I want to help shape the future and not be passive and just take what is thrown at us," she tells me from her home in Edmonton, Alberta, where when I reach her via Skype. "The people who talk to me are 99 percent—You're crazy. You're crazy amazing or you're crazy and stupid. But I don't want to blindly go through life without trying to make it *my* life; that doesn't sound appealing."[1]

It all started in 2013, when Foley came across Dutch millionaire Bas Lansdorp's plan to establish a colony on Mars. To achieve this goal, Lansdorp had cofounded a nonprofit organization called Mars One and was raising money and, even better, accepting applicants. I should note here that Christy Foley is hardly the only person who believes in the importance of getting to Mars. So agreeable is this notion that at least two very rich men are currently vying to own Mars—the aforementioned Bas Lansdorp and the billionaire entrepreneur Elon Musk. Musk once described Mars as a "fixer-upper planet" and even, at one point, put a ten-year timeline on colonizing and transforming the planet with as many as 80,000 people.[2] Indeed, Musk is on record for noting that the whole reason he started his private space exploration company SpaceX was that he discovered he was unable to rent a rocket that could fulfill an initial plan of landing living plants on the red planet, presumably in an attempt to jump-start atmospheric production.[3] At any rate, Foley was among roughly 200,000 people around the world who applied to be considered for the opportunity to go to Mars. The application process included an essay, a video, various questionnaires, and a thirty-three-dollar entry fee. Both Christy and her husband applied. Foley got good news late in 2013, between Christmas and the New Year. "I was goofing off because it was just after Christmas, and I was on Facebook and I read that [the e-mails] were going out. So I hit refresh on my e-mail over and over again and then I screeched, and my coworker next door to me was like—'What what what?'" Moments later, an e-mail from her partner for the last ten years also arrived. It was a forward of the Mars One rejection letter.

The two of them quickly worked out an arrangement. They would stay together, and Foley's husband would help her do everything she needed to do to fulfill her dream. And when and if the time came for her to leave forever they would divorce and, as she tells me, "he gets everything. Easiest divorce ever!"

And so the plan is hatched. Christy's plan and the plan of the Mars One masterminds, who have been releasing a steady rain of press releases documenting their progress including an initial purchase of satellites and plans to raise the estimated six billion dollars necessary to send waves of equipment, then people, on a one-way trip to live out the rest of their lives on Mars.

The selection of candidates is a big part of the plan. Henceforth, Mars One is hoping to raise money and further support by turning the selection process into a reality TV broadcast, which could even continue after they've left Earth, with cameras onboard to chronicle their arrival and establishment of the colony. But that's a decade down the road. For now, Christy is one of 1,058 people selected from around the world for the next phase. (There are 75 Canadians and 301 Americans tapped for further consideration.) I ask Christy what comes next as her life and the Mars One plan begin to intersect. She says she's waiting to find out. (At the time of our conversation, it had been three months or so since her selection.) So far, not much has been established beyond the hazy plan to turn the whole thing into a TV show. I ask Christy if she knew she was signing up for a reality TV production. "That's not my favorite part," she says flatly. But she'll persevere. She's hired a personal trainer. She's taking classes online to increase her scientific know-how. She's doing interviews, practicing her ability to be a Mars One ambassador, anticipating that she'll be expected to, as she puts it, "evangelize for the project."

I ask Christy to tell me more about what good she thinks will come out of all of this. I mean, it's not as if there is much of a future for a human colony on Mars, a planet with no breathable atmosphere (as of yet!), a planet where everything from drinking water to seeds and soil will have to be carted from home, a planet we can send people to, but can't bring them back from. Christy tells me about her motivations. First off, is, of course, the chance to go into space. Ever since Christy met Canadian astronaut Roberta Bondar in grade school, she's dreamed of being an astronaut. "In my elementary school year book, I said I wanted to colonize the moon. That's not going to happen, but Mars will be just fine."

But beyond the personal fulfillment of her dreams, what good will the trip do for the world at large? Christy talks about the insurance policy element of the plan. If things don't work out on Earth, at least there will be people off planet to carry on the species. She describes herself as an environmentalist and says that she has "a bit of a state-of-the-Earth complex." But overall she's hopeful that it won't come to that. In fact, the real benefit settling Mars will bring to humanity will be new ways to approach the challenges facing Earth. Who knows what kinds of technological boons might come from figuring out how to make the trip happen? "Space travel has always been a catalyst in developing new things," Foley tells me. "While we are trying to figure out how to feed ourselves on Mars, maybe we develop a food that will help stop hunger, maybe a new way to process water to stop the water wars, an inoculation against unknown bacteria and we get rid of antibiotic resistance, maybe we can cure the common cold." She says that last part jokingly, but she's serious. Going to Mars will change everything.

And what about the sacrifices she will have to make, leaving everything and everyone behind? "I don't see it as a sacrifice in the sense of losing my family," Christy tells me. "I will be communicating with them, and there will be the new family, my team. There is going to be a feeling of loss, but the accomplishment and the daily grind of surviving and thriving on Mars will make up for that."

I hope she's right. I hope what she gives away—her marriage, her chance to raise and know children, whatever more prosaic contributions she might have made to her community here on Earth—will be worth it. For now, the future beckons, the personal trainer is waiting, and it's time for Christy to go.

o o o o o o

There are two, or maybe three, ways we are trying to escape the future by actively attempting to break out of the perplexingly infinite loop of our new era. The first exit plan is the now mainstream option most of us are caught up in. And that's to believe in bringing our quest for future to its conclusion by actually reaching the promised end-of-future. Call it the Trees-on-Mars option. Mars is just one of many symbolic stand-ins. It's a metaphor for the singular moment of arrival when we all will live happily (for)ever after—on colonized Mars, or downloaded into computers, or even on an Earth transformed by platoons of robot servants who do all the work, anticipate our every need and are powered by rechargeable solar batteries. Mars and its many incarnations are the pop/consumer spectacle merging with the forever promise of techno-science that now dominates how we think about the world around us. Christy Foley's ambition is a stark reminder of how chasing the future has now become utterly mainstream. We all have to be doing our bit to get to the (end of) future, whether that's going to Mars, helping your wife get to Mars, or investing your millions in putting trees and people on Mars. So that's option number one for exiting the permanent future: to chase the future until we finally arrive there. We've heard a lot about option number one in this book, and we'll hear just a bit more about it before this book is over.

But now, I'd like to introduce the second prevailing way people are currently seeking to exit the era of permanent future. In this less popular, but nevertheless fairly persistent and increasingly predominant scenario, there is no and-we-all-go-to-Mars-and-it's-great-there! end. For those who embrace option number two, there is the outright rejection of the notion that relentless pursuit of the future is going to bring about the inevitable utopian conclusion to the human project.

Every dominant, mass media broadcast–ready version of reality has a counter to it. At first, perhaps, it's a zone for defeated drop-outs, a place where the inevitable misfits can go to announce themselves and find a community of similar people who, for whatever reason, found themselves left behind or left out of the prevailing narrative. When celebrity culture held full sway in the age before broadband, I wrote about the zinesters, the collagists, the samplers, the remixers, the underground artist do-it-yourself creatives and even the furries and sci-fi conventioneers who injected themselves into a popular culture they often disdained and desperately craved.[4] They wanted out of the prevailing ideology that rewarded people not for what they did but for how much attention they got for doing it. But they also wanted in—a way to *be*, a way to acknowledge their shared obsession and develop a sense of ownership over a popular culture that, no matter how much they railed against it, would always remain their only meaningful collective cultural touchstone. We can see a similar progression as the future-first era coalesces into a forceful interlocking ideology. Many of those who feel shut out or left behind are grappling for a new way to be part of the future-present and its imperatives. It's not a rejection of the prevailing order per se, but rather a different kind of acceptance of the predominant phenomenon, a restating of the terms of the relationship—we're not the ones going to be left behind; you are.

Meet Tom Martin, a long-distance trucker and a founder and vice president of the American Preppers Network. I reach Tom a good distance from his home in northern Idaho. He's talking to me, via the miracle of cellular technology, from the front of his cab as he trucks a long-haul load across the crisscrossing highways of America. As he drives, he tells me about the need to be ready, a need he feels in the pit of his stomach the way another man might feel hunger. Tom's hungry for Americans to realize just how vulnerable and weak they are. He's hungry for us to start getting ready for what he sees as the inevitable collapse. For Tom, each stretch of new highway, each change in the passing landscape as fallow corn fields give way to patchy forest then rolling hills, is a new challenge. He thinks about it as he drives. What if it happens right now? How far is he from a likeminded peer with a cache of food, water, medicine, and ammunition? How long till he reaches a bunker or hunting shack, somewhere Tom can weather the first few turbulent weeks until he can start working his way back to his own built-to-endure self-sufficient outfit at home?

"I keep about three months of food in my truck plus my bugout gear," Martin tells me. "I've got all the stuff I need. . . . I know enough people around the country that if I was in Florida and wanted to get to Idaho in the midst of a disaster I would carry enough of what I need to barter with from place to place so I would have places to stay, with people that I know. I could cross the country by foot if had to."[5] Tom tells me that he's also a member of an organization called ANTS—Americans Networking To Survive. "Once you join," he says, "you pretty much make a promise to help out other members if they need it during a disaster and they promise to help you." The stated goal of ANTS is to have at least one member in every city and town in America, so that when it all goes down, there remains a supply and communications chain. I think of ants and cockroaches, the only creatures left standing. Tom tells me that back home he's got everything prepared to survive for at least six months. He has a 3,000-square-foot garden his brother looks after, plus six months' worth of food in storage and a wide range of other gear.

Tom is a relative newcomer to the movement known as survivalism or, as some prefer to call it, prepping. He tells me he first started thinking about it when he delivered bottled water to a Texas disaster zone. "I did disaster relief delivering water after Hurricane Ike and it baffled my mind. People were lined up to get bottled water and I'm thinking, 'Why do so many people need water, why don't they have water stored prior to a hurricane?'" Faced with the specter of so many helpless people, Tom was jarred out of his own state of passivity. "I started doing research and I just got to realize that the vast majority of Americans simply are not prepared for any disaster. They are very complacent and think that everything is going to be okay and just fine, and they get warned about a pending disaster like a hurricane or tornado warning, then they all rush to the store at the last minute. . . . I think that's a very dangerous mentality for people to have." After his experience in Texas, Tom became involved in the prepper movement and eventually started APN. "I thought it would be a good idea to have this website where we can teach about getting prepared and how to get prepared."

Tom talks to me about "companies like Monsanto creating genetically modified food and commercial farming techniques destroying the soil and the water and that's all because people are dependent on buying their food from the grocery store." He notes that more and more people are "interested in growing their own food, urban gardening, growing food in their apartment." I find myself nodding along to his answers. What he's saying connects with my thinking and that of my friends, former hipsters who now spend weekends with their kids spreading homemade compost on their tiny but productive backyard plots. As Tom puts it: "I think we should localize not globalize."

Tom's preaching to the converted so far. And the prepper movement's seeming embrace of the values shared by environmentalists and anticorporate activists is corroborated by outside reports. A journalist visiting a Tulsa, Oklahoma, prepper convention writes that he was expecting it to be "peopled with right-wing zealots with a taste for guns and gold, or what survivalists like to call 'the bullet-and-bullion set.'" But aside from being harangued by a fellow promoting the movement to impeach President Obama, what he mostly finds are "organic gardeners, homeopathic healers and publishers selling books on the commercial uses of hemp."[6] If a skeptic like me can be drawn to at least some of what the prepper is all about, then what's the overall appeal here? How many people, I ask Tom, identify themselves as preppers and survivalists? "We have over 30,000 members on our forum, 35,000 newsletter subscribers," Tom tells me. But that's just his forum, one of hundreds in the US and thousands around the world. Tom goes on: "I would guess in the tens if not hundreds of millions of people worldwide are interested in preparedness." Though there is no solid number of how many people in North America or even the world consider themselves preppers/survivalists, it's clear from the proliferation of organizations, websites, conferences, and products that this is a vital, growing, and increasingly (counter)mainstream movement. "Preppers," goes a *Newsweek* article, "are what you might call survivalism's Third Wave: regular people with jobs and homes."[7] But for Tom, it's not enough. It's a drop in the bucket. "What concerns me," he explains, "is how many people are not interested in preparedness. Those are the people we have to worry about rescuing after a disaster—able-bodied people who become a burden to our first responders."

But, I ask Tom, isn't telling everybody to be prepared for every kind of collapse just preying on people's fears? How much of being a prepper is involved with worrying about major disasters and overall system failure that nobody can really do anything about anyway? Tom dismisses this question brusquely. "The vast majority of preppers are the least fearful people there are. I don't know any preppers that are fearful, I'm not fearful of anything." Why would he be fearful? After all, he's prepared. Tom returns, this time a bit more forcefully, to the subject of the lack of preparedness of the average person. He cites Hurricane Katrina and "people who just sat down in the streets because people just did not know what to do. . . . I'm paying into the tax system and then you say, 'Why are we taking care of people who are fully capable of taking care of themselves?' Rather than putting up their food storage, they are out putting their money in entertainment or whatever." Tom's mention of taxes—which he clearly does not approve of—is code for government, which many, if not all, preppers believe is a corrupt institution deliberately coddling people until they become too weak to resist their enslavement. The tax riposte precedes a more elaborate digression into how the United States was once a collection of more-or-less sovereign regions: "A state by definition is a country, so it was originally intended to be the united countries of America. Every state has a state capital and a state government, and that's one of the things that changed over the course of time, going from a plural country to a singular country."

What is this actually about? What does the increasingly popular prepper movement really want? Veggie gardens in the front yard, bottled water and your bugout kit in the basement and the right for Texas to secede from the nation? It goes deeper than that, of course. The prepper movement appeals as a solution, a way to exit the anxiety endemic to the future era. The movement restates and reestablishes ownership of future. It gives people a way out. The stuff that seems to be leaving you behind, don't even bother about it. It's not even going to be around in ten or twenty or fifty years. Vast swathes of America, shut out of the promise of future both materially and spiritually, are very open to envisioning a different future in which those consolidating power in the information age lead us to collapse while those who seem powerless and left behind now turn out to be right all along.

Another prepper I speak with, Jerry Young, a sixty-year-old living in Reno, Nevada, whom I meet on the Internet, pulled in by a series of stories he's written about various collapse scenarios, summarizes the appeal of the lifestyle: "A sense of empowerment is a major part of what a lot of people get into it for. A lot of people think preppers and survivalists are scared to death all the time. We're not. We are prepared for something that is going to happen. We're not fearful people, we're confident people, because we know we can handle what comes up. People sit at home and wring their hands. We don't dwell on it, we go out and do something about it, which is a positive function. People who are fearful all the time, I don't see how they live."[8] Jerry neatly sums up the empowering nature of this countermovement. Do you think things are getting worse and not likely to get better? Do you feel like you are being left out of the future of endless techo-upgrade? Do you feel like institutions—from the government to the education system to the corporations—have let you down or left you behind? Then instead of dreading what's coming or what you feel is already happening, do something about it. As Jerry says, "The government isn't going to help you." You have to help yourself.

At some point in exploring the various strands of this approach to escaping the permanent future, I start asking myself: What's the difference between Patrick Tucker's evocation of the twenty-first–century future-enabled techno-individualist who no longer wants or needs to rely on the government or the education system or any institutional organization, really, and the twenty-first–century prepper who no longer believes they can or should have to rely on the government or the education system? Isn't Jerry saying exactly what many denizens of the Silicon Valley technocracy are saying? Not unlike among the Silicon Valley elite, there's the rhetoric of self-reliance, the self-fulfilling prophecy of institutional ineffectuality, and an enthusiasm for all things gadget, especially those things that supposedly enable people to solve their problems themselves. Patrick Tucker has his tricorders and legions of futurists building and operating their own drones, Tom Martin and the preppers have their bugout kits, smoke bombs, and portable greenhouses. At the further fringes of prepperdom, there are militias that want to actively bring about the end-time, overthrow the government, end the corruption and forced enfeeblement of the citizenry. Again, I'm reminded of the Silicon Valley leaders, walling themselves off from the rest of society to focus on solving the problem of online media revenue management and mobile phone drink orders while pouring billions into dubious life extension schemes and envisioning the Bay Area seceding from California and the USA to become its own zone governed by the logic-infused fiat of data-empowered CEOs. At their core, both the technologists and the preppers have secular belief systems rooted in a sense of superiority over others. Both have a lifestyle of products and gatherings revolving around the endlessly arriving future. Their core ideology is very similar: *The future is coming, everything is going to change, you'd better be getting ready or you'll be swept away. The institutions can't help you, you have to do it yourself. We are prepared. We understand. Why don't you?* Their approach and message is the same, and both groups—one increasingly representing mainstream society, one pulling in ever larger numbers of the disaffected, disappeared, and left behind—think almost exclusively about the future.

So the big difference here is the way the two groups see us exiting from this period of relentless and now engrained destabilization into a new era, possibly the final era. The techno-futurists, whose ideas now dominate mainstream ideology, argue that the more things fall apart, the more they can be (and are being) put together again better than before. They see destabilizing fragmentation as an inevitable part of the perfect thing we (they) will soon achieve. The survivalists also seem to relish the prospect of things falling apart, but unlike the techno-libertarians, who see collapse as inevitable progress toward the end of history and arrival of the end of future and even time, preppers don't really yearn for future—they yearn for past. For them, collapse isn't progress because they don't really believe in or want progress; they want return. The prepper movement yearns for a return to a mythical time long past when things were simple, when small towns and small farms dotted the land, when fish bobbed plentifully in the lake, when people, or even a people, stood on solid ground, in control of their destiny. At the core of a prepper lifestyle inextricably lodged in a slowly decaying middle class is a longing for an antediluvian America where people weren't data, weren't fodder for corporate takeover, weren't mortgaged, weren't subject to the perpetually changing future at all. This is where the preppers divide starkly from the future-era technologists. The dominant techno-upgrade philosophy sees past and its ways as nothing more than an anchor tied around the collective neck of humanity, pulling us down, practically forcing us to cut loose. They argue that if we jettison the past and invest fully and completely in the coming technologically mediated future, we can and will get there before it's too late. The pervasive counter-ideology of preppers, survivalists, and other purveyors of apocalypse-soon culture, on the other hand, envision the escape from future as a return to a fictional past we lost and need to find once more. Their second way of escaping from the permanent future is a marker of how damaging the notion of a permanent future really is. For many, the real toll isn't just found in unemployment or rising levels of mental turmoil, it's in a total collapse of their ability to believe in progress at all. Instead, they heap their hope on the past—the idyll of what was becomes their hopeful escape from the endless false promise of future.

o   o   o   o   o

The instinctive counterproposal to our eventual arrival at techno utopia is a told-you-so collapse; this collapse proves itself appealing not just to the growing subset of preppers and survivalists, but to society at large in the form of the apocalyptic fantasy/science-fiction narrative. This immensely popular narrative—giant tidal waves, human-made plagues run amok, nuclear decimation, rise of the apes—is pretty much the only socially acceptable place where we can explore our sense that things, as amazing and incredible as they are, are also systematically spiraling farther and farther out of the control of communities and individuals. Even as we push further down the road dotted by driverless cars occupied by people halfway living in virtual worlds, there is a part of us that mourns what we're losing. There is a part of us that seeks solace in the fact that if it all goes wrong, some semblance of a renewed tribal life emerging from the ruins of modernity might yet be attainable.

In a small café in a little sun-strewn town an hour or so from Los Angeles, I meet up with Lissa Price, the author of the young adult science-fiction books *Starters* and *Enders*, a two-book series with the premise that a virus has killed off everyone between the ages of twenty and sixty. The story is told from the point of view of a sixteen-year-old who has to deal with the death of her parents and loss of the family home, all the while keeping her younger brother safe from the many dangers of this strange new reality.

Price herself is a sort of dream story—a self-assured middle-aged woman who wrote several novels, couldn't get anywhere with her writing, but never gave up. Her first agent didn't believe in her new YA series and cut her loose. Then another agent picked her up and secured her a six-figure advance from the biggest publishing company in the world. On the surface, it's the fairytale ending that seems to be the exact opposite of the end-of-the-world scenario she creates in the book. But the two stories are both predicated on uncertainty, on the random, on the idea that anything can happen at any moment. Once upon a time, the story Price would have told was the one her life has (sort of) followed: rags to riches, work hard, believe in yourself, and you will get what you deserve.

But today, stories resonating with optimistic faith in the system—like, say, the 2014 Will Smith–backed botched remake of *Annie*—do not tend to garner much favor. The tales that resonate are on the flipside—collapse, disillusion, corruption and conspiracy. So where does Price think this interest in stories about collapse comes from? "It's because if you look at our world today," she tells me, "every other restaurant and brand name store is closing. It's kind of shocking. We lost Borders, Gelson's grocery store, a coffee shop in my neighborhood, so I think people are worried from all this stuff that's going on. So maybe there's some appeal in reading a fantasy or science fiction . . . I think people feel helpless. I couldn't stop Borders from being closed, there's nothing I could do, so I think of course people feel that way . . ."9

Relentless change on the surface, no matter how seemingly mundane, creates foreboding and anxiety on a much deeper level. Like *The Hunger Games*, Cormac McCarthy's *The Road*, and so many other popular stories of collapse and dystopia, *Starters* and *Enders* aren't really about the future at all. Price wasn't necessarily intending it, but her personal story and the story she's written are both anxiety-ridden love letters to our decaying middle-class lives. The impetus for the narrative is the creepy terror of watching things that we always believed would be here slip away. For preppers, it's self-reliance, it's the family farm, it's fair pay for fair work. For Price and her upscale middle class, it's the loss of entire careers, entire industries, entire lifestyles centered around high-end grocery stores and bookstores serving up frothy americanos and all the magazines you could ever imagine flipping through. Either way, you get the sense of destabilizing change for no apparent purpose. Where did everything go? Price's desperate heroine, in between flashbacks of her bucolic suburban home life before the viral flood, ends up renting her body out to enders paying exorbitant sums to occupy young flesh (via the wonders of mind-meld technology). On many levels this is a story about what once was and where it all went. Nostalgia dosed with anxiety and dread, these narratives are about extremely unlikely survival in increasingly more fantastic scenarios, but their real appeal is the way they tap into the cold uncertainty seeping through our chests and into our once warm hearts. What we had is slowly being taken away. Why? Nobody knows.

And what's the solution? The solution is to keep doing what we're doing and alleviate our fear by exploring the subject as fiction. What if the robots attack? What if the germs get loose and turn us into zombies? What if a giant tsunami wipes us out? What if everyone dies and only a small hardy band survive to live and start over? We watch horror films to see our worst nightmares projected back at us, to pretend we aren't frightened by the bogeyman that secretly just confirms our fears. Similarly, the horror subset of apocalypse narratives reveal just how much we dread and yearn for these scenarios. We are terrified of the collapse, but also we like the idea that these stories will eventually come true. If things don't work out, if our technology fails us or we fail to redeem our faith in technology, then at least we'll be freed from technocratic society and returned to a time when human destiny was in human hands. In the end, there will be heroes—at least, we very much hope so.

o o o o o o

It all comes back to hope, or in this case, the false hope of technological redemption and/or redemption through the premise of collapse then return. We believe in these things because, as we have already explored, they are psychologically enticing: they confirm our antediluvian instinct, the conflation of survival and imagined future that allowed us to become the dominant species. Owning the future means mastery over our enemies, total control over whatever comes next. Who doesn't want to believe in the great big solar-powered 3-D printer in the sky, churning out snacks and creature comforts for all? Every day, we see the evidence that the great hope of future is just around the corner, and we are all too willing to believe.

Let me unpack this with the example of the "solar-powered outlet." I first come across it in a web magazine called *Inhabitat* (a clever malapropism) dedicated to "green" design. A short article extols the promise of this solar-powered outlet. It suctions to a window, captures the sun, and powers your devices. The article sports large pictures of this amazing, sleek-looking, innovative way to bring free solar energy to billions of people. Look at the pictures, read the headline—"Window Socket: Portable Solar-Powered Outlet Sticks to Windows, Charges Small Electronics"—and prepare to be hopeful.[10] Below the piece are the by now de rigueur comments—people talking about how amazing this thing is and asking where they can buy the device. The answer is nowhere. Read the fine print and you find out that the device isn't actually a commercial product. It's a prototype that takes five to eight hours to charge and still doesn't have enough juice to power up even the smallest electronic item. No matter. When creators Yanko Design put up the device on a web page in 2013 and started, uh, plugging it, their tweet was retweeted more than 1,600 times, and a Facebook post was liked more than 18,000 times.[11] Ah ha! Free energy to power the devices dividing like Tribbles over every available surface. Problem? Solution. Hope!

No matter what side you're on, this post-industrial shell game is pushing us to the brink and beyond. Going to Mars isn't a solution, it's a fatal distraction, a chimera as pointless as a Google Glass that actually works or a scheme to download our minds onto computer chips. So too is the idea that we can somehow personalize our disasters and emerge, with the right bugout gear and good old-fashioned American know-how, from the other end of collapse better, stronger, freer. Smoke grenades and hydroponics, trees on Mars and self-driving electric cars, solar outlets and solar panels, it's all just exacerbating our problems and distracting us from the reality of our situation.

The reality is that we are choosing Mars over Earth. There are many examples of this, but here's one of the most ironic and tangible: a twenty-minute drive from the center of the inner Mongolian city of Baotou lies a massive, manmade "lake." Once a sleepy town of 97,000, Baotou is now the epicenter of Chinese rare mineral production, an industrial city of two and a half million people supplying the crucial ingredients for the factories across China and the world assembling our most cutting-edge technology. It's in the mines that surround Baotou where 95 percent of the rare earth elements the world uses are dug out of the ground and refined at a considerable price to the natural world. Consider cerium oxide, primarily used to polish the touch screens of smartphones and tablets. This delightful stuff is made by "crushing mineral mixtures and dissolving them in sulfuric and nitric acid," which has to be done on an "industrial scale" and results in "a vast amount of poisonous waste."[12] What to do with this waste? Welcome to Baotou's "lake," for lack of a better word. In fact, there are no children frolicking on this body of water's shores, there are no fish gliding silently through its cool depths, there are no marshes, boats, frogs, terns or even dragonflies. There is only a massive ten square kilometer "tailings pond," a brackish dumping ground consisting of the toxic sludge piped and dumped there by the mines and processing facilities that have transformed Baotou into a key part of the early lifecycle of the most futuristic of our gadgets. I haven't been to this "lake," but I've seen pictures and videos. I've read about how the shore is made up of a black crust so thick you can walk on it, and how clay taken from the "lake" tested "at around three times background radiation." When BBC journalist Tim Maughan made the trip, he stood on its banks, at a loss for words, contemplating this man-made apparition, almost too horrible to be real. Finally, in keeping with the perverse irony of the situation of humankind in the grip of future frenzy, he took out his iPhone and tried to capture a photograph of what he would later describe as "a terrible toxic lake that stretches to the horizon."[13]

The rare earth minerals mined and processed in the distant Inner Mongolian city of Baotou are used in everything from laptops to tablets to GPS systems to cheap solar panels to electric cars. But these are not benevolent technologies showered on nice neighborhoods like manna from a God eager to reward our willingness to think green. Even the most well-meaning devices seeking to harness technology for the goal of a greener future come with a hidden price that someone, somewhere, is already paying. The future is coming for us, of that there's no doubt; in fact, if you look closely enough, you'll find ample evidence that it's already here.

The planet is warming at an unprecedented rate. The year 2014 was the hottest year on Earth ever recorded. On the same day that little kernel of news emerged, a paper in the journal *Science*, authored by eighteen imminent scientists, was also being reported on. The paper announced that four environmental thresholds had now been definitively crossed. For the record, the thresholds in question are "the extinction rate; deforestation; the level of carbon dioxide in the atmosphere; and the flow of nitrogen and phosphorous (used on land as fertilizer) into the ocean." As a result of crossing those thresholds, the scientists hold that we are now entering zones of extreme unpredictability with outcomes ranging from definitely bad to likely horrible to possibly catastrophic. Or, as they gently put it: "The planet is likely to be much less hospitable to the development of human societies."[14]

Well, we've been warned. We live in the era of endless disruption on the way to, supposedly, owning and shaping an ever more imminent future. But the promise of getting to the future is a Trojan horse. It's a sneaky way to keep doing what we've been doing for at least the last two hundred or even two thousand years, despite ample evidence that we are on a collision course with our own impulses. Under the rubric of constant change, we don't have to really change. And yet, while the future promises more of the same only much, much better (personal drones controlled by our smartphones, etc.), the present promises something else altogether: a downward path to the edge of a cliff we seem determined to plunge over. Unfortunately, the promise of the future overwhelms the reality of the present day. Nothing stays the same, and everything doesn't change.

o o o o o o

When I first embarked on this project, I imagined a last chapter that followed the pattern of almost all books chronicling a major problem in contemporary society. Call it the default hope chapter. From the plight of the African elephant to the overmedication of children to the power of corporate money to manipulate democracy to cures for global warming, the last chapter in the book almost always sounds that hopeful, encouraging note. I'd do it too, of course. I'd mix specific policy recommendations with assurances that every little bit counts. I'd promise that it's not too late and if we all raise our voices and work together for change we can break out of the crazy cyclone of chasing a future we can never get to. It wouldn't have been hard to pick and choose from different scenarios to make a bit of a case for good old default hope. There is still, after all, lots of good being done with technological advances, big and small. I'd point to an app helping people in poor countries get micro-loans to buy goats; or a newly designed mosquito net saving millions of kids; a home desalinization kit; doctors using big data to cure infections in premature babies before the fever even gets a chance to register on the thermometer; a tiny Northern European country using wizard-like technology to lower its carbon output to practically nothing. Others have toured the planet for its best sustainable ideas and written about them. There are thinkers and doers in almost every field whose works amount to a rethink or even a challenge to the tunnel vision of future now. There are economists rethinking what innovation actually means. There are engineers and scientists determined to "do" innovation differently. There are farmers reinventing how tractors are made and crops are grown and sold. There are bloggers desperately trying to preserve and even bring back the artifacts of fast-disappearing analogue life. There are new kinds of open-source videogame makers and new kinds of crowd-funded ways to make art. There's the slow food movement, the local movement, the do-it-yourself movements, the Maker movement, even the Occupy and Tea Party movements. They all want to change the direction we are moving in. In all of them we can find the seed of protest and the sprout of some possible solution. All of these powerful memes in society link together. They reflect a real need for things to be slower, truer, more linked, more whole, more about living life in genuine communities.

But if I'd written that chapter, I'd have been lying to myself and to you. Those movements, ideas, and products are not the overall reality, nor even a predominant trend; they aren't shaping our world any more than organic food at the Walmart Supercenter points to true sustainability or the Tesla electric car connotes a carbon neutral tomorrow. The future is sabotaging the future. We are ignoring the solutions that could improve our planet and our lives in the present day and leave a legacy our children might actually be able to follow. Despite all the good ideas and good things happening in the world, it would be a pernicious lie to argue that we are moving toward a collective present of real innovation grounded in the only thing that is really going to make a difference to our children's future: altering our pattern of consume-and-move-on by substantially cutting back on the things we now think we need to live—constant connectivity; same-day shipping; meat for breakfast, lunch and dinner; twelve-lane highways for our two-hour commutes. It's obvious that we need to develop sustainable, far more prudent patterns. But let's face it, this isn't happening; it isn't even starting to happen. Instead, we have the far easier downward path of hopes and future trances: a billionaire Dutch dude plans to be the first to people Mars; Christy Foley plans to be among the first to live there; and Elon Musk plans to be already up there, living in a shack in the woods.

So if I'm not going to offer solutions, am I saying that we should, shudder to think, give up on so-called progress? Could I actually be proposing that we reject technology, go Luddite, go underground? That's not what I'm saying—though, yes, to be honest, I think we should give up on the increasingly more malignant idea of all of us wandering around with phones, glasses, watches, and eventually brains hooked in to some central Skynet. But that's a whole other can of virtual worms. What I'm saying is that our typical reaction to the intractable problem of our consumptive urge is hope.

It's hope, not technology, that lies at the heart of our collective future phantasmagoria. As long as we stick with the equation that technology plus future equals, as if by default, *hope*, we will never change. (For the preppers, the equation is technology plus the end of the future, but the sum still somehow comes out to the same thing: hope.) We need a new calculation, one that at its most heart-wrenchingly basic level, subtracts hope from the equation. Is there another, third way that can help us escape the self-destructive ideology of future-first?

o o o o o o

One summer weekend in 2013, the Sustainability Centre in Hampshire, United Kingdom, was home to an event called Uncivilization.

It was described as "a gathering of people searching for answers to questions about our collective future in a rapidly changing and depleting world." At first glance, it didn't seem all that much different from a prepper conference. Uncivilization attracted around 400 people to sessions including a wild food foraging workshop and a talk on moving beyond a monetary based economy. But at Uncivilization the practical skills seemed to be on the periphery of the experience; more significant were events that allowed for the seemingly inexpressible. There was a session in which attendees were asked to imagine then discuss "how it might have been to live during the Mesolithic period." There was a discussion in which the impact of the "inevitable romanticism of rural life" was addressed. There was music, kid's stories, and slow yoga under the trees. And it all culminated in a ceremonial storytelling circle described as a "liturgy of loss." Searching for ways that people are grappling with the era of future first, Uncivilization caught my eye. Here was an event neither prepper-apocalyptic nor techno-futuristic. Here was a gathering that seemed to be asking that utterly ignored but increasingly important question: how to live in a present dominated by the specter of a future that might not turn out to be all that "abundant" after all?

The Uncivilization festival was organized by the Dark Mountain Project, a cooperative founded in 2009 with an annual journal and ongoing blog. One of Dark Mountain's primary sustainers is Paul Kingsnorth, a forty-something, Oxford-educated, disillusioned former environmental journalist who has come to the conclusion that we are in an inexorable period of "slow collapse." To Kingsnorth and his Dark Mountain followers—the website has around 50,000 visitors a year and their 2009 manifesto has been reprinted in book form three times—the problems are intractable. There is no turning back, no halting climate change, no ending our lifestyle of rampant overconsumption rooted in environmental destruction. Like me, they see that the core of the human pattern—consume and move on, consume and move on—is neither sustainable nor likely to be significantly altered in time for any kind of meaningful reversal to occur. The Dark Mountain goal, then, is to give a forum to voices willing to acknowledge that no matter how ardent we are about recycling and voting green, we will still be living in a time of disintegration, a time of ongoing loss. "It's happening already," Kingsnorth tells me when I reach him in the UK via Skype. "It's not an apocalypse, it's a slow collapse."[15] Dark Mountain was started by Kingsnorth and his collaborators because, as Kingsnorth puts it, he had "become disillusioned, feeling like the things that I had been doing were not working." In an essay called "Dark Ecology," Kingsnorth writes about teaching a course on using the scythe. He notes that the scythe has been replaced by the gas or electric powered brushcutter, which "is more cumbersome, more dangerous, no faster and far less pleasant to use than the tool it replaced." So why did the brushcutter replace the scythe? "Brushcutters," Kingsnorth writes, "are not used instead of scythes because they are better, they are used because their use is conditioned by our attitudes to technology. Performance is not really the point, and neither is efficiency. Religion is the point; the religion of complexity. The myth of progress manifested in tool form."[16] Progress as myth equals churning out endlessly more elaborate devices to get simple tasks done. Obviously returning a small number of people to the scythe isn't going to dent the world or even the lawn care appliance industry's dedication to what Kingsnorth aptly dubs "the religion of complexity." Paul Kingsnorth is fully aware of that. Acknowledging that point is what Dark Mountain is all about. For Kingsnorth, the point is to stop believing that technology is going to save us; the point is to stop yearning for a simpler time we can return to in which we lived in harmony in nature (we have never lived in harmony with nature). The point isn't even learning how to scythe. Kingsnorth isn't trying to teach survival skills for the coming time when cheap fuel and empty calories aren't the norm. He's trying, instead, to connect people to a story—the story of a time when everything changed in contradictory ways that nobody could fully grasp. A story of the time when we used hope as an excuse to relentlessly repeat the mistakes we refused to recognize. As Kingsnorth said in regards to his excellent novel *The Wake*, set in eleventh-century Britain, it's about "the falling apart of a way of life, it's about unstoppable change being unleashed which individuals have to deal with."[17] Kingsnorth is trying to etch a story into the fringes of our cultural narrative, tattoo it into our skin and let the ink seep into our souls.

So the number one point is to stop living a lie. Stop acting like every-thing is going to get straightened out either by future tech or a neat little collapse that eradicates the weak and their Android apps and cleanses the earth in order to return us to our bucolic, natural past. Give it up, Dark Mountain is saying. Neither of these things is going to happen. As Paul Kingsnorth puts it in our conversation: "We are going to have to live through it, we can't do much about it. We aren't going to stop the global economy. Those of us fighting to build a different kind of world and values are losing and we have to live with that and deal with that and ask ourselves—what then? Many people, ex-activists, say, 'I'm very glad you said this, because this is how I've been feeling.'"

And where, I ask Paul, does this leave us? How exactly do we live? What do we aim for? "What's worth doing, that's something you have to work out for yourself," he tells me. "But at Dark Mountain what we are not talking about is preparing for apocalypse. We're talking about a society that is already falling apart. What do you do to live with that? It's not so much of a question about preparing for anything, it's a question of adjusting our expectations to live through something that's already happening."

Living through what's already happening. Adjusting our expecta-tions. I leave my conversation with Paul relieved and unnerved. He is saying something I've long felt, but didn't think I was able to, or was even allowed to, express. It isn't that there is no joy or happiness or beauty or comfort to be found in our world. It isn't that it's time to just totally give up on the human project. It's that all of that joy and comfort can and must be leavened with sadness and acknowledgment of the stark truth. "Apocalypse," writes the great cultural critic Susan Sontag, "is now a long running serial: not 'Apocalypse Now' but 'Apocalypse From Now On.' Apocalypse has become an event that is happening and not happening."[18] If we're going to exit the future era, the first step is to acknowledge the reality of the present by deleting hope from the equation. The forces put in motion are unstoppable. Dark Mountain points toward that third way to escape the permanent future: speak truth about our present, mourn it, let its stark reality ache in our hearts; tell the story of what is happening, and how and why it happened; let that storytelling be part of our commitment to love what remains of a once resplendent planet and its tired, but ever still rapacious, landlords.

Around the same time I discover Kingsnorth's Dark Mountain Project I come across a short book by journalism professor and activist Robert Jensen, who teaches at the University of Texas at Austin. Entitled *We Are All Apocalyptic Now*, the work is a manifesto. In it, Jensen argues that "responsible intellectuals need to think apocalyptically." For Robert Jensen, thinkers of all stripes and types need to reclaim the apocalypse from survivalists, fanatics, and pop culture. As he writes: "Thinking apocalyptically can help us confront honestly the crises of our time and strategize constructively about possible responses."[19] Intrigued, I arrange to meet Jensen when I'm in Austin watching the endless pitch sessions and congratulatory panel discussions of SXSWi. Jensen is a man in his later fifties sporting a soldier's buzz cut and peering intensely through his glasses with a look constantly veering between anger and consternation. He takes me to a vegetarian restaurant on the edge of the city, which is packed with what he theorizes are Austinites fleeing the downtown chaos of people commingling in the long line-up to shake the paw of Grumpy Cat. We eat, and Jensen talks, and the seed of what I'm coming to think of as the third way continues to sprout in my mind.

I ask Robert Jensen how he came to the conclusion that we all need to embrace apocalypse. "If you look at the data with any sort of rational agency," he tells me, "everything is in decline. The only good new environmental news is some local improvements in air and water. Otherwise, long-term prognosis is bad beyond belief."[20] Furthermore, he goes on, we live at a time when the "only intervention is technological fundamentalism" which he does not believe will succeed. Is there no hope whatsoever? I ask Jensen. He shakes his head and glares at me. "If every society in the world fully mobilized to dramatically reduce carbon output—maybe we could turn this around." We both know that isn't going to happen. The consume-and-move-on imperative is far too strong. "So," he tells me, "we have to start getting ready for a different kind of future." I ask Jensen why so few people have come to these conclusions, why most have adopted the belief that constant technological upgrade is the solution. "Well," he says with his characteristic frankness, "it's devastating to come to terms with this, which is why most people don't want to look at it." What about the survivalists? What about, even, religious fundamentalists finding signs in the Bible that we are in the period of discord prefiguring the Second Coming and the Rapture? Are they, I ask Jensen, taking a more realistic approach to the future than the FitBit-wielding suburbanite power walking to the Panera? Jensen thinks about this for a moment and then tells me that they fall into the category of having an "irrational response to a rational observation." It occurs to me that the entire techno-future ideology falls into that category. Is it rational to believe that we can innovate our way out of the corner that innovation has forced us into? Is now finally the time when it's actually rational to predict not salvation but destruction? "People have been predicting the end of the world forever," Robert Jensen tells me. "But," he says, "I'm not predicting the end of the world." What is he predicting? Following Kingsnorth, he's predicting deterioration—inevitable and at times imperceptible decline. "On the Left," Jensen notes acidly, "we're supposed to be science-based, except when the science is too painful."

Unlike Paul Kingsnorth and Dark Mountain, Jensen is more than willing to talk specifically about the coming apocalypse, the time after the fall. I listen intently as he sketches his vision. When we reach a certain level of environmental degradation, resource scarcity, and wealth imbalance, things will start to break down. We'll eventually enter a phase of pure survival during which many will inevitably die—perhaps fewer than the disaster movie industry depicts in their bloated CGI epics, but still, there will be bodies in the streets. Most critically for Jensen, there will come a time when those who are left start to emerge and rebuild. During this fraught period, we'll be asking, Jensen says, "What survives? Who are we?" Jensen takes a sip of water and deadpans a relieved aside—"I'll be dead by that part," he says, grimacing into a smile. "But," he continues, "if I can do anything in my life it's to try and contribute to that moment when we will need to keep some aspect of humanity intact." For Jensen, as with Kingsnorth, the most important thing in this time of global decline and overwhelming tech-fantasy ideology is "doing things to retain your humanity" pre-collapse. Our task is not to hoard food and erect elaborate bugout caches. Nor is our task to fight for or against the Trojan horse of endless upgrade on the way to the perfect future. Instead our sole remaining task is to live in the present, telling the story of what it's like for us and what we can remember of how we got here. Our task is to help who we can when we can while telling the story of who we are and could have been. When we tell the story of the human, we keep humanity alive in the face of the looming systematic forces that threaten not just our environment and livelihoods, but the very notion of personhood.

Is there any chance of this approach becoming a movement? I ask Jensen with something as close to enthusiasm as the subject allows. Any chance that the Dark Mountaineers, the disaffected academics, the disillusioned environmentalists, the community organizers, the leftie nature lovers with mid-level management jobs, the start-up dropouts running organic food trucks and writing novels will come together? Jensen looks at me like I'm a hyper little boy. "I don't think it's a movement," he says. "It's recognition that every system that regulates modern life is no longer up to the task. And there's no way to reform that. There's no revolution coming. The majority of people will not engage this."

o o o o o o

Don't get your hopes up, Robert Jensen is telling me. "The majority of people will not engage this." Decoupling from hope is what we need to do, but it's not something likely to happen based on my recommendation or even the ideas of my much smarter and more influential peers. As I've argued in this book, we change because we have to, not because we want to. So when we finally do decouple technology from hope, it will be because we were forced to. At some point, it's going to be impossible to ignore the increasingly debilitating circumstances brought about by the consumptive frenzy we like to call progress. The tide will rise, we'll be swept out to sea, and we will have to figure out if we want to sink like our smartphones or swim to nowhere in particular. The question isn't: How do we decouple from de facto hope and chart a path to a real sustainability not reliant on the chimera of technological progress? We're going to decouple from hope by staying on the path we've pretty much refused to leave for centuries. It's hardly going to be pleasant, but it's going to happen. The path will be obliterated by the coming flood and we will finally have to admit that we were lost all along. So the question we need to be asking then is: What to do in the meantime? How do we live in a present dominated by this false hope, this Trojan horse of future upgrade? What do we work toward and live for while we wait for the end that may or may not be some kind of new beginning?

Robert Jensen and Paul Kingsnorth are both groping for a path forward. By acknowledging a gradual collapse and creating space for us to mourn and talk about that collapse, they do the unthinkable: they reject hope. Hope sustains the fantasy of future perfect or future-perfect collapse. But if we want to accept where—and what—we really are, we will be required to embrace what Nietzsche called "a strict, hard factuality"; not hope, but *"courage* in the face of reality."[21]

The reality is that no matter how many new livers and kidneys the labs will grow, how many versions of the tricorder we come up with, how many houses will be conjured from 3-D printers the size of dragons, it's becoming increasingly more difficult to situate hope in visions of a techno-utopian future nearer to us every day. Even Peter Thiel seems to be getting impatient with the bets he has made. "Moore's Law is good if you're a computer," he said at a 2012 public discussion. "But the question is, how good is it for human beings, and how does this translate into economic progress for humans?"[22]

The answer to Thiel's question based on the data we have, right now, in the present, is that Moore's law is not translating into progress, economic or otherwise, for the people or other living things of our planet. If we can accept that truth and stop putting our faith in the hope that this most damning fact will soon be irrelevant due to some great renewing collapse or singularity, then we will finally be making at least some small modicum of "progress."

But then what exactly? Then we must each, at first individually and eventually collectively, stumble toward some other kind of meaning for our lives and the remaining time human beings will be on this planet. I have argued that the human impulse toward future—one of our great survival mechanisms—has run amok and created a situation where we are psychologically susceptible to any and every promise regarding our future ability to know and own tomorrow. This, to me, does not mean that we are without agency, subject exclusively to pre-programmed physiology we are helpless to resist. When we are made aware of our biases and tendencies and their consequences, we can and do resist them. But this process doesn't simply happen. We don't just read a book, come to a new realization and agree to subtract hope from the equation. Human beings do not tend to do well when they have nothing to live for.

So what do we replace hope with? There isn't, I'm sorry to say, one easy answer. Like Paul Kingsnorth and Robert Jensen, I'm reluctant to make sweeping prescriptions regarding how we should live in an age of inescapable decline we can do almost nothing about. But that doesn't mean I think we should just while away our days playing *Angry Birds* and *Clash of Clans* while waiting for the batteries to run out. With our without hope, we human beings are creatures that need narrative, that are miserable without some kind of story to tell ourselves and each other. And so how should we live in the shadow of ongoing collapse, liberated from the false promise of future's last minute redemption? We should live by struggling to make sense of it all, by never ceasing to find purpose and meaning in our broken world. Erase hope and make room in your mind for a less reflexive, far more difficult striving: the striving for meaning.

In this, I am inspired by Viktor Frankl's classic 1946 book *Man's Search for Meaning.* "As a professor in two fields, neurology and psychiatry," writes the Austrian-born doctor, "I am fully aware of the extent to which man is subject to biological, psychological and sociological conditions. But in addition to being a professor in two fields I am a survivor of four camps—concentration camps, that is—and as such I also bear witness to the unexpected extent to which man is capable of defying and braving even the worst conditions conceivable."[23] For Frankl, human beings are always capable of making choices and meanings. Even the "worst conditions," which Frankl experienced firsthand in the Auschwitz death camp, leave room for individual choice, for each person to decide how they will respond, who they will become in the face of whatever trials and torments they are being put through. In some cases, as Frankl relates poignantly in his book, the prisoners interned in the camps behaved little better than their captors. Frankl doesn't blame them for doing what they felt they needed to do to survive. He only notes that the actions of other prisoners clearly show that there was choice, for he cites many examples of remarkable sacrifice, prisoners sharing their meagre rations, shielding each other from beatings, caring for the sick, providing what comfort and mental succor they could muster. Ultimately, finds Frankl, those that were able to cobble some kind of meaning out of their ordeal were more likely to find the mental will to survive than those who submerged themselves in the ideology of their captors and accepted their fate as subhumans, or those who clung to the irrational hope that they would be rescued and their ordeal ended, even as years passed and millions of people were murdered all around them. Those who never gave up trying to make meaning, who never stopped trying to use what little they had left to reframe what was happening to them, those were the ones who—whether they ultimately survived or not—died or lived as human beings whose lives continue to resonate as the ultimate rejection of the Nazi ideology of Aryan supremacy. It is this hard-won observation that allows Frankl to write that "man's search for meaning is the primary motivation of his life. . . . This meaning is unique and specific in that it must and can be fulfilled by him alone; only then does it achieve a significance which will satisfy his own will to meaning."[24]

Acknowledge what is true and try to find meaning in that painful truth. Abandon the easy promise of hope. Embrace hope's uncertain corollary: will to meaning. Frankl is not alone in seeing this as the only way to make sense of that which makes so little sense. From the ancient Greek philosophy of Stoicism to the modernist theory of Existentialism, the idea that we each must make our own meaning in hard times and good has come in and out of favor. "Who, then, is the invincible human being?" asks foundational Stoic Epictetus, former slave turned philosopher. "One who can be disconcerted by nothing that lies outside the sphere of choice."[25] And what about those things that do lie within our "sphere of choice"? Viktor Frankl talks about those who believe that the goal of life is to achieve some kind of harmony, "equilibrium or, as it is called in biology, homeostasis." This reminds me of Ray

Kurzweil's singularity and other similar quests to advance technology to a point where human beings can transform into immortal beings presumably in perfect equilibrium with their host machines. It also reminds me of the prepper fantasy: the return to our "natural" state, liberated human beings eking out a living through harmonious interaction with the benevolent, abundant Earth. But what meaning does such an equilibrium provide? If we ever get there, what will we then have to ponder and think about? What will we live for? Frankl writes: "What man actually needs is not a tensionless state, but rather the striving and struggling for a worthwhile goal, a freely chosen task."[26]

One of the strange by-products of the modern has been an ongoing series of totalitarian ideologies, systems of belief that systematically replace the will to meaning with the yearning for an oxymoronic future return to mythical equilibrium. How to oppose them? Perhaps the answer has always been to, as Robert Jensen puts it, "keep some aspect of our humanity intact." In other words, find meaning in what is good about the human project and give that meaning prominence in our lives. Prepare ourselves and those around us for whatever comes next by focusing on making the present matter. Speaking the truth about the present and mourning for the future we should have had is not a movement and it's definitely not a revolution. This is not an action plan. It is in fact that rarest of things: an admission of failure. But in admitting failure, we are able to get closer to individually assessing and understanding who we are and what motivates us; we begin the difficult process of finding meaning outside future-now. We focus, instead, on maintaining humanity, on telling the story of who we are and how we got here. Embrace the real. Speak the truth. Tell the story of how we chased a chimera and didn't see that the faster and longer we ran, the more the ground beneath us was starting to fissure until suddenly we were falling into the cracks.

That's it, that's all I have for you: storytelling, preparing for the fall, embracing what good there is and doing what good we can while acknowledging that the fatal flaws of humanity got the best of us, at least this time around.

I know that for many, this lack of a plan, this failure to end the book with the compulsory chapter promising corporations to boycott, politicians to e-mail, and nonprofits to send money to will be read as a cop-out. He's giving up, you may sigh, disgusted.

But that's not it at all. There are many ways to make meaning, many ways to oppose the ideology of future perfect. Political advocacy, protests, petitions, forming a human chain around the last forest sheltering the last pack of proud timber wolves, small acts of human kindness, all these things also make meaning and tell the story of what we became and what we tried to do about it. The actions we take will fail. Infected with false hope, we have long since set sail on a final cruise with high-speed WiFi, massive buffets, and awe-inspiring vistas of giant drifting icebergs of ethereal plastic trash. But that doesn't mean what we do to register our dissent won't matter. Everything we do makes meaning—to us, and to those around us. Not in the future, but right now, when we need meaning more than anything.

And so I write, not, admittedly, out of hope, but rather out of a *refusal* to give up on the possibility of making meaning now that might resonate in whatever present my daughters and their daughters will ultimately have handed down to them. For me, mourning our lost future while doing our best to remember the past and celebrate what good remains in our present is not an act of capitulation; it is a profound, near-tragic act of defiance. We can carry on without the pretense of pretending. We don't have to believe. We don't have to hope. We can wish Christy Foley all the luck in the world, but know in our hearts that Mars is just a big dead red ball. It can't save us. We can't even save ourselves.

Acknowledgments

I gratefully acknowledge the funding support of the Ontario Arts Council and the Access Copyright Foundation. I am also grateful to the Mabel Pugh Taylor Writer-in-Residence program for selecting me as a resident and giving me time and space to work on this book at McMaster University's Department of English and Cultural Studies and the Hamilton Public Library.

Ariel Teplitsky gave me substantial feedback as the book developed and fuelled my efforts with his fancy rum. Rob Wineberg very generously lent his time and professional poise as moderator of the future focus group. Matt Gorbet sent me the link to the solar outlet. Gord Wiebe helped me think things through while we sat in the park and watched our kids make up theatrical dances. Elizabeth Brennan at Warehouse Workers United was a great help in arranging for interviews with the workers of the Inland Empire, and Shantal Contreras was my capable translator during those interviews. Veronica Liu, my editor at Seven Stories Press, offered her excellent advice and encouragement throughout, even as she got ready for future adventures. Lauren Smythe, my agent, gave me valuable feedback and believed in this project from the beginning.

I'm grateful, as ever, to my parents, Sam and Nina Niedzviecki, for their love and enthusiasm, not to mention babysitting and sleepovers.

Finally, I'd like to thank my wife, Rachel Greenbaum, whose support never wavers and who offered critique and insight throughout. Her expertise was particularly valuable to the second part of this book. And I'd like to thank my kids, Noa and Elly, who remind me every day that what we do is who we are, now and forever.

Notes

INTRODUCTION

1. Barack Obama, *State of the Union Address*, January 25, 2011, www.whitehouse.gov/the-press-office/2011/01/25/remarks-president-state-union-address.
2. Tony Blair, "Keynote Speech to the Labour Party's 2005 Conference," *BBC*, September 27, 2005, sec. UK Politics, http://news.bbc.co.uk/2/hi/uk_news/politics/4287370.stm.
3. Fareed Zakaria, "The Future of Innovation: Can America Keep Pace?," *Time*, June 5, 2011, http://content.time.com/time/nation/article/0,8599,2075226,00.html.

CHAPTER 1

1. "Statistics for SXSW Interactive 2014," n.d., http://sxsw.com/sites/default/files/attachments/STATISTICS%20FOR%20SXSW%20%202014%20%281%29.pdf.
2. Mara Lewis, Mara Lewis Interview, March 2013.
3. 24,800,000 results on April 10, 2015.
4. "Canadian Youth Business Foundation Announces YOU Innovate Canada Tournament National Champion," November 21, 2011, http://www.futurpreneur.ca/en/press-media/you-innovate-national-champion/. The winners were four students from Brandon University in Manitoba – Stephanie Fung, Jeanette Hudon, Stephen Chychota and Kayvon Razzaghi. Their Grow Mug Project proposed using personalized recycled mugs to grow herbs and teach children about plants and healthy eating. The quotes from Branson and Fox were part of the GEC promotional website for the 2012 Liverpool event, no longer accessible via search. Liverpool courted the Global Enterpenership Congress with aims of rebranding

itself as an innovation hub, see Martin Wainwright, "Liverpool Summons Richard Branson to Help Its 'Capital of Entrepreneurship' Campaign," *The Guardian*, accessed April 10, 2015, http://www.theguardian.com/uk/the-northerner/2012/jan/19/liverpool-richard-branson.

5. Greg Krauska, "Does Your Club Have a Growth Mindset?," *Innovate Rotary!*, March 7, 2011, http://changeagentgroup.typepad.com/innovate_rotary/2011/03/does-your-club-have-a-growth-mindset.html.

6. Jonathan Bell, "'The Future Is Here' Exhibition at the Design Museum, London," *Wallpaper*, July 24, 2013, http://www.wallpaper.com/technology/the-future-is-here-exhibition-at-the-design-museum-london/6657.

7. Steven Russolillo, "Apple Reports Blowout Earnings, Shares Surge After Hours," *WSJ Blogs - MarketBeat*, January 24, 2012, http://blogs.wsj.com/marketbeat/2012/01/24/apple-reports-blowout-earnings-stock-halted/.

8. "Apple Profit Doubles, Thanks Largely to 37 Million iPhone Sales in Three Months," *The Globe and Mail*, accessed January 31, 2012, http://www.theglobeandmail.com/globe-investor/apple-profit-doubles-thanks-largely-to-37-million-iphone-sales-in-three-months/article2313464/.

9. Eric Reguly, "Apple Is Sacrificing Innovation on the Altar of Shareholder Value," *The Globe and Mail*, accessed April 10, 2015, http://www.theglobeandmail.com/report-on-business/apple-is-sacrificing-innovation-on-the-altar-of-shareholder-value/article14056389/.

10. Leslie Kwoh, "You Call That Innovation?," *Wall Street Journal*, May 23, 2012, http://online.wsj.com/article/SB10001424052702304791704577418250902309914.html?goback=%2Egde_160628_member_118254490.

11. James Gleick, *The Information: A History, a Theory, a Flood* (New York: Knopf Doubleday Publishing Group, 2011), 361.

12. Ibid.

13. "U.S. Patent Statistics Chart Calendar Years 1963 - 2014," n.d., http://www.uspto.gov/web/offices/ac/ido/oeip/taf/us_stat.htm.

14. Enrico Moretti, *The New Geography of Jobs* (Boston: Houghton Mifflin Harcourt, 2012), 38.

15. Sarah McBride, "Startups Jostle for Funding, Attention at South by Southwest," *Reuters*, March 11, 2014, http://www.reuters.com/article/2014/03/11/us-venture-capital-sxsw-idUSBREA2A17F20140311.

16. "Annual Venture Capital Investment Tops $48 Billion In 2014, Reaching Highest Level In Over A Decade, According To The Moneytree Report," *PwC*, accessed April 13, 2015, http://www.pwc.com/us/en/press-releases/2015/annual-venture-capital-investment-tops-48-billion.jhtml.

17. "BMWi3 Advertisement," *Corporate Knights*, July 1, 2014.

18. Kwoh, "You Call That Innovation?"

19. Don Peck, "They're Watching You at Work," *The Atlantic*, December 1, 2013, http://www.theatlantic.com/magazine/archive/2013/12/theyre-watching-you-at-work/354681/.

20. "The Art of Innovation: Lessons in Creativity from IDEO, America's Leading Design Firm," *Amazon.com*, accessed April 28, 2015, http://www.amazon.com/The-Art-Innovation-Creativity-Americas/dp/0385499841.

21. Quentin Hardy, "How Tech Remakes Space, Food and Urgency," *The New York*

Times, September 4, 2013, http://bits.blogs.nytimes.com/2013/09/04/how-tech-remakes-space-food-and-urgency/.

22. Eric Jackson, "6 Things Jeff Bezos Knew Back in 1997 That Made Amazon a Gorilla," *Forbes*, accessed April 13, 2015, http://www.forbes.com/sites/ericjackson/2011/11/16/6-things-jeff-bezos-knew-back-in-1997-that-made-amazon-a-gorilla/.

23. Moretti, *The New Geography of Jobs*, 11.

24. "Americans Predict a Future Like Science Fiction," *Bits Blog*, accessed April 22, 2014, http://bits.blogs.nytimes.com/2014/04/22/americans-predict-a-future-like-science-fiction/.

25. You can see the full conference schedule at "WorldFuture 2012 Conference Highlights," accessed April 13, 2015, http://www.wfs.org/worldfuture-2012.

26. Patrick Tucker, Patrick Tucker Interview, April 23, 2012.

27. Jessica Vascellaro, "Interns Are Latest Target In Battle for Tech Talent," *The Wall Street Journal*, December 22, 2011, http://online.wsj.com/article/SB10001424052970204879004577108672160430712.html.

28. Cheryl Wakslak, Cheryl Wakslak Interview, November 19, 2013.

29. Aaron Smith, "Future of Technology," *Pew Research Center's Internet & American Life Project*, April 17, 2014, http://www.pewinternet.org/2014/04/17/us-views-of-technology-and-the-future/.

30. Ibid.

31. Patricia Vieira and Michael Marder, "What Do We Owe the Future?," *The New York Times*, October 13, 2013, http://opinionator.blogs.nytimes.com/2013/10/13/what-do-we-owe-the-future/.

32. Sarah Gray, "Walter Isaacson: 'Innovation' Doesn't Mean Anything Anymore," *Salon.com*, August 5, 2014, http://www.salon.com/2014/08/05/walter_isaacson_innovation_doesnt_mean_anything_anymore/.

33. Thomas Frank, "TED Talks Are Lying to You," *Salon.com*, October 13, 2013, http://www.salon.com/2013/10/13/ted_talks_are_lying_to_you/.

34. Daniel Kahneman, *Thinking, Fast and Slow* (Toronto: Doubleday Canada, 2011).

35. "*Time* Person of the Year," *Wikipedia, the Free Encyclopedia*, April 13, 2015, http://en.wikipedia.org/w/index.php?title=Time_Person_of_the_Year&oldid=656202490.

36. Quentin Hardy, "Someday Worth Billions, but Now, They Need a Desk," *The New York Times*, September 3, 2013, http://www.nytimes.com/2013/09/04/realestate/commercial/someday-worth-billions-but-now-they-need-a-desk.html.

37. Quentin Hardy, "The Monuments of Tech," *The New York Times*, March 1, 2014, http://www.nytimes.com/2014/03/02/technology/the-monuments-of-tech.html.

38. Hardy, "How Tech Remakes Space, Food and Urgency."

39. Jill Peterson, "Creating a Park like No Other - Fortune," September 25, 2012, http://fortune.com/2012/09/25/creating-a-park-like-no-other/.

40. Marge Macris, "Marin Voice: Choosing the Future We Want for Marin," September 12, 2012, http://www.marinij.com/opinion/20120912/marin-voice-choosing-the-future-we-want-for-marin.

41. Ban Ki-moon, "United Nations Secretary-General Ban Ki-Moon," September 25, 2012, http://www.un.org/sg/statements/index.asp?nid=6312.

42. Quentin Hardy, "Growing Numbers of Start-Ups Are Worth a Billion Dollars," *The New*

York Times, February 4, 2013, sec. Technology, http://www.nytimes.com/2013/02/05/technology/growing-numbers-of-start-ups-are-worth-a-billion-dollars.html.

43. David Streitfeld, "Amazon Delivers Some Pie in the Sky," *The New York Times*, December 2, 2013, sec. Technology, http://www.nytimes.com/2013/12/03/technology/amazon-delivers-some-pie-in-the-sky.html.

44. Ibid.

45. Michelle Riggen-Ransom, "Meet the 6-Year-Old Entrepreneur Who Just Wowed Startup Weekend," *GeekWire*, May 21, 2012, http://www.geekwire.com/2012/meet-6yearold-entrepreneur-wowed-startup-weekend/. Oh and you can follow the little tike on Twitter @gaptoothkid.

46. Somini Sengupta, "Mark Zuckerberg Remains the Undisputed Boss at Facebook," *The New York Times*, February 2, 2012, sec. Technology, http://www.nytimes.com/2012/02/03/technology/from-earliest-days-zuckerberg-focused-on-controlling-facebook.html.

47. Laura M. Holson, "Sean Parker Brings Facebook-Style Skills to New York Social Scene," *The New York Times*, December 17, 2011, sec. Fashion & Style, http://www.nytimes.com/2011/12/18/fashion/sean-parker-brings-facebook-style-skills-to-new-york-social-scene.html.

48. Sengupta, "Mark Zuckerberg Remains the Undisputed Boss at Facebook."

49. William Alden, "Jack Ma to Join Tech Moguls in Backing Medical Research Prize," *DealBook*, September 27, 2013, http://dealbook.nytimes.com/2013/09/27/jack-ma-to-join-tech-moguls-in-backing-medical-research-prize/.

50. George Packer, "Change the World," *The New Yorker*, May 27, 2013, http://www.newyorker.com/reporting/2013/05/27/130527fa_fact_packer?currentPage=all.

51. David Streitfeld, "A Screaming Comes Across the Sky: Google vs. the Counterforce," *The New York Times*, February 10, 2014, http://bits.blogs.nytimes.com/2014/02/10/a-screaming-comes-across-the-sky-google-vs-the-counterforce/.

52. Jill Lepore, "The Disruption Machine," *The New Yorker*, June 23, 2014, http://www.newyorker.com/reporting/2014/06/23/140623fa_fact_lepore?currentPage=all.

53. Steve Coll, "Citizen Bezos," *The New York Review of Books*, July 10, 2014, http://www.nybooks.com/articles/archives/2014/jul/10/citizen-bezos-amazon/.

54. Brendan Keenan, "The Future...? It's Not What It Used to Be," *Belfast Telegraph*, January 3, 2012, http://www.belfasttelegraph.co.uk/business/opinion/view-from-dublin/the-future-itrsquos-not-what-it-used-to-be-16098561.html.

55. McBride, "Startups Jostle for Funding, Attention at South by Southwest."

56. Ibid.

57. Ryan Konicek, Ryan Konicek Interview, March 2013.

58. Brian Singerman, Brian Singerman Interview, May 28, 2013.

59. Packer, "Change the World."

60. Mara Lewis does eventually settle on a Plan B. A year or so later she resurfaces as the Managing Director of Memphis-based Start Co., a so-called "start-up accelerator" that mentors and advises tech start-ups. http://neverstop.co/.

CHAPTER 2

1. "Joan and Irwin Jacobs Give $133M to Name Cornell Tech Institute | Cornell Chronicle," accessed April 13, 2015, http://news.cornell.edu/stories/2013/04/joan-and-irwin-jacobs-give-133m-name-cornell-tech-institute.

2. "Cornell NYC Tech Launches Connective Media Degree," accessed April 13, 2015, http://mediarelations.cornell.edu/2013/10/01/cornell-nyc-tech-launches-connective-media-degree/.
3. Daniel Huttenlocher and Adam Shwartz, Daniel Huttenlocher and Adam Shwartz Interview, April 25, 2014.
4. Ry Rivard, "Cornell Tech Rethinks How Universities Invest in Software Start-Ups | InsideHigherEd.com," February 25, 2014, https://www.insidehighered.com/news/2014/02/25/cornell-tech-rethinks-how-universities-invest-software-start-ups.
5. Jaron Lanier, *Who Owns the Future?* (New York: Simon & Schuster, 2013).
6. "Chapman University Banner Advertisement," *Inside Higher Ed*, February 25, 2014.
7. "Humanities+," accessed April 13, 2015, http://humanities.byu.edu/about-the-college/humanitiesplus/.
8. "USC Jimmy Iovine and Andre Young Academy," accessed April 13, 2015, http://iovine-young.usc.edu/.
9. John Schwartz, "Socrates Takes a Back Seat to Business and Tech," *The New York Times*, August 1, 2014, http://www.nytimes.com/2014/08/03/education/edlife/socrates-takes-a-back-seat-to-business-and-tech.html.
10. "CAL Digital Humanities :: Undergraduate Specialization," accessed April 13, 2015, http://dh.cal.msu.edu/index.php/curriculum/undergrad/.
11. "The Digital Humanities Initiative," accessed April 13, 2015, http://isites.harvard.edu/icb/icb.do?keyword=k15573.
12. "Digital Humanities : University of Rochester | The Andrew W. Mellon Foundation," accessed April 13, 2015, http://mellon.org/grants/grants-database/grants/university-of-rochester/31300609/.
13. Adam Kirsch, "Technology Is Taking Over English Departments," *The New Republic*, May 2, 2014, http://www.newrepublic.com/article/117428/limits-digital-humanities-adam-kirsch.
14. Ibid.
15. Ibid.
16. Matthew Kirschenbaum, "What Is Digital Humanities and What's It Doing in English Departments?," *ADE Bulletin*, November 15, 2010.
17. Tamar Lewin, "Stanford Fund-Raising Topped $1 Billion in 2012," *The New York Times*, February 20, 2013, http://www.nytimes.com/2013/02/21/education/stanfords-fund-raising-topped-1-billion-in-2012.html.
18. George Packer, *The Unwinding: An Inner History of the New America*, First edition (New York: Farrar, Straus and Giroux, 2013), 439.
19. Jefferson Graham, "Stanford Students, Apple iPad Apps Just Go Together," *USATODAY.COM*, accessed April 13, 2015, http://www.usatoday.com/tech/columnist/talkingtech/story/2012-03-13/stanford-students-apps/53516698/1.
20. "Stanford Will Start New Joint Computer Science Programs @insidehighered," accessed January 28, 2015, https://www.insidehighered.com/news/2014/03/07/stanford-will-start-new-joint-computer-science-programs.
21. Tamar Lewin, "As Interest Fades in the Humanities, Colleges Worry," *The New York Times*, October 30, 2013, sec. Education, http://www.nytimes.com/2013/10/31/education/as-interest-fades-in-the-humanities-colleges-worry.html.

22. Ibid.

23. Tom Kroll, "California Education's Painful Decline," *Salon.com*, October 2, 2012, http://www.salon.com/2012/10/02/california_educations_painful_decline/.

24. "A Few States Are Spending More on Higher Ed than before the Recession Hit | Inside Higher Ed," accessed April 21, 2014, http://www.insidehighered.com/news/2014/04/21/few-states-are-spending-more-higher-ed-recession-hit.

25. Lewin, "As Interest Fades in the Humanities, Colleges Worry."

26. Lexi Belculfine, "Edinboro University to Lay off 30-plus on Faculty," *Pittsburgh Post-Gazette*, accessed April 15, 2015, http://www.post-gazette.com/news/state/2013/10/26/Edinboro-University-to-lay-off-30-plus-on-faculty/stories/201310260096.

27. Jennifer Levitz and Douglas Belkin, "Humanities Fall From Favor," *Wall Street Journal*, June 6, 2013, sec. US, http://www.wsj.com/articles/SB10001424127887324069104578527642373232184.

28. Colleen Flaherty, "Where Have All the English Majors Gone? @insidehighered," accessed January 28, 2015, https://www.insidehighered.com/news/2015/01/26/where-have-all-english-majors-gone.

29. Michael C. Bender, "Scott: Florida Doesn't Need More Anthropology Majors," *Tampa Bay Times*, October 10, 2011, http://www.tampabay.com/blogs/the-buzz-florida-politics/content/scott-florida-doesnt-need-more-anthropology-majors.

30. Louis Efron, "Tackling The Real Unemployment Rate: 12.6%," *Forbes*, accessed April 15, 2015, http://www.forbes.com/sites/louisefron/2014/08/20/tackling-the-real-unemployment-rate-12-6/.

31. John Williams quoted in Alex Henderson, "10 Ways America Has Come to Resemble a Banana Republic," *AlterNet*, September 5, 2013, http://www.alternet.org/economy/10-ways-america-has-come-resemble-banana-republic.

32. "Google: Global Annual Revenue 2014 | Statistic," *Statista*, accessed April 15, 2015, http://www.statista.com/statistics/266206/googles-annual-global-revenue/.

33. Mike Swift, "Google Will Hire at Least 6,000 Workers 'across the Board' in 2011," accessed April 15, 2015, http://www.mercurynews.com/ci_17194423?nclick_check=1.

34. Patrick Mcgeehan, "Half of New York's Tech Workers Lack College Degrees, Report Says," *The New York Times*, April 1, 2014, http://www.nytimes.com/2014/04/02/nyregion/half-of-new-yorks-tech-workers-lack-college-degrees-report-says.html.

35. "Where the Jobs Are | Inside Higher Ed," accessed April 24, 2014, http://www.insidehighered.com/quicktakes/2014/04/23/where-jobs-are#sthash.J4L8nNW5.dpbs.

36. Arlene Dohm and Lynn Shniper, "Occupational Employment Projections to 2016," *Monthly Labor Review*, November 1, 2007, http://www.bls.gov/opub/mlr/2007/11/art5full.pdf.

37. Brian Vastag, "U.S. Pushes for More Scientists, but the Jobs Aren't There," *The Washington Post*, July 7, 2012, sec. National, http://www.washingtonpost.com/national/health-science/us-pushes-for-more-scientists-but-the-jobs-arent-there/2012/07/07/gJQAZJpQUW_story_2.html.

38. Thomas L. Friedman, "How to Get a Job at Google," *The New York Times*, February 22, 2014, http://www.nytimes.com/2014/02/23/opinion/sunday/friedman-how-to-get-a-job-at-google.html.

39. Thomas L. Friedman, "How to Get a Job," *The New York Times*, May 28, 2013, sec. Opinion, http://www.nytimes.com/2013/05/29/opinion/friedman-how-to-get-a-job.html.

40. Ibid.

41. Dan Schawbel, "Dale Stephens: Ditch College And Create Your Own Educational Experience," *Forbes*, March 5, 2013, http://www.forbes.com/sites/danschawbel/2013/03/05/dale-stephens-ditch-college-and-create-your-own-educational-experience/.

42. Friedman, "How to Get a Job at Google."

43. "Close the Innovation Deficit," n.d., http://www.innovationdeficit.org/.

44. Steven Leckart, "The Hackathon Fast Track, From Campus to Silicon Valley," *The New York Times*, April 6, 2015, http://www.nytimes.com/2015/04/12/education/edlife/the-hackathon-fast-track-from-campus-to-silicon-valley.html.

45. Alex Williams, "Saying No to College," *The New York Times*, November 30, 2012, sec. Fashion & Style, http://www.nytimes.com/2012/12/02/fashion/saying-no-to-college.html.

46. "Undrip ~ Mobile App for Content Discovery," accessed April 28, 2014, http://undrip.com/.

47. Valerie Strauss, "Netflix's Reed Hastings Has a Big Idea: Kill Elected School Boards (update)," *Washington Post*, March 14, 2014, http://www.washingtonpost.com/blogs/answer-sheet/wp/2014/03/14/netflixs-reed-hastings-has-a-big-idea-kill-elected-school-boards/.

48. "Rocketship: A Network of Elementary Charter Schools Eliminating the Achievement Gap In Our Lifetime," accessed April 15, 2015, http://www.rsed.org/.

49. TechnoBuffalo, "Apple Sold More Than 8 Million iPads to Schools," *TechnoBuffalo*, accessed April 15, 2015, http://www.technobuffalo.com/2013/03/03/apple-8-million-ipad-school/.

50. Brenda Iasevoli, "After Bungled iPad Rollout, Lessons from LA Put Tablet Technology in a Time Out," *Hechinger Report*, December 18, 2013, http://hechingerreport.org/content/after-bungled-ipad-rollout-lessons-from-la-put-tablet-technology-in-a-time-out_14123/.

51. Carlo Rotella, "No Child Left Untableted," *The New York Times*, September 12, 2013, sec. Magazine, http://www.nytimes.com/2013/09/15/magazine/no-child-left-untableted.html.

52. Susan Pinker, "Can Students Have Too Much Tech?," *The New York Times*, January 30, 2015, http://www.nytimes.com/2015/01/30/opinion/can-students-have-too-much-tech.html.

53. Brian Bergstein, "Former Microsoft Research Executive Says Technologists Overestimate Their Ability to Drive Social Progress," *MIT Technology Review*, April 15, 2015, http://www.technologyreview.com/qa/536701/putting-technology-in-its-place/.

54. Larry Cuban, Larry Cuban Interview, April 25, 2014.

55. Iasevoli, "After Bungled iPad Rollout, Lessons from LA Put Tablet Technology in a Time out."

56. Pat Shellenbarger, "Rural Poverty Continues to Be Tough Problem for Michigan to Solve," *MLive.com*, August 5, 2014, http://www.mlive.com/politics/index.ssf/2014/08/down_and_out_in_lake_county.html.

57   Gale Holland, "L.A. County Leads California in Poverty Rate, New Analysis
      Shows," *Los Angeles Times*, September 30, 2013, http://articles.latimes.com/2013/
      sep/30/local/la-me-poverty-20131001.

CHAPTER 3

1.   "Guidelines Qualcomm Tricorder XPrize," *Qualcomm Tricorder XPRIZE*, accessed
      April 15, 2015, http://tricorder.xprize.org/about/guidelines.
2.   Mark Winter, Mark Winter Interview, December 5, 2013.
3.   "DARPA Announces Cyber Grand Challenge," October 22, 2013, http://www.dar-
      pa.mil/NewsEvents/Releases/2013/10/22.aspx.
4.   Bureau of Public Affairs Department Of State. The Office of Website Manage-
      ment, "Innovation in Arms Control Challenge," August 28, 2012, http://www.
      state.gov/t/avc/innovationcompetition/.
5.   "DOL Fair Labor Data Challenge," *DOL Fair Labor Data Challenge*, accessed April
      15, 2015, http://fairlabor.challengepost.com/.
6.   "Presenting Arts Data Artfully," *Presenting Arts Data Artfully*, accessed April 15,
      2015, http://artsdata.challengepost.com/.
7.   "Reinvent the Toilet," *Bill & Melinda Gates Foundation*, accessed April 15, 2015,
      http://www.gatesfoundation.org/What-We-Do/Global-Development/Rein-
      vent-the-Toilet-Challenge.
8.   "Hult Prize: Start-up Accelerator for Social Entrepreneurship," accessed April 15,
      2015, http://www.hultprize.org/en/about/mission/.
9.   "Hult Prize 2013 Finals," accessed April 15, 2015, http://www.hultprize.org/en/
      compete/2013-prize/2013-finalists/.
10.   "Smart Tech Challenges Foundation," *Smart Tech Challenges Foundation*, accessed
      April 15, 2015, https://smarttechfoundation.org/.
11.   Chuck Salter, "Silicon Valley's Smart Tech Foundation Launches $1 Million
      Competition For Safer Guns," *Fast Company*, accessed April 15, 2015, http://
      www.fastcompany.com/3021232/silicon-valley-trio-launches-1-million-competi-
      tion-for-smarter-safer-guns-exclusive.
12.   Hugo Miller and Erlichman, "BlackBerry Inventor Starts Fund to Make Star Trek
      Device Reality," *Bloomberg.com*, accessed April 15, 2015, http://www.bloomberg.
      com/news/articles/2013-03-19/blackberry-inventor-starts-fund-to-make-star-trek-
      device-reality.
13.   William J. Broad, "Billionaires With Big Ideas Are Privatizing American Science,"
      The New York Times, March 15, 2014, http://www.nytimes.com/2014/03/16/sci-
      ence/billionaires-with-big-ideas-are-privatizing-american-science.html.
14.   Salter, "Silicon Valley's Smart Tech Foundation Launches $1 Million Competition
      For Safer Guns."
15.   Packer, "Change the World."
16.   Robert Hromas, Janis L. Abkowitz, and Armand Keating, "Facing the NIH Fund-
      ing Crisis," *JAMA : The Journal of the American Medical Association* 308, no. 22
      (December 12, 2012): 2343–44, doi:10.1001/jama.2012.45067.
17.   "Fact Sheet: Impact of Sequestration on the National Institutes of Health," ac-
      cessed April 15, 2015, http://www.nih.gov/news/health/jun2013/nih-03.htm.
18.   "Full Committee Hearing: Driving Innovation through Federal Investments |
      Senate Appropriations Committee," April 29, 2014, http://www.appropriations.

senate.gov/hearings-and-testimony/outside-witness-testimony-federal-innovation-hearing.

19. Joanna Rothkopf, "Lack of Science Funding Is Seriously Threatening U.S. National Security, according to MIT Report," April 27, 2015, http://www.salon.com/2015/04/27/lack_of_science_funding_is_seriously_threatening_u_s_national_security_according_to_mit_report/.

20. David Edgerton, *The Shock of the Old: Technology and Global History since 1900* (Oxford ; New York: Oxford University Press, 2007), 118.

21. Ibid., 169.

22. Ibid.

23. David Brooks, "Goodbye, Organization Man," *The New York Times*, September 15, 2014, http://www.nytimes.com/2014/09/16/opinion/david-brooks-goodbye-organization-man.html.

24. Coll, "Citizen Bezos."

25. "Google Lunar XPRIZE," *Google Lunar XPRIZE*, accessed April 16, 2015, http://lunar.xprize.org/.

26. NASA is building the Orion spacecraft which is designed for "deep space destinations such as an asteroid and eventually Mars." Mark Garcia, "Orion," Text, *NASA*, (July 8, 2013), http://www.nasa.gov/exploration/systems/orion/index.html.

27. Quentin Hardy and Conor Dougherty, "Google and Fidelity Put $1 Billion Into SpaceX," *The New York Times*, January 20, 2015, http://www.nytimes.com/2015/01/21/technology/google-makes-1-billion-investment-in-spacex.html.

28. "Paleofuture," *Paleofuture*, accessed April 16, 2015, http://paleofuture.gizmodo.com/.

29. Matt Novak, Matt Novak Interview, April 1, 2013.

30. Matt Novak, "Googie: Architecture of the Space Age," *Smithsonian*, accessed April 16, 2015, http://www.smithsonianmag.com/history/googie-architecture-of-the-space-age-122837470/.

31. "Tomorrowland," *Wikipedia, the Free Encyclopedia*, April 14, 2015, http://en.wikipedia.org/w/index.php?title=Tomorrowland&oldid=656422696.

32. Virginia I. Postrel, *The Future and Its Enemies: The Growing Conflict over Creativity, Enterprise, and Progress* (New York: Simon & Schuster, 1999), 14.

33. Robert W. Rydell, "Century of Progress Exposition," *Encyclopedia of Chicago* (Chicago: Chicago History Museum and the Newberry Library, 2005), http://encyclopedia.chicagohistory.org/pages/225.html.

34. Robert Buderi, *Engines of Tomorrow: How the World's Best Companies Are Using Their Research Labs to Win the Future* (New York: Simon & Schuster, 2000), 78.

35. Matt Novak, "This Automated Drive-In Market Was Pretty Retro, Even For 1956," *Paleofuture*, accessed April 16, 2015, http://paleofuture.gizmodo.com/this-automated-drive-in-market-was-pretty-retro-even-f-1379535551.

36. Edgerton, *The Shock of the Old*, 12.

37. Ibid.

38. Tim Wu, *The Master Switch the Rise and Fall of Information Empires* (New York: Alfred A. Knopf, 2010), 160, http://www.contentreserve.com/TitleInfo.asp?ID={2BDB149B-1432-4B87-867F-7ACFAD6999AA}&Format=410.

39. Ibid.

40. Ibid.

41. Postrel, *The Future and Its Enemies*, 39.
42. John Jordan, *Machine-Age Ideology Social Engineering and American Liberalism, 1911-1939*, n.d., 66.
43. Alexander Waugh, *Time: From Micro-Seconds to Millennia, a Search for the Right Time* (London: Headline Book Pub., 1999).
44. Buderi, *Engines of Tomorrow*, 15.
45. David Hillel Gelernter, *1939, the Lost World of the Fair* (New York: Avon Books, 1996).
46. Postrel, *The Future and Its Enemies*, 82.
47. Packer, *The Unwinding*, 249.
48. Ibid., 152.
49. Ibid., 240.

CHAPTER 4

1. "Jack Dangermond," *Forbes*, accessed April 16, 2015, http://www.forbes.com/profile/jack-dangermond/.
2. Peter Eredics, Peter Eredics Interview, July 16, 2013.
3. Simon Thompson, Simon Thompson Interview, July 16, 2013.
4. David Pierce, "Location Is Your Most Critical Data, and Everyone's Watching," *WIRED*, April 27, 2015, http://www.wired.com/2015/04/location/.
5. Chris Ovens, Chris Ovens Interview, July 16, 2013.
6. "Richmond, Virginia Police Department," accessed April 16, 2015, http://www.cwhonors.org/Search/his_4.asp.
7. Viktor Mayer-Schönberger and Kenneth Cukier, *Big Data: A Revolution That Will Transform How We Live, Work, and Think* (Boston: Houghton Mifflin Harcourt, 2013), 152.
8. Ryan Prox, "How Vancouver Tapped Big Data Analytics to Fight Crime," *A Smarter Planet Blog*, accessed April 16, 2015, http://asmarterplanet.com/blog/2013/07/how-vancouver-tapped-big-data-analytics-to-fight-crime.html.
9. Mayer-Schönberger and Cukier, *Big Data*, 6.
10. Ibid., 183.
11. Ibid., 15.
12. Ibid.
13. Ibid., 6.
14. Ibid., 9.
15. Ariana Eunjung Cha, "'Big Data' from Social Media, Elsewhere Online Redefines Trend-Watching," *The Washington Post*, June 7, 2012, sec. Business, http://www.washingtonpost.com/business/economy/big-data-from-social-media-elsewhere-online-take-trend-watching-to-new-level/2012/06/06/gJQArWWpJV_story_2.html.
16. Evgeny Morozov, *To Save Everything, Click Here: The Folly of Technological Solutionism* (PublicAffairs, 2013), 7.
17. Mayer-Schönberger and Cukier, *Big Data*, 135.
18. Will Knight, "Why Is Google Buying So Many Robot Startups?," *MIT Technology Review*, December 4, 2013, http://www.technologyreview.com/view/522251/why-is-google-buying-so-many-robot-startups/.
19. Adam Fisher, "Google's Road Map to Global Domination," *The New York Times*,

December 11, 2013, sec. Magazine, http://www.nytimes.com/2013/12/15/maga-zine/googles-plan-for-global-domination-dont-ask-why-ask-where.html.

20. Alexis C. Madrigal, "The Trick That Makes Google's Self-Driving Cars Work," *The Atlantic*, May 15, 2014, http://www.theatlantic.com/technology/archive/2014/05/all-the-world-a-track-the-trick-that-makes-googles-self-driving-cars-work/370871/.

21. Mayer-Schönberger and Cukier, *Big Data*, 57.

22. "The Pregnancy Is Gone, but the Promotions Keep Coming," *Motherlode Blog*, accessed February 4, 2014, http://parenting.blogs.nytimes.com/2014/02/02/the-pregnancy-is-gone-but-the-promotions-keep-coming/.

23. Michael Beyman, "Big Data's Powerful Effect on Tiny Babies," *CNBC*, accessed April 17, 2015, http://www.cnbc.com/id/101032950.

24. Mayer-Schönberger and Cukier, *Big Data*, 57.

25. Ibid., 132.

26. Ibid., 57.

27. Ibid., 132.

28. Quentin Hardy, "How Urban Anonymity Disappears When All Data Is Tracked," *The New York Times*, April 19, 2014, http://bits.blogs.nytimes.com/2014/04/19/how-urban-anonymity-disappears-when-all-data-is-tracked/.

29. Wolfgang Hall, Wolfgang Hall Interview, July 16, 2013.

30. Mayer-Schönberger and Cukier, *Big Data*, 89.

31. Peck, "They're Watching You at Work."

32. Ibid.

33. Ibid.

34. Ibid.

35. Ibid.

36. Ibid.

37. Ibid.

38. Ibid.

39. Ibid.

40. Marshall Kirkpatrick, "Green Goose Wows the Crowd & Raises $100K On Launch Conference Stage," *ReadWrite*, accessed April 17, 2015, http://readwrite.com/2011/02/23/green_goose_wows_the_crowd_raises_100k_on_launch_c.

41. In my book The Peep Diaries I discuss why people now think of privacy as more of a commodity than a human right. Hal Niedzviecki, *The Peep Diaries: How We're Learning to Love Watching Ourselves and Our Neighbors* (San Francisco, CA: City Lights Books, 2009).

42. Lanier, *Who Owns the Future?*.

CHAPTER 5

1. Claudia Hammond, *Time Warped: Unlocking the Mysteries of Time Perception* (Toronto: House of Anansi Press, 2012), 18.

2. Waugh, *Time*.

3. Ibid.

4. Ibid.

5. Marshall McLuhan, Eric McLuhan, and Frank Zingrone, *Essential McLuhan*, 1st ed (New York, NY: BasicBooks, 1995), 240.

6. Thomas Hobbes, *Leviathan, or The Matter, Forme and Power of a Commonwealth*,

Ecclesiasticall, and Civill, 1886th ed. (London: George Routledge and Sons, 1651), 299.

7. Daniel Innerarity, *The Future and Its Enemies in Defense of Political Hope* (Stanford, California: Stanford University Press, 2012), 43.

8. Ibid, 45.

9. Ibid., 42.

10. Hammond, *Time Warped: Unlocking the Mysteries of Time Perception*, 140.

11. Ibid., 158.

12. Ibid., 77.

13. Ibid., 100.

14. Ibid., 141.

15. Ibid., 144.

16. Ibid., 158.

17. Benedict Carey, "How the Brain Stores Trivial Memories, Just in Case," *The New York Times*, January 21, 2015, http://www.nytimes.com/2015/01/22/health/study-shows-brain-stores-seemingly-trivial-memories-just-in-case.html.

18. Hammond, *Time Warped: Unlocking the Mysteries of Time Perception*, 150.

19. Carey, "How the Brain Stores Trivial Memories, Just in Case."

20. John Coates, "The Biology of Risk," *The New York Times*, June 7, 2014, http://www.nytimes.com/2014/06/08/opinion/sunday/the-biology-of-risk.html.

21. Hammond, *Time Warped: Unlocking the Mysteries of Time Perception*, 142.

22. Jared M. Diamond, *The World until Yesterday: What Can We Learn from Traditional Societies?* (New York: Viking, 2012), 243.

23. Innerarity, *The Future and Its Enemies in Defense of Political Hope*, 43.

24. Chrystia Freeland, "The Advent of the Global Brain," *Reuters Blogs - Chrystia Freeland*, accessed September 27, 2013, http://blogs.reuters.com/chrystia-freeland/2011/09/23/the-advent-of-the-global-brain/.

25. Ray Kurzweil, *The Singularity Is Near: When Humans Transcend Biology* (New York: Penguin, 2006).

26. Ibid.

27. David Segal, "Dmitry Itskov and the Avatar Quest," *The New York Times*, June 1, 2013, sec. Business Day, http://www.nytimes.com/2013/06/02/business/dmitry-itskov-and-the-avatar-quest.html.

28. Ibid.

29. Claire Cain Miller and Andrew Pollack, "Tech Titans Form Biotechnology Company," *The New York Times*, September 18, 2013, http://bits.blogs.nytimes.com/2013/09/18/google-and-former-genentech-chief-announce-new-bio-tech-company/.

30. Ibid.

31. Packer, *The Unwinding*, 436.

32. Ibid.

33. Jessica Roy, "The Rapture of the Nerds," *Time*, April 17, 2014, http://time.com/66536/terasem-trascendence-religion-technology/.

34. Ibid.

35. Ibid.

CHAPTER **6**

1. Gleick, *The Information*, 43.
2. A.R. Luria, *Cognitive Development: Its Cultural and Social Foundations* (Cambridge, Mass., USA: Harvard University Press, 1976). And: Gleick, *The Information*, 43.
3. Innerarity, *The Future and Its Enemies in Defense of Political Hope*, 30.
4. "IARPA Home Page," accessed April 20, 2015, http://www.iarpa.gov/.
5. David Ignatius, "More Chatter than Needed," *The Washington Post*, November 2, 2013, sec. Opinions, http://www.washingtonpost.com/opinions/david-ignatius-more-chatter-than-needed/2013/11/01/1194a984-425a-11e3-a624-41d661b0bb78_story.html.
6. Philip E. Tetlock, Philip Tetlock Interview, November 19, 2013.
7. Philip E. Tetlock and Dan Gardner, "Who's Good at Forecasts?," *The Economist*, accessed November 20, 2013, http://www.economist.com/news/21589145-how-sort-best-rest-whos-good-forecasts.
8. Ibid.
9. Ignatius, "More Chatter than Needed."
10. "SciCast Predict Home Page," accessed April 20, 2015, https://scicast.org/#!/.
11. "About the Millennium Project," accessed April 20, 2015, http://www.millennium-project.org/millennium/overview.html.
12. Wakslak, Cheryl Wakslak Interview.
13. Denis Diderot, *The Encyclopédie* (Paris, 1751) as cited in Gleick, *The Information*, 351..
14. Gleick, *The Information*, 351.
15. Martin Davis, *The Universal Computer: The Road from Leibniz to Turing*, Turing centenary ed (Boca Raton, Fla: CRC Press, 2012), 16.
16. George Dyson, *Turing's Cathedral: The Origins of the Digital Universe*, 1st ed (New York: Pantheon Books, 2012), 104.
17. Ibid., 105.
18. Charles Babbage, *Charles Babbage and His Calculating Engines: Selected Writings* (Dover Publications, 1961), 247.
19. Ibid., 252.
20. Pierre-Simon Laplace, *A Philosophical Essay on Probabilities* (Wiley, 1902).
21. Dyson, *Turing's Cathedral*, 2012, 130.
22. "The Atlantic Telegraph," *The New York Times*, August 6, 1858.
23. Marshall McLuhan, *Understanding Media: The Extensions of Man*, 1st MIT Press ed (Cambridge, Mass: MIT Press, 1994).
24. John Archibald Wheeler, "It from Bit," in *At Home in the Universe: The Search for Laws of Self-Organization and Complexity*, ed. Stuart A Kauffman (New York: Oxford University Press, 1996), 298.
25. Ibid, 296.
26. Meehan Crist and Tim Requarth, "Why IQs Rise," *The New Republic*, October 26, 2012, http://www.tnr.com/book/review/are-we-getting-smarter-rising-IQs-james-flynn.
27. Mayer-Schönberger and Cukier, *Big Data*, 183.
28. Ariel Garten, Ariel Garten Interview, June 14, 2013.
29. Mika Turim-Nygren, "Meet the Woman Making Brainwave Control Look More like Meditation and Less like the Matrix," *Digital Trends*, February 9, 2013, http://www.digitaltrends.com/computing/spotlight-on-ariel-garten-the-ceo-behind-interaxons-thought-controlled-brainchild/.

30. Barry L. Beyerstein, "Brainscams: Neuromythologies of the New Age," *International Journal of Mental Health* 19, no. 3 (1990): 27–36.

31. Frederic Lardinois, "InteraXon Raises $6M Series A Round From Horizon, A-Grade And Others For Its Brainwave-Sensing Headset," *TechCrunch*, August 15, 2013, http://social.techcrunch.com/2013/08/15/interaxon-raises-6m-series-a-round-from-horizon-a-grade-and-others-for-its-brainwave-sensing-headset/.

CHAPTER 7

1. Steven Johnson, *Where Good Ideas Come from the Natural History of Innovation* (New York: Riverhead Books, 2010), 77, http://www.contentreserve.com/TitleInfo.asp?ID={16F9BDC1-134C-49E0-B2B9-EC7813E3F7C8}&Format=50.

2. Ibid.

3. Johnson, *Where Good Ideas Come from the Natural History of Innovation*.

4. Frank, "TED Talks Are Lying to You."

5. Jeanne Arnold, Jeanne Arnold Interview, July 30, 2013.

6. J. B MacKinnon, *The Once and Future World: Nature as It Was, as It Is, as It Could Be* (Toronto: Random House Canada, 2013), 58.

7. MacKinnon, *The Once and Future World*, 62.

8. Clive Ponting, *A New Green History of the World: The Environment and the Collapse of Great Civilizations*, Rev. ed (New York: Penguin Books, 2007).

9. MacKinnon, *The Once and Future World*, 23.

10. Edgerton, *The Shock of the Old*, 145.

11. Ibid., 148.

12. Ibid.

13. Ibid., 150.

14. Ibid.

15. Amy Novogratz and Mike Velings, "The End of Fish," *The Washington Post*, June 3, 2014, http://www.washingtonpost.com/posteverything/wp/2014/06/03/the-end-of-fish/.

16. Edgerton, *The Shock of the Old*, 156.

17. Ibid.

18. "Poultry Facts - Purdue Food Animal Education Network," accessed April 21, 2015, http://www.ansc.purdue.edu/faen/poultry%20facts.html.

19. Lanier, *Who Owns the Future?*, 143.

20. Ronald Wright, *A Short History of Progress*, CBC Massey Lectures Series (Toronto: House of Anansi Press, 2004).

21. Richard Dawkins, *The Selfish Gene*, 30th anniversary ed (Oxford ; New York: Oxford University Press, 2006), xxi.

22. Gleick, *The Information*, 277.

23. Dawkins, *The Selfish Gene*, 25.

24. Edgerton, *The Shock of the Old*, 181.

25. MacKinnon, *The Once and Future World*, 30–31.

26. Benoit Godin, Benoit Godin Interview, September 20, 2013.

27. Aristotle, *Aristotle's Politics*, trans. Carnes Lord, Second edition (Chicago: The University of Chicago Press, 2013).

28. Plato, *Plato, Protagoras*, ed. Nicholas Denyer, Reprinted, Cambridge Greek and Latin Classics (Cambridge: Cambridge Univ. Press, 2011).

29. Benoit Godin, "'Meddle Not With Them That Are Given to Change': Innovation as Evil," *Project on the Intellectua L History of Innovation Working Paper No. 6*, 2010, http://www.csiic.ca/PDF/IntellectualNo6.pdf.
30. Ibid., Heylin, 1637.
31. Ibid., Edward VI, 1548.
32. Ibid., Charles I, 1626.
33. Godin, "'Meddle Not With Them That Are Given to Change': Innovation as Evil."
34. Ibid.
35. Ibid., Burton, 1636 .
36. Ibid., Heylin, 1637.
37. George Dyson, *Turing's Cathedral: The Origins of the Digital Universe* (Pantheon, 2012), 12.
38. Godin, "'Meddle Not With Them That Are Given to Change': Innovation as Evil," Anonymous, 1696.
39. Ibid., Berkeley, 1785.
40. Eula Biss, *On Immunity: An Inoculation* (Minneapolis, Minnesota: Graywolf Press, 2014).
41. Floyd Norris, "Population Growth Forecast From the U.N. May Be Too High," *The New York Times*, September 20, 2013, sec. Business Day, http://www.nytimes.com/2013/09/21/business/uns-forecast-of-population-growth-may-be-too-high.html.
42. Dyson, *Turing's Cathedral*, 2012, 10.
43. Ibid., 7–8, 187, 220.
44. Ibid., 329.
45. Ibid., 62.
46. Plato, *Plato's Cratylus*, trans. Benjamin Jowett (Serenity Publishers, 2008).

CHAPTER 8

1. Roger Vincent, "Inland Empire Warehouse Deals," *Los Angeles Times*, November 15, 2007, http://articles.latimes.com/2007/nov/15/business/fi-warehouses15.
2. David Kelly, "Inland Growth to Continue," *Los Angeles Times*, April 10, 2008, http://articles.latimes.com/2008/apr/10/local/me-growth10.
3. Jeff Horseman, "Region: Inland Welfare, Food Stamp Usage Soars," *Press Enterprise*, August 19, 2012, http://www.pe.com/articles/county-653361-welfare-percent.html.
4. Juana Ibanez, Juana Ibanez Interview, July 15, 2013.
5. Marc Lifsher, "Chino Warehouse Operator Fined for Alleged Overtime Violations," *Los Angeles Times*, January 29, 2013, http://articles.latimes.com/2013/jan/29/business/la-fi-warehouse-fine-20130129.
6. Raul, Raul Interview, 20013-07-15.
7. Javeir Rodriques, Javeir Rodriques Interview, July 15, 2013.
8. Jose Martinez, Jose Martinez, July 15, 2013.
9. Charles Duhigg and David Barboza, "Apple's iPad and the Human Costs for Workers in China," *The New York Times*, January 25, 2012, sec. Business Day, http://www.nytimes.com/2012/01/26/business/ieconomy-apples-ipad-and-the-human-costs-for-workers-in-china.html.
10. Thomas B. Edsall, "The Downward Ramp," *The New York Times*, June 10, 2014, http://www.nytimes.com/2014/06/11/opinion/the-downward-ramp.html.

11. Ibid.

12. Ibid.

13. David Autor and David Dorn, "How Technology Wrecks the Middle Class," *The New York Times*, August 24, 2013, http://opinionator.blogs.nytimes.com/2013/08/24/how-technology-wrecks-the-middle-class/.

14. Mark Bittman, "Fast Food, Low Pay," *The New York Times*, July 25, 2013, http://opinionator.blogs.nytimes.com/2013/07/25/fast-food-low-pay/.

15. Neil Irwin, "Why American Workers Without Much Education Are Being Hammered," *The New York Times*, April 21, 2015, http://www.nytimes.com/2015/04/22/upshot/why-workers-without-much-education-are-being-hammered.html.

16. Hope Yen, "Exclusive: Signs of Declining Economic Security," *Associated Press*, July 28, 2013, http://bigstory.ap.org/article/exclusive-4-5-us-face-near-poverty-no-work-0.

17. Ibid.

18. Moretti, *The New Geography of Jobs*, 8.

19. Ross Douthat, "A World Without Work," *The New York Times*, February 23, 2013, sec. Opinion / Sunday Review, http://www.nytimes.com/2013/02/24/opinion/sunday/douthat-a-world-without-work.html.

20. Edgerton, *The Shock of the Old*, 56.

21. Ibid.

22. Ibid., 58.

23. Ibid., 66.

24. Ibid., 69.

25. Ibid., 58.

26. Autor and Dorn, "How Technology Wrecks the Middle Class."

27. Erik Brynjolfsson and Andrew McAfee, *Race Against the Machine* (Lexington, Massachusetts: Digital Frontier Press, 2011).

28. Ibid.

29. Ibid.

30. Autor and Dorn, "How Technology Wrecks the Middle Class."

31. Brynjolfsson and McAfee, *Race Against the Machine*.

32. Moisés Naím, "America's Coming Manufacturing Revolution," *The Atlantic*, April 21, 2014, http://www.theatlantic.com/business/archive/2014/04/americas-coming-manufacturing-revolution/360931/.

33. Ibid.

34. Brynjolfsson and McAfee, *Race Against the Machine*.

35. "Working for the Few," *Oxfam International*, accessed April 23, 2015, https://www.oxfam.org/en/research/working-few.

36. Ibid.

37. Brynjolfsson and McAfee, *Race Against the Machine*.

38. Mayer-Schönberger and Cukier, *Big Data*, 140.

39. Jeremy Rifkin, "The Rise of Anti-Capitalism," *The New York Times*, March 15, 2014, http://www.nytimes.com/2014/03/16/opinion/sunday/the-rise-of-anti-capitalism.html.

40. Don Tapscott, "Davos: Delight over the Recovery, Fear for the Bigger Picture," *The Globe and Mail*, January 28, 2014, http://www.theglobeandmail.com/report-on-business/international-business/davos-delight-over-the-recovery-fear-for-the-bigger-picture/article16540650/.

41. Brynjolfsson and McAfee, *Race Against the Machine*.
42. Lanier, *Who Owns the Future?*, 60.
43. Paul Beaudry, David A. Green, and Benjamin M. Sand, *The Great Reversal in the Demand for Skill and Cognitive Tasks*, Working Paper (National Bureau of Economic Research, March 2013), http://www.nber.org/papers/w18901.
44. Graph used by permission, taken from Paul Beaudry, David A. Green, and Benjamin M. Sand, *The Great Reversal in the Demand for Skill and Cognitive Task*.
45. Autor and Dorn, "How Technology Wrecks the Middle Class."
46. "The American Dream, RIP?," *The Economist*, September 21, 2013, http://www.economist.com/news/united-states/21586581-economist-asks-provocative-questions-about-future-social-mobility-american.
47. Brynjolfsson and McAfee, *Race Against the Machine*.
48. "Kodak's Growth and Decline: A Timeline," *Rochester Business Journal*, January 19, 2012, http://www.rbj.net/print_article.asp?aID=190078.
49. "The Rise and Fall of Kodak," *PhotoSecrets*, accessed April 23, 2015, http://photosecrets.com/the-rise-and-fall-of-kodak.
50. Lanier, *Who Owns the Future?*, 13.
51. Lawrence Summers, "Thomas Piketty Is Right About the Past and Wrong About the Future," *The Atlantic*, May 16, 2014, http://www.theatlantic.com/business/archive/2014/05/thomas-piketty-is-right-about-the-past-and-wrong-about-the-future/370994/.
52. Mitch Potter, "A Dark Shadow Is Falling upon next Week's Edition of Black Friday," *The Toronto Star*, November 24, 2013, http://www.thestar.com/news/world/2013/11/24/black_friday_and_the_digital_rumble_of_americas_working_poor.html.
53. Mayer-Schönberger and Cukier, *Big Data*, 55.
54. Michael Maiello, "Walmart's Wage Hike Still About Greed," *The Daily Beast*, February 20, 2015, http://www.thedailybeast.com/articles/2015/02/20/walmart-s-wage-hike-still-about-greed.html.
55. Robert Reich, "Wal-Mart and McDonald's: What's Wrong with U.S. Employment," November 30, 2012, http://www.salon.com/2012/11/30/wal_mart_and_mcdonalds_whats_wrong_with_u_s_employment/.
56. Postrel, *The Future and Its Enemies*, 95.
57. Packer, "Change the World."
58. "World's Most Admired Companies 2015," accessed April 23, 2015, http://fortune.com/worlds-most-admired-companies/apple-1/.
59. "Remarks by the President on Jobs for the Middle Class," *The White House*, July 30, 2013, https://www.whitehouse.gov/node/228621.
60. Greg Bensinger, "Amazon Wants to Ship Your Package Before You Buy It," *WSJ Blogs - Digits*, January 17, 2014, http://blogs.wsj.com/digits/2014/01/17/amazon-wants-to-ship-your-package-before-you-buy-it/.
61. Daniel D'Addario, "Amazon Is Worse than Walmart," *Salon*, July 30, 2013, http://www.salon.com/2013/07/30/how_amazon_is_worse_than_wal_mart/.
62. Simon Head, "Worse than Wal-Mart: Amazon's Sick Brutality and Secret History of Ruthlessly Intimidating Workers," *Salon*, February 23, 2014, http://www.salon.com/2014/02/23/worse_than_wal_mart_amazons_sick_brutality_and_secret_history_of_ruthlessly_intimidating_workers/.

63. Mark Landler and Jackie Calmes, "Obama Proposes Deal Over Taxes and Jobs," *The New York Times*, July 30, 2013, http://www.nytimes.com/2013/07/31/us/politics/obama-offers-to-cut-corporate-tax-rate-as-part-of-jobs-deal.html.

64. Richard Kirsch, "Amazon Won't Revive the Economy," *Salon*, August 3, 2013, http://www.salon.com/2013/08/03/amazon_wont_revive_the_economy_partner/.

65. D'Addario, "Amazon Is Worse than Walmart."

66. David Jackson, "Amazon Touts New Jobs a Day before Obama Visit," *USA Today*, July 29, 2013, http://www.usatoday.com/story/theoval/2013/07/29/obama-amazon-jobs-chattanooga-tennessee/2595859/.

67. Brandon Bailey, "Amazon Robot army, 15,000 Strong, Is Ready for the Holiday Rush (+video)," *Christian Science Monitor*, December 2, 2014, http://www.csmonitor.com/Business/Latest-News-Wires/2014/1202/Amazon-robot-army-15-000-strong-is-ready-for-the-holiday-rush-video.

68. Lanier, *Who Owns the Future?*, 100.

69. Douthat, "A World Without Work."

70. Jeremy Rifkin, *The End of Work: The Decline of the Global Labor Force and the Dawn of the Post-Market Era*, A Jeremy P. Tarcher/Putnam Book (New York: Putnam, 1995).

71. Martin Ford, *The Lights in the Tunnel: Automation, Accelerating Technology and the Economy of the Future* (U.S.: Acculant Publishing, 2009).

72. Paul Williams, "Self-Driving Fleets Are Steering Big Rig Operators toward Obsolescence," *The Globe and Mail*, February 19, 2014, http://www.theglobeandmail.com/globe-drive/new-cars/auto-news/self-driving-fleets-are-steering-big-rig-operators-toward-obsolescence/article16937157/.

73. Ibid.

74. Jesse Mckinley, "With Farm Robotics, the Cows Decide When It's Milking Time," *The New York Times*, April 22, 2014, http://www.nytimes.com/2014/04/23/nyregion/with-farm-robotics-the-cows-decide-when-its-milking-time.html.

75. Farhad Manjoo, "Silicon Valley's Next Great Company," *Slate*, September 26, 2012, http://www.slate.com/articles/technology/technology/2012/09/square_jack_dorsey_s_payments_firm_is_silicon_valley_s_next_great_company_.single.html.

76. Lanier, *Who Owns the Future?*, 186.

77. Tapscott, "Davos."

78. Jodi Kantor, "Working Anything but 9 to 5," *The New York Times*, August 13, 2014, http://www.nytimes.com/interactive/2014/08/13/us/starbucks-workers-scheduling-hours.html.

79. Packer, "Change the World."

80. Lanier, *Who Owns the Future?*, 186.

81. Natasha Singer, "In the Sharing Economy, Workers Find Both Freedom and Uncertainty," *The New York Times*, August 16, 2014, http://www.nytimes.com/2014/08/17/technology/in-the-sharing-economy-workers-find-both-freedom-and-uncertainty.html.

82. Ibid.

83. Ibid.

84. Ibid.

85. Lanier, *Who Owns the Future?*, 186.
86. Dyson, *Turing's Cathedral*, 2012.
87. Lanier, *Who Owns the Future?*, 155.
88. Ibid., 17.
89. "The Secrets of Generation Flux," *SXSW Schedule 2013*, accessed April 24, 2015, http://schedule.sxsw.com/2013/events/event_IAP4957.
90. Ibid., full audio is available online at link.
91. Quentin Hardy, "The Most Dangerous Word in Tech," *The New York Times*, April 12, 2014, http://bits.blogs.nytimes.com/2014/04/12/the-most-dangerous-word-in-tech/.
92. Lanier, *Who Owns the Future?*, 167.
93. Ibid., 117.

CHAPTER 9

1. Robert Benzie, "Ontario's Youth Unemployment Is Higher than Rust Belt States and Quebec, New Study Finds," *The Toronto Star*, September 27, 2013, http://livenews.thestar.com/Event/Youth_Unemployment_in_Ontario.
2. Future Focus Group Interviews, May 28, 2013.
3. Patty Winsa, "National Survey of Post-Secondary Students in Canada Shows Stress and Anxiety Are Major Factors in Mental Health," *The Toronto Star*, June 17, 2013, http://www.thestar.com/news/gta/2013/06/17/national_survey_of_postsecondary_students_in_canada_shows_stress_and_anxiety_are_major_factors_in_mental_health.html.
4. Jake New, "Incoming Students' 'Emotional Health' at All-Time Low, Survey Says," *Inside Higher Ed*, February 5, 2015, https://www.insidehighered.com/news/2015/02/05/incoming-students-emotional-health-all-time-low-survey-says.
5. Walter Hamilton, "Employers Have Negative View of Gen Y Workers, Study Finds," *Los Angeles Times*, September 3, 2013, http://www.latimes.com/business/la-fi-mo-employers-negative-gen-y-millennials-20130903-story.html.
6. David Brooks, "The Streamlined Life," *The New York Times*, May 5, 2014, http://www.nytimes.com/2014/05/06/opinion/brooks-the-streamlined-life.html.
7. "Any Anxiety Disorder Among Adults," *NIMH*, accessed April 24, 2015, http://www.nimh.nih.gov/health/statistics/prevalence/any-anxiety-disorder-among-adults.shtml.
8. Marcia Angell, "The Epidemic of Mental Illness: Why?," *The New York Review of Books*, June 23, 2011, http://www.nybooks.com/articles/archives/2011/jun/23/epidemic-mental-illness-why/.
9. Ibid.
10. William Kremer and Claudia Hammond, "Hikikomori: Why Are so Many Japanese Men Refusing to Leave Their Rooms?," *BBC News*, accessed April 24, 2015, http://www.bbc.com/news/magazine-23182523.
11. Kristin Rushowy, "Toronto Students Worry about Family, School and Future, Survey Finds | Toronto Star," February 12, 2013, http://www.thestar.com/yourtoronto/education/2013/02/12/toronto_students_worry_about_family_school_and_future_survey_finds.html.
12. Brooks, "The Streamlined Life."
13. Alan Schwarz, "More College Freshmen Report Having Felt Depressed," *The New*

York Times, February 5, 2015, http://www.nytimes.com/2015/02/05/us/more-college-freshmen-report-having-felt-depressed.html.

14. Stephanie Nolan, "Suicide among India's Young Adults at 'crisis' Levels," *The Globe and Mail*, June 21, 2012, http://www.theglobeandmail.com/news/world/suicide-among-indias-young-adults-at-crisis-levels/article4362016/.

15. Lorianna De Giorgio, "What Chronic Stress Does to Your Brain," *The Toronto Star*, July 15, 2012, http://www.thestar.com/news/world/article/1225370--what-chronic-stress-does-to-your-brain.

16. Alvin Toffler, *Future Shock* (New York: Bantam Books, 1990).

17. Ibid., 2.

18. Toffler, *Future Shock*.

19. Ibid.

20. Ibid., 375.

21. Ibid., 379.

22. Ibid., 377.

23. Toffler, *Future Shock*.

24. Ibid., 379.

25. Moretti, *The New Geography of Jobs*, 33.

26. Edgerton, *The Shock of the Old*.

27. Lucas Mearian, "IBM Smashes Moore's Law, Cuts Bit Size to 12 Atoms," *Computerworld*, January 12, 2012, http://www.computerworld.com/article/2501259/data-center/ibm-smashes-moore-s-law--cuts-bit-size-to-12-atoms.html.

28. "AT&T Next - Get A New Smartphone Every Year from AT&T Wireless," accessed April 24, 2015, http://www.att.com/shop/wireless/next.html.

29. Moretti, *The New Geography of Jobs*, 104.

30. Innerarity, *The Future and Its Enemies in Defense of Political Hope*, 42.

CHAPTER 1 0

1. Christy Foley, Christy Foley Interview, December 10, 2014.

2. Dana Hull and Patrick May, "Rocket Man: The Otherworldly Ambitions of Elon Musk," *San Jose Mercury News*, April 11, 2014, http://www.mercurynews.com/business/ci_25541126/rocket-man-otherworldy-ambitions-elon-musk.

3. Hardy and Dougherty, "Google and Fidelity Put $1 Billion Into SpaceX."

4. Hal Niedzviecki, *We Want Some Too: Underground Desire and the Reinvention of Mass Culture* (Toronto, Ont. : New York, N.Y: Penguin Books ; Penguin Putnam, 2000).

5. Tom Martin, Tom Martin Interview, May 10, 2013.

6. Alan Feuer, "At Survivalists Expo, Items for Everything Short of the Zombie Apocalypse," *The New York Times*, April 6, 2014, http://www.nytimes.com/2014/04/07/us/at-survivalists-expo-items-for-everything-short-of-the-zombie-apocalypse.html.

7. Jessica Bennet, "Rise of the Preppers: America's New Survivalists," *Newsweek*, December 27, 2009, http://www.newsweek.com/rise-preppers-americas-new-survivalists-75537.

8. Jerry Young, Jerry Young Interview, April 10, 2013.

9. Lissa Price, Lissa Price Interview, July 17, 2013.

10. Charley Cameron, "Window Socket: Portable Solar-Powered Outlet Sticks to Windows, Charges Small Electronics," *Inhabitat*, June 27, 2014, http://inhabitat.com/

window-socket-portable-solar-powered-outlet-sticks-to-windows-charges-small-electronics/.

11. Chris Clarke, "Viral 'Solar Window Outlet' Cannot Possibly Work," *KCET*, May 3, 2013, http://www.kcet.org/news/redefine/rewire/solar/photovoltaic-pv/viral-solar-window-outlet-cant-possibly-work.html.

12. Tim Maughan, "The Dystopian Lake Filled by the World's Tech Lust," *BBC Future*, April 2, 2015, http://www.bbc.com/future/story/20150402-the-worst-place-on-earth.

13. Ibid.

14. Joel Achenbach, "Scientists: Human Activity Has Pushed Earth Beyond Four of Nine 'Planetary Boundaries,'" *The Washington Post*, January 15, 2015, http://www.washingtonpost.com/national/health-science/scientists-human-activity-has-pushed-earth-beyond-four-of-nine-planetary-boundaries/2015/01/15/f52b61b6-9b5e-11e4-a7ee-526210d665b4_story.html?tid=pm_pop.

15. Paul Kingsnorth, Paul Kingsnorth Interview, July 30, 2013.

16. Paul Kingsnorth, "Dark Ecology," *Orion Magazine*, 2013, https://orionmagazine.org/article/dark-ecology/.

17. Mark Brown, "Paul Kingsnorth's The Wake: A Novel Approach to Old English," *The Guardian*, November 9, 2014, http://www.theguardian.com/books/2014/nov/09/paul-kingsnorth-the-wake-novel-approach-old-english.

18. Susan Sontag, *Illness as Metaphor ; AIDS and Its Metaphors*, 1st Picador USA ed (New York: Picador USA, 2001).

19. Robert Jensen, *We Are All Apocalyptic Now: On the Responsibilities of Teaching, Preaching, Reporting, Writing, and Speaking Out*, 2013.

20. Robert Jensen, Robert Jensen Interview, March 10, 2013.

21. Friedrich Wilhelm Nietzsche et al., *Twilight of the Idols: And, The Anti-Christ*, Penguin Classics (London ;New York, N.Y: Penguin Books, 2003).

22. Packer, *The Unwinding*, 432.

23. Viktor Emil Frankl, *Man's Search for Meaning*, Mini book ed. (Boston: Beacon Press, 2006), 130.

24. Ibid., 99.

25. Epictetus, *Discourses, Fragments, Handbook*, trans. Robin Hard, Oxford World's Classics (Oxford ; New York, NY: Oxford University Press, 2014).

26. Frankl, *Man's Search for Meaning*, 105.

Bibliography

Aristotle. *Aristotle's Politics*. Translated by Carnes Lord. Second edition. Chicago: The University of Chicago Press, 2013.

Babbage, Charles. *Charles Babbage and His Calculating Engines: Selected Writings*. Dover Publications, 1961.

Biss, Eula. *On Immunity: An Inoculation*. Minneapolis, Minnesota: Graywolf Press, 2014.

Brynjolfsson, Erik, and Andrew McAfee. *Race Against the Machine*. Lexington, Massachusetts: Digital Frontier Press, 2011.

Buderi, Robert. *Engines of Tomorrow: How the World's Best Companies Are Using Their Research Labs to Win the Future*. New York: Simon & Schuster, 2000.

Davis, Martin. *The Universal Computer: The Road from Leibniz to Turing*. Turing centenary ed. Boca Raton, Fla: CRC Press, 2012.

Dawkins, Richard. *The Selfish Gene*. 30th anniversary ed. Oxford ; New York: Oxford University Press, 2006.

Diamond, Jared M. *The World until Yesterday: What Can We Learn from Traditional Societies?*. New York: Viking, 2012.

Dyson, George. *Turing's Cathedral: The Origins of the Digital Universe*. 1st ed. New York: Pantheon Books, 2012.

Edgerton, David. *The Shock of the Old: Technology and Global History since 1900*. Oxford; New York: Oxford University Press, 2007.

Epictetus. *Discourses, Fragments, Handbook*. Translated by Robin Hard. Oxford World's Classics. Oxford ; New York, NY: Oxford University Press, 2014.

Ford, Martin. *The Lights in the Tunnel: Automation, Accelerating Technology and the Economy of the Future*. U.S.: Acculant Publishing, 2009.

Frankl, Viktor Emil. *Man's Search for Meaning*. Mini book ed. Boston: Beacon Press, 2006.

Gelernter, David Hillel. *1939, the Lost World of the Fair*. New York: Avon Books, 1996.

Gleick, James. *The Information: A History, a Theory, a Flood*. New York: Knopf Doubleday Publishing Group, 2011.

Godin, Benoit. *Innovation Contested: The Idea of Innovation over the Centuries*. Routledge Studies in Social and Political Thought. New York, NY: Routledge, 2014.

Hammond, Claudia. *Time Warped: Unlocking the Mysteries of Time Perception*. Toronto: House of Anansi Press, 2012.

Innerarity, Daniel. *The Future and Its Enemies in Defense of Political Hope*. Translated by Sandra Kingery. Stanford, California: Stanford University Press, 2012.

Jensen, Robert. *We Are All Apocalyptic Now: On the Responsibilities of Teaching, Preaching, Reporting, Writing, and Speaking out*, 2013.

Johnson, Steven. *Where Good Ideas Come from the Natural History of Innovation*. New York: Riverhead Books, 2010.

Kahneman, Daniel. *Thinking, Fast and Slow*. Toronto: Doubleday Canada, 2011.

Kingsnorth, Paul. *The Wake*. London: Unbound, 2014.

Kurzweil, Ray. *The Singularity Is near: When Humans Transcend Biology*. New York: Penguin, 2006.

Lanier, Jaron. *Who Owns the Future?* New York: Simon & Schuster, 2013.

Laplace, Pierre-Simon. *A Philosophical Essay on Probabilities*. Wiley, 1902.

Luria, A.R. *Cognitive Development: Its Cultural and Social Foundations*. Cambridge, Mass., USA: Harvard University Press, 1976.

Sontag, Susan. *Illness as Metaphor ; AIDS and Its Metaphors.* 1st Picador USA ed. New York: Picador USA, 2001.

Tetlock, Philip E. *Expert Political Judgment: How Good Is It? How Can We Know?* Princeton, NJ: Princeton Univ. Press, 2006.

Thomas Hobbes. *Leviathan, or The Matter, Forme and Power of a Commonwealth, Ecclesiasticall, and Civill.* 1886th ed. London: George Routledge and Sons, 1651.

Toffler, Alvin. *Future Shock.* New York: Bantam Books, 1990.

Waugh, Alexander. *Time: From Micro-Seconds to Millennia, a Search for the Right Time.* London: Headline Book Pub., 1999.

Wright, Ronald. *A Short History of Progress.* CBC Massey Lectures Series. Toronto: House of Anansi Press, 2004.

Wu, Tim. *The Master Switch the Rise and Fall of Information Empires.* New York: Alfred A. Knopf, 2010.

Index

About the Author

One of North America's smartest and most explosive contrarians, HAL NIEDZVIECKI is a writer, speaker, and culture commentator known for challenging preconceptions and exploring the new patterns of tech-infused everyday life. He is the author of three previous books of nonfiction, including *The Peep Diaries: How We're Learning to Love Watching Ourselves and Our Neighbors* and *Hello, I'm Special: How Individuality Became the New Conformity*. *The Peep Diaries* was made into a television documentary entitled *Peep Culture*, produced for the CBC and shown at festivals and on television in six countries. Niedzviecki's articles on contemporary life have appeared in newspapers, periodicals, and journals across the world including *New York Times Magazine*, *Playboy*, *Utne Reader*, and the *Globe and Mail*. He serves as publisher and fiction editor of *Broken Pencil*, the seminal indie culture publication that he founded in 1995. Niedzviecki grew up in the suburbs of Washington DC, and currently lives in Toronto with his wife and two daughters. For more information, see his website, AlongCameTomorrow.com.

About Seven Stories Press

Seven Stories Press is an independent book publisher based in New York City. We publish works of the imagination by such writers as Nelson Algren, Russell Banks, Octavia E. Butler, Ani DiFranco, Assia Djebar, Ariel Dorfman, Coco Fusco, Barry Gifford, Martha Long, Luis Negrón, Hwang Sok-yong, Lee Stringer, and Kurt Vonnegut, to name a few, together with political titles by voices of conscience, including Subhankar Banerjee, the Boston Women's Health Collective, Noam Chomsky, Angela Y. Davis, Human Rights Watch, Derrick Jensen, Ralph Nader, Loretta Napoleoni, Gary Null, Greg Palast, Project Censored, Barbara Seaman, Alice Walker, Gary Webb, and Howard Zinn, among many others. Seven Stories Press believes publishers have a special responsibility to defend free speech and human rights, and to celebrate the gifts of the human imagination, wherever we can. In 2012 we launched Triangle Square books for young readers with strong social justice and narrative components, telling personal stories of courage and commitment. For additional information, visit www.sevenstories.com.